EXPLORING BRITAIN
COUNTRY TOWNS

COUNTRY TOWNS
WAS EDITED AND DESIGNED BY
THE READER'S DIGEST ASSOCIATION LIMITED, LONDON

FIRST EDITION COPYRIGHT © 1984
THE READER'S DIGEST ASSOCIATION LIMITED, 25 BERKELEY SQUARE,
LONDON W1X 6AB

COPYRIGHT © 1984
READER'S DIGEST ASSOCIATION FAR EAST LIMITED
PHILIPPINES COPYRIGHT 1984
READER'S DIGEST ASSOCIATION FAR EAST LTD

PRINTED IN GREAT BRITAIN

CONTRIBUTORS

MAIN TEXT BY DAVID WARD
GAZETTEER BY JOHN BISHOP

EXPLORING BRITAIN
COUNTRY TOWNS

PUBLISHED BY THE READER'S DIGEST ASSOCIATION LIMITED
LONDON NEW YORK MONTREAL SYDNEY CAPE TOWN

—C O N T E N T S—

A–Z GUIDE TO COUNTRY TOWNS
8 – 159

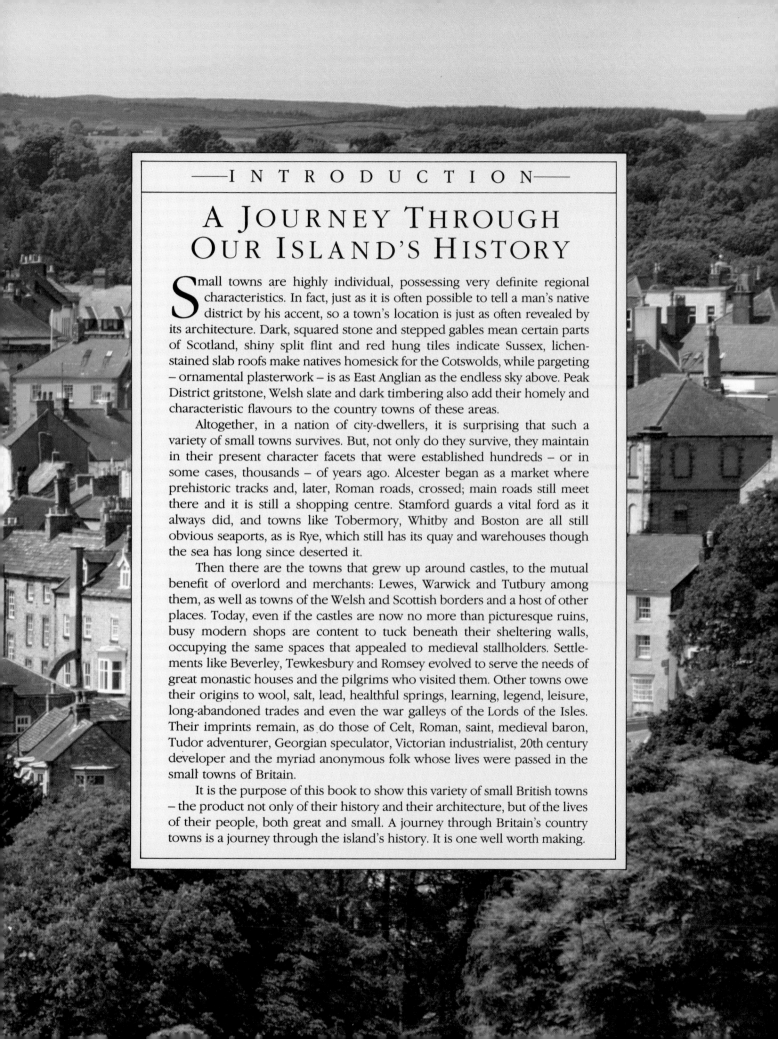

A Journey Through Our Island's History

Small towns are highly individual, possessing very definite regional characteristics. In fact, just as it is often possible to tell a man's native district by his accent, so a town's location is just as often revealed by its architecture. Dark, squared stone and stepped gables mean certain parts of Scotland, shiny split flint and red hung tiles indicate Sussex, lichen-stained slab roofs make natives homesick for the Cotswolds, while pargeting – ornamental plasterwork – is as East Anglian as the endless sky above. Peak District gritstone, Welsh slate and dark timbering also add their homely and characteristic flavours to the country towns of these areas.

Altogether, in a nation of city-dwellers, it is surprising that such a variety of small towns survives. But, not only do they survive, they maintain in their present character facets that were established hundreds – or in some cases, thousands – of years ago. Alcester began as a market where prehistoric tracks and, later, Roman roads, crossed; main roads still meet there and it is still a shopping centre. Stamford guards a vital ford as it always did, and towns like Tobermory, Whitby and Boston are all still obvious seaports, as is Rye, which still has its quay and warehouses though the sea has long since deserted it.

Then there are the towns that grew up around castles, to the mutual benefit of overlord and merchants: Lewes, Warwick and Tutbury among them, as well as towns of the Welsh and Scottish borders and a host of other places. Today, even if the castles are now no more than picturesque ruins, busy modern shops are content to tuck beneath their sheltering walls, occupying the same spaces that appealed to medieval stallholders. Settlements like Beverley, Tewkesbury and Romsey evolved to serve the needs of great monastic houses and the pilgrims who visited them. Other towns owe their origins to wool, salt, lead, healthful springs, learning, legend, leisure, long-abandoned trades and even the war galleys of the Lords of the Isles. Their imprints remain, as do those of Celt, Roman, saint, medieval baron, Tudor adventurer, Georgian speculator, Victorian industrialist, 20th century developer and the myriad anonymous folk whose lives were passed in the small towns of Britain.

It is the purpose of this book to show this variety of small British towns – the product not only of their history and their architecture, but of the lives of their people, both great and small. A journey through Britain's country towns is a journey through the island's history. It is one well worth making.

ABINGDON *Oxfordshire*

Any town with the infant Thames for company is already at an advantage. There is a pleasant formality in having an ancient bridge for an entrance, and a sense of pleasurable busyness in the coming and going of cabin cruisers. While on spring and summer evenings the scents of lilac, may and cow-parsley mingle with the smell of the river in one glorious bouquet. Then is the time to see Abingdon, from the meadows side of the bridge, as the slanting light picks out the individuals among its distinguished congregation of roofs. There is the pretty, 17th-century cupola of the Market House, with its lattice windows and gilded weather-vane, in delicate contrast to the octagonal tower of the Old Gaol. To the left, over the willows, the buttressed spire of St Helen's Church rises above the red-tiled roofs of its attendant almshouses. A line of neatly pollarded trees stands between their stone walls and the river. The scene is very English.

Abingdon grew up about the gates of an abbey that, in its 15th-century heyday, was about the form and size of Wells Cathedral. Not a vestige of it remains, but here and there in the town its offshoots spring up, like those from some long-forgotten root buried deep in the garden. Just across the bridge, for example, there is the Nag's Head Inn, and beyond that, The Broad Face which stands on the corner of Thames Street. This runs alongside a duck-haunted backwater that was the mill-stream created by monks in the 10th century; at its end, beyond a venerable red-brick bridge, the mill-race still thunders beside a medieval mill that has been converted into one of the most attractive hotels in the Thames Valley. Beside it is a small group of stone buildings that were once abbey offices – the Bakery, the Checker (counting-house), the Granary and the Long Gallery, which was probably accommodation for counting-house clerks. The Bakery and Granary are now an abbey museum, while the Checker has been turned into a little jewel of an aproned-staged Elizabethan-style theatre. A rare 13th-century chimney rises above the buildings, and the great stone fireplaces still exist.

At the top of Thames Street and over Bridge Street is the fortress-like Old Gaol, still with massive black bars blocking the windows. Just round the corner is the Market Place. The great Gatehouse of the abbey opened on to it, and still does in fact, though there is now no abbey beyond. Here was the nucleus of the town, where merchants bought and sold their wares, and where fairs were held. Since this was abbey land, the abbot charged large fees for these privileges and, it seemed to the townsfolk, gave precious little in return. Relations were never amicable, and in 1327 the town rioted and, with the aid of some Oxford students, sacked the abbey. Savage retribution followed, but little reconciliation, and nearly two centuries before the Dissolution of the Monasteries the author of *Piers Plowman* was darkly prophesying: *'And thanne shal the Abbot of Abyndoun and alle his issue for evere Have a knokke of a kyng and*

OPEN PLAN *The upper storey of the Long Gallery was originally divided into several rooms used as dwellings – cold comfort since the long windows bordering the side passageway were never glazed. The building was used by a brewery for 300 years, until 1895, and changes made during that time and recent restoration have opened up a spacious view of the superb timber roof.*

CIVIC PRIDE *Abingdon was proud of its gaol when it was built in 1812, and is even prouder now that it has been converted to a sports and social centre.*

incurable the wounde.' And so it came about. In 1538, Henry VIII pensioned off the abbot and monks, and building contractors fell upon the abbey and stripped lead, timber and stone until there was nothing left at all. But, oddly enough, there is still an Abbot of Abingdon; it is one of the titles traditionally conferred upon the vicar of the Church of St Paul in the Vatican.

The complex of buildings to the right of the gate are mostly 15th century with later additions and alterations. The Corporation bought them at the Dissolution, and what had been the gatehouse and the abbey Hospital of St John, were used down the years as prison, council chambers, courtroom and grammar school. The school was founded by John Roysse in 1563, and the magnificent 63 ft schoolroom where 63 free pupils were taught can still be seen.

Within the same complex but on the other side of the gate is a low Norman doorway which is the entrance to the Church of St Nicholas, once part of the abbey. After the Dissolution, it became the church of a small parish, and more than a century ago was attached to the main church of St Helen. The interior is plain – the early glass was smashed by Parliamentarian troopers – but the font is medieval and there is a fine Jacobean pulpit. The monuments include a charming one to John and Jane Blacknall and their two daughters, all represented by kneeling black-robed, white-ruffed figures. Mr and Mrs Blacknall both died on the same day, August 21, 1625, presumably of the plague, and left large sums of money to the church and to the poor of the parish.

As if to demonstrate that great architecture did not expire with the Middle Ages, there stands on the other side of Market Place one of the loveliest municipal buildings in England, the Market House or County Hall, as it is just as often called. Of worn, pale stone, it was built about 1680 by Christopher Kempster, one of Wren's masons during the building of St Paul's

Cathedral, and the clean lines of the hall are worthy of the master himself. It consists of an open, high-arched ground floor that is still sometimes used as a covered market and, above, a line of wonderfully tall latticed windows completely surrounding the building, which is topped off by a cupola with no other purpose except to charm. The first floor now houses Abingdon Museum, which has some fine archaeological collections and displays of town life down the years, including a case of sad little relics of MG cars, which were made in Abingdon from 1929 to 1980. Due to an initial distaste for the smoke and noise, Abingdon lost the Great Western Railway to Reading and with it, within a few years, its position as county town of Berkshire. Then, in 1974, during the reshufflings of local government, it was ousted from Berkshire altogether, and is now in the Vale of White Horse District of Oxfordshire.

The Market House, and the medieval buildings opposite, look upon the High Street, which further along its course becomes Ock Street. These, and other streets in the town, are of that very English blur consisting of colour-wash buildings Victorian and older, some modern shop fronts, illuminated here and there by some good Georgian work. Ock Street has its own unofficial mayor, elected in June each year from among the street's Morris dancers.

East St Helen Street is the most obviously attractive in the town, a charming jumble of Tudor gables and overhangs and 18th-century elegance. The street leads to the river, and to St Helen's Church, part of which dates from the 13th century and is unusual in being rather broader than it is long. There are wonderful panels in the Lady Chapel and some interesting monuments, including one to a man who helped build the bridge in 1416. John Roysse, the founder of the Grammar School is also there, lying, under a slab taken from his London garden.

In the churchyard there are three groups of almshouses, the oldest of which is Long Alley Almshouses, fronted by a long, oak-pillared gallery and a number of improving texts from the Scriptures. They were founded in 1446 by the Fraternity of the Holy Cross, a charitable lay organisation that also built Abingdon Bridge; despite later alterations and widenings, much of the present bridge remains as their monument. At the Dissolution the Fraternity was also disbanded, and the responsibility for the Almshouses was taken over by the Master and Governors of Christ's Hospital. It was they who built the rather cheerier red-brick Twitty and Brick Alley Almshouses in the 18th century.

Delightful though all this is, it would be wrong to give the impression that Abingdon is gently subsiding beneath a weight of past glories. To the north there are vast industrial estates, cash-and-carries and super-supermarkets; these continue, interspersed with wide fields and views of distant woods, almost to the point where the distant spires and pylons of Oxford lift over the horizon.

RIVERSIDE CHARM *On St Helen's Wharf, the slender spire of St Helen's Church, the tall chimneys of Long Alley Almshouses poking skywards from lichen-stained roofs, and the cheery red-and-white face of the Old Anchor Inn combine comfortably in a serene blend of medieval dignity and Georgian elegance.*

ALCESTER *Warwickshire*

Alauna, Alyncester, the town's ancient names, as well as its present one, are derived from the River Alne, which at this point joins the Arrow before their waters flow united to the Avon. It was this confluence of rivers that brought about Alcester's beginnings, long ago, perhaps in the Iron Age. Then, when the Romans were building their network of roads across the land, two of their most important routes – Ryknield Street and the Salt Way from Droitwich – intersected at the old British settlement. A market grew up at the crossroads, and a walled town, but of this Roman Alcester almost nothing remains on the surface other than a sculpted torso in a wall near the Rectory. The remainder lies beneath the present town.

Marketing and catering for the needs of travellers remained Alcester's principal occupations for a very long time. It has an annual fair, 'The Mop', that dates back to 1446, and a Court Leet – a body of elected officials such as Ale Taster, Flesh Taster, Bread-weigher, Constable and Brooklooker – has been responsible for the affairs of the market since the 13th century. The Court Leet still meets in the handsome Town Hall presented by Sir Fulke Greville in 1618, but the market itself no longer functions. As for the town's other role, as a transport centre, there are two Georgian houses in Church Street that were once a well-known coaching inn, but when the railways came it lost its purpose and was divided into two pleasant town houses.

The town was put together, with careless grace, over many years, and the evidence is apparent in every street. Malt Mill Lane, with its beautifully restored Malthouse and its companions, is early Tudor, but Henley Street and the grouping about the Town Hall are mostly 17th and 18th century. In the High Street, Georgian fronts often mask buildings of the 16th and 17th centuries, as may be seen by glancing down the little dividing alleys and courts where the original black-and-white structure is revealed.

At the junction of Henley Street and High Street, and skirted to the west by pretty, narrow Butter Street, is St Nicholas's Church. Some of it, the tower particularly, dates from the 13th century, but it was given a classical interior after a fire in 1727, and the Victorians added their rather heavy-handed contribution in 1871.

It is contrary to nature, or at least to the inclinations of their inhabitants, that great houses should exist within the purlieus of towns. But Alcester has two within a couple of miles and both are well worth a visit. Ragley Hall, the home of the Marquesses of Hertford, was built in a Blenheim-like scale about 1680, but both in its surroundings – laid out by Capability Brown – and in its superb interiors it typifies the free and noble spirit of the 18th-century Age of Reason.

Coughton Court, on the other hand, is dark-panelled and has a faintly sad and weary air. It belongs to the National Trust now, but from 1509 until very recently it was the property of the Throckmortons who, down the generations, steadfastly maintained their allegiance to the Catholic faith, as a number of secret hiding places for priests bear witness. It was there, in 1605, that the wives of the conspirators in the Gunpowder Plot heard of the plot's failure and their husbands' indictment for high treason.

ALDEBURGH *Suffolk*

From a distance, it cannot be said for certain whether the town belongs to sky or sea or land. The sky is vast, blue-white or dark and racing, with the town as a tiny centrepiece; the sea too is huge, either a shimmering silver backdrop at the streets' edge or a terrifying charge of grey-white horses. The land appears to play the least part, a narrow line of no particular significance and no great permanence, either, since Aldeburgh is part of that strange part of Suffolk that is gently dissolving into the North Sea.

Not that there is any great urgency in the sense of borrowed time. The Celts and the Romans both knew the place, and when the Saxons gave it a name, it was one that meant 'the old town' or perhaps 'the old fort'. The sea's encroachment is therefore fairly leisurely, and it is not until the positioning of the town's oldest secular building is considered that it is apparent that it occurs at all. When the Moot Hall, or council hall, was built in 1512, there were three streets between it and the sea. Now it stands almost on the shingle, a handsome but lonely Tudor building of timber, herringbone brick and red tile, backed by pretty colour-washed houses of the early 19th century.

Overshadowed by the port of Orford to the south, Aldeburgh had but a modest share in the great Suffolk wool boom of the Middle Ages, and it was not until Tudor times that it became significant as a trading and shipbuilding centre. It is to this period of prosperity that the Moot Hall belongs, and much of the parish church of St Peter and St Paul too, though the tower at least is 14th century. The church, grand in the East

FIT FOR A PRINCE *The Prince Regent was a frequent visitor to Ragley Hall, and the bed specially made for him stands in the Prince Regent's Bedroom. The curtains are of 17th-century hand-painted silk, and the gilded Prince of Wales's crest of feathers leaves no doubt as to whose bed it was. A portrait of the prince hangs above the fireplace.*

Anglian style, was considerably knocked about by the Puritans, the work being carried out by a Captain Johnson, whose deeds are recorded on a black marble slab in the chancel. Nevertheless, some fine furnishings escaped his attentions, and there are memorials to the town's most famous sons, one native and the other adopted. George Crabbe (1754–1832), the poet who was born in the town, is commemorated by a bust, while near by there is a window by John Piper dedicated to the memory of the composer Benjamin Britten. In the churchyard lies Elizabeth Garrett Anderson, England's first woman doctor of medicine.

After its Tudor heyday, Aldeburgh fell into a slow decline. Its significance as a port was eclipsed by that of London, its trade further threatened by Dunkirk pirates, its very existence endangered by the inroads of the sea. During most of the 18th century it was little more than a fishing village, clinging to life by its fingertips. This was the Aldeburgh described by George Crabbe, who had been a labourer on Aldeburgh quay while he struggled to become first a surgeon and then a curate. He knew of the bitterness, squalor and meanness that poverty creates, and he recalled the lives of his neighbours with a sardonic pen. One of the people he wrote about was Peter Grimes, the savage, tortured fisherman haunted by the ghosts of the apprentices he had murdered. Nearly

150 years later, Benjamin Britten made Grimes the subject of his great opera.

Aldeburgh was saved in the middle of the 19th century by the urban middle classes who suddenly noticed the sunniness and dryness of its climate, and the bracing quality of its salt air. It is to this gracious period that much of the present building belongs, and the town has been a pleasant and intimate seaside resort, the kind that families come back to year after year and generation after generation. Confined by the sea, and the marshes on either side, Aldeburgh could not expand even if it wished to, and has in consequence made ingenious use of whatever is available for holiday accommodation – including a windmill and a Martello tower.

The greatest test of the town's resources takes place in June every year with the Aldeburgh Festival – the brilliant conception of Peter Pears, Benjamin Britten and their friends. From humble beginnings in the Jubilee Hall in 1948, the music festival has now extended to the parish church, and to those of neighbouring Orford, Blythburgh and Framlingham as well. The heart of the proceedings, however, is the complex carved out of the majestic 19th-century Maltings, in the neighbouring village of Snape, which includes a concert hall, an art gallery, a craft centre and a school for advanced musical studies.

TOWN ON THE BRINK *The sea and its ally, the ever-shifting shingle, have swallowed up most of Aldeburgh during the last three centuries. Now it stands defiant, only three streets wide and within yards of its mortal enemy. Unable to expand on to the surrounding marshland, Aldeburgh makes the most of what it has – and therein lies its charm.*

ALNWICK *Northumberland*

As with other towns in the 'Debatable Land' where England marches with Scotland, there is an air of the frontier about Alnwick. The defences here, one feels, are serious, from the Hotspur Tower gate that forces all traffic into single file, to the great barbican of the castle and the battlemented front of St Michael's Church. And well they might be, since for centuries, until the Union of the Crowns in 1603, de Vescys, Percys, Douglases and the rest raided across the Border in both directions, and if the enemy was safely locked up in his castle, they would harry his lands instead.

Harrying, a deceptively mild term, meant the slaughter of every living thing that did not hide and the burning of all crops and buildings. And although this might be regarded as a summer sport of the aristocracy, there were also the royal armies of England and Scotland that passed through on their way to do battle with one another. Sometimes it seemed hardly worth while to plant a crop at all, while Alnwick itself, which had the misfortune to stand on the only suitable crossing point of the River Aln, was razed at least twice. Such days now are only the stuff of ballads, but if the town still retains an atmosphere of watchfulness, it can hardly be blamed.

The visitor from the south is left in no doubt as to whose country he is in, for his greeting is an 83 ft tall pillar guarded by four Trafalgar Square-type lions, and topped by the stiff-tailed heraldic lion of the Percys. This is the Percy Tenantry Column, erected in 1816 by the Duke of Northumberland's tenants in gratitude for his lowering rents during a period of agricultural depression. Near by is the Hotspur Tower, a square, 15th-century block of masonry riven through by the tunnel of the town's only complete medieval gate. It is named after Harry Percy, celebrated by Shakespeare in *Henry IV, Part One*, and killed at the Battle of Shrewsbury in 1403. He gained the nickname 'Hotspur' by his spirited and courageous conduct at the siege of Berwick Castle; he was 12 years old at the time.

Beyond the tower, the town begins immediately with Bondgate Within, a street of mainly 18th-century brick and stone, whose clean lines, rising above the partly cobbled roadway, seem particularly well suited to the crisp, clear light of the Borders. Several of Alnwick's street names have this ending of 'gate', which has nothing to do with openings in the town walls, but comes instead from the Old Norse word meaning a way, or path. Bondgate was the area where the bondsmen lived, the poorer folk who owed service to the Lord of the Manor, Bailiffgate was the way to the castle's outer bailey, Walkergate was where the fullers cleaned fleeces by treading them, Canongate was the way the White Canons took to the abbey across the river.

Above Bondgate is the Market Place, with its cross on whose steps John Wesley preached, and the Town Hall, built by the Freemen – officers of the craft Guilds – in 1771. The Freemen – in effect the town corporation – owe their authority to a charter that dates back to 1160. Their hall, however, is rather dwarfed by Northumberland Hall on the other side of the square. This was built by the then Duke of Northumberland in 1826 as a shopping arcade to replace the ancient shambles, or meat market. The hall was topped by Assembly Rooms, salons dedicated to genteel entertainment and elegant conversation, without which no late Georgian town was complete. The interior of the ballroom in the nearby White Swan Hotel was extracted all of a piece from RMS *Olympic*, sister ship of the *Titanic*, in about 1930.

Bondgate runs into the aptly named Narrowgate, which has some charming old houses including the red-brick town house of the Forsters of Bamburgh. It is generally called 'Dorothy Forster's House' in memory of the girl who in 1715 rescued her brother, a somewhat incompetent Jacobite general, from London's Newgate Prison. She also made a vain attempt to save her lover, the gallant Earl of Derwentwater, but he died on the scaffold a few months later.

Narrowgate opens out to Castle Square and to St Michael's Church, destroyed in one of the periodical sackings and rebuilt by means of grants made by Henry VI in 1464. It has a fortified look due, no doubt, to lessons hard-learned, and is one of the finest parish churches in the north of England. It has a 14th-century Flemish chest, some good medieval monuments and a pair of curious, much-restored little statues, reputedly representations of Henry VI and St Sebastian. Another church worth visiting is St Paul's, some distance off, in St Michael's Lane. It contains a vast, pre-Raphaelite east window depicting St Paul preaching at Antioch, and an awesome effigy of the 3rd Duke of Northumberland, who built and presented the church to the town in the middle of the last century; he is depicted in Garter robes and a coronet.

Bailiffgate, running off Castle Square, has some pleasant buildings, including the 18th-century Duchess's School, but the eye is at once riveted by the tremendous castle barbican at its far end. The worn stones reflect its years – it was built in 1310 – and the threatening aspect of the great gateway flanked by two massive towers is hardly diminished by the stone

MONUMENTAL FOLLY *The Percy Tenantry Column is known locally as Farmers' Folly because, it is said, the 2nd Duke of Northumberland, in whose honour it was erected, raised the rents of his tenants when he became aware they could afford such an extravagance. It stands 83 ft high and has an internal staircase leading to a gallery at the top.*

TRADITIONAL FAIR *Mobcapped ladies tend their wares at Alnwick Fair, a revived event dating back to 1297. The fair is held in the Market Place during the last week in June and re-creates the colour and atmosphere of its 13th-century origins. A weekly market has been held there for more than 800 years, since the building of Alnwick Castle.*

soldiers that stand on the battlements. Carved in the 18th century, they probably replaced much older ones; it was the custom to place such figures on castle walls, especially in the north, as a means of warding off the evil eye. Behind them is a narrow, easily defended passage leading to the gatehouse, beyond which are the mighty towers, baileys, courts and keep of the castle itself. Of Windsor-like proportions and looks, it stands just as nobly above the Aln as Windsor does over the Thames, though it lacks Windsor's slightly fairy-tale aspect. Alnwick Castle is more business-like, a place that was made not only for splendid living, but for serious soldiering too.

The first lord of Alnwick was Gilbert Tyson, William the Conqueror's standard-bearer, but whether he built a castle there is not known; if he did, it would have been no more than a wooden tower on a mound. The first true castle was built by Eustace Fitzjohn in the opening decades of the 12th century, and despite its early date it was much the same design as the present one; a good deal of the early masonry still remains. It was later held by the de Vescys, during whose residence it was besieged at least twice, on the second occasion by the Scottish King William the Lion who, unable to get at the castle's owner, massacred 300 of his tenants who had taken refuge in a church.

The de Vescys died out at the beginning of the 14th century, and in 1309 the castle was acquired by Henry Percy. Despite wars, murders, attainders, executions and female lines, his descendants have held it ever since, first as Earls then as Dukes, of Northumberland.

After the Union of the Crowns, Alnwick Castle was largely abandoned and fell gradually into decay; a famous painting by Canaletto, executed about 1752, depicts its then romantically overgrown state. A few years later, the 1st Duke began to restore it and the work was completed by the 4th and 6th Dukes. Now, if the exterior still looks like a grim Border fortress, the interior is a palace, containing priceless antiquities, paintings, books and furniture. It is open to the public during the summer.

So, too, is the park, landscaped by Capability Brown and embracing legacies of Border history. There is the gatehouse of Alnwick Abbey, founded in 1147 by Eustace Fitzjohn, and the ruins of the 13th-century Hulne Priory, with its massive tower, built as a place of refuge against the Scots. The two bridges over the Aln, one of which bears a Percy lion, were both by John Adam in about 1716; they are the goals for the annual Shrovetide football match, in which the whole town joins. There is also a stone that marks where William the Lion was captured by chance after his massacre of the tenants in 1174, while another monument indicates where Malcolm Canmore, King of Scotland and Macbeth's successor, was murdered in 1093. Border memories are long, it seems.

DAUNTING PROSPECT *A Percy lion prowls the undergrowth, and across open meadows stands the great fortress of the Percys themselves, a sight that must have daunted even the most resolute attackers. Yet despite its seeming impregnability, Alnwick Castle was besieged and captured many times during its turbulent history.*

ALSTON Cumbria

Burly roofs of split millstone grit keep Alston cosy, and indefatigable cobbles on the steep streets keep its feet dry, despite its exposed position on the hunched north shoulder of Cross Fell. Standing about 1,000 ft up on the hillside, it is the loftiest market town in England, and owes its situation to the silver and lead found in the surrounding hills. Most of what can be seen now was built during the great local lead boom of the 18th and early 19th centuries.

The Romans knew about the lead in Alston Moor, and about its silver too; it could be that the great Roman fort now known as Whitley Castle, which governs Maiden Way, one of the main routes to Hadrian's Wall, was also the centre of Roman mining activities. Carlisle Mint was supplied with Alston silver during Henry I's reign, and in the 12th century Windsor Castle was roofed with Alston lead. In the 18th century the mining rights were leased to the London Lead Company, more popularly known as the Quaker Company, since its directors were of that persuasion. During the next 100 years or so, the Quakers utilised part of their profit to provide social welfare for the miners, which included disablement and sickness benefits, schools, a library and public baths. By 1885, however, the known deposits were almost exhausted, foreign competition made further exploration uneconomic, and the mines began to close. No mining is currently carried out.

The heart of the town is the Market Place, a close-knit gathering of stone buildings all much of a size and height, many of which have outside staircases up to the first floor. This feature is fairly common in Alston, and is partly due to earlier townsfolk keeping livestock on the lower floors while they lived above, and partly to the providing of further accommodation, by dividing single houses into two flats, during the boom mining years.

The attractive Market Cross was originally the gift of William Stephenson, a local boy who rose in the world and became Lord Mayor of London in 1764. Unfortunately, the present Market Cross is a copy of a copy, due to its predecessors' fatal attraction for runaway lorries. But it has been well done, and both cross and buildings have been much enhanced by a highly original paving scheme within the market area, in which flags, cobbles and setts are attractively combined in patterns to guide pedestrians and traffic.

Front Street is Alston's high street, wherein stands the 17th-century Quaker Meeting House. Considering the enormous influence that the Quakers had upon the town, it looks oddly small and self-effacing among the surrounding buildings. Not far off is the Angel Inn, Alston's oldest pub, which dates from 1611. Next door is Church Gaytes, another 17th-century building, with an ornate outside staircase. As its name implies, it stands at one of the entrances to the churchyard of St Augustine's which, like the Market Cross, is a replacement of replacements and dates only from 1864. The dedication, however, is ancient and abiding enough, since St Augustine was very highly thought of hereabouts. He it was who is said to have exorcised the demons on Cross Fell by planting a cross upon it; before that it was known as Fiends' Fell. Or so it is said. The church clock and bell are considerably older than the building. They came from Dilston Hall, the home of the Earl of Derwentwater, and along with all his other property were forfeit to the State when he died under the headman's axe on Tower Hill after 'coming out' in the Jacobite rising of 1715.

Backing on to one side of the churchyard is a rather curious three-storey terrace, a clue to whose purpose may be seen in the rounded staircase that climbs to the building's full height. It is a very early form of tenement, and was occupied by miners and their families in the 17th and 18th centuries. To the north of the churchyard, and reached by a series of little courts, is The Butts, in which there is hardly a house much later than 1700. As the name suggests, this was where the townsmen practised archery under an ancient law which demanded that all males over 16 should be proficient with the bow.

From The Butts, a track leads down to the River Nent, and to a stone bridge over a force known locally as Gossipgate, from the many tongues of water that flow down and through the rocks. It is a charming place, and a splendid introduction to the many walks and rambles in the neighbourhood.

VENERABLE INN *Alston's Angel Inn dates from the early 17th century, though there are signs of later additions. A distinct Flemish flavour is given by the rounded dormer window. The style was probably influenced by early Flemish settlers who came to work in the lead mines.*

AMERSHAM Buckinghamshire

More than a century ago, a citizen wrote:

*'O Amersham! What voice is this that wakes
   you up so rudely?'
The line is coming through thy midst ere long
The Metropolitan Extension Railway
O turn aside, do not this cruel wrong.'*

The emotion was not shared by everyone. True, Squire Drake, whose family had owned the town and all the land about since the days of Elizabeth I was

violently opposed; he saw the coming of the railway as the New Age's final blow – the first being the abolition of Amersham's two Parliamentary seats under the Reform Act of 1832. But the innkeepers were generally for it, and the headmaster of the school 'for the sons of liberal gentlemen' was enthusiastic. He could envisage new platoons of liberal gentlemen coming down by train from London to beat a path to his door.

In the end, a compromise was reached. The old town was by-passed, and the railway went to Amersham Common instead. Inevitably, a town grew up beside it, a decorous town of good shops and pleasant houses whose occupants mostly worked in the City.

Old Amersham breathed a sigh of relief, for it had the best of both worlds; new prosperity and new shops to hand, while its ancient charm was retained virtually unscathed. High Street is a very pretty street, of all kinds of periods from the 15th to the 19th centuries. Mostly it is brick, in some cases creeper-clad, but there is also the King's Arms which, not so long ago, had its Georgian brick cladding stripped away to reveal its timbered, 17th-century frontage beneath. Other inns and ex-inns, too, hint at Amersham's importance in the coaching network – the Elephant and Castle, Red Lion House, the Crown Hotel with its pretty porch flying over the pavement, the Griffin Hotel, and next door a house that used to be part of an inn.

The most eye-catching building, however, is the neat brick oblong of the Market Hall, the gift of Sir William Drake in 1682. It has a smart, white bell-tower, and in the open ground floor is the old lock-up and the town pump. Amersham's right to hold a weekly market was granted in 1200, the same year that its annual fair was confirmed. This still continues, along the whole length of the street, on September 19 and 20.

There is plenty to see down the side streets too. A narrow passage by the King's Head leads to the stately Baptist Church of 1783, while down Whielden Street is the attractive 17th-century Friends' Meeting House, and the not so attractive workhouse, now a hospital. The Platt, probably the oldest thoroughfare in Amersham, climbs up and gives a good view over the red roofs of the town. It has some old, pretty cottages and passes Shardiloes, a mansion built in 1766 for the Drake family; it contains some of Robert Adam's earliest known work, and the park, with its lake, was landscaped by Humphry Repton.

The parish church of St Mary is, unsurprisingly, in Church Street. Its outer casing of Victorian flint serves as a disguise, for St Mary's is a very old church indeed, having been endowed by Geoffrey de Mandeville, 1st Earl of Essex, in 1140, and part of the building dates from this period. It has been added to down the centuries almost to the present day, strong proof of the affection in which the town has always held it. There is some good 17th-century glass, and an

CHILTERN TOWN *Old Amersham lies in the valley of the Misbourne, the 'Gateway to the Chilterns' that follows the tiny meandering river northwards and westwards through the undulating Buckinghamshire countryside and carries the old London to Aylesbury coach road.*

FLIGHTS OF ANGELS *Henry Curwen, who died aged 14 in 1636, was a pupil of the Rector of St Mary's Church, Amersham. His monument, magnificently carved in alabaster and adorned with cherubs and angels, was placed in the chancel by his parents, Sir Patrick and Lady Isabella Curwen of Workington, Cumberland.*

extraordinary range of monuments dating from the 1430s onwards.

Despite Amersham's snug and serene appearance, there was always a streak of nonconformity in it. William Penn, the Quaker founder of Pennsylvania, courted his sweetheart, Guilema Springett, whom he later married, in the porch of Bury Farm in Amersham on the Hill, though other old farms in the vicinity, since demolished, have also been credited as being the site of this tender scene. Not far off is the Martyrs' Memorial, a monument to seven Lollards, followers of John Wycliff, burned to death on the spot in the 16th century; for many years it was lost in the undergrowth, but it was cleared and restored in the 1950s.

AMPTHILL *Bedfordshire*

Bedfordshire is a comfortable county, and Ampthill is a comfortable town. It is built on the least-complex of plans, simply four cross-ways, with a little web of indeterminate streets that go nowhere except into each other, off Dunstable Street to the south. The general impression is Georgian, though there is a good deal of later building, and not very much earlier; which is strange, for Ampthill has been a market town since at least 1219. The four main roads – Woburn Street, Bedford Street and Church Street, as well as Dunstable Street – meet at Moot Hall, a brick building of 1852 that bears a cupola-topped tower that looks a couple of sizes too big for it. This is because it once belonged to an earlier Moot Hall on the same site, and before that to nearby Park House, until it was presented to the town by the Earl of Upper Ossory in 1784. The obelisk covering the town pump near by was also his gift, as were the group of thatched and timbered estate cottages in Woburn Street.

The White Hart at the corner, which has an 18th-century front veiling a much older building, is a good introduction to Dunstable Street, which has some very attractive 18th and early 19th-century houses, and even a gazebo of 1740, though they are somewhat at odds with a large supermarket. Beyond is The Cedars, now a council home but formerly a workhouse built in 1835.

The most attractive street, and one that is entirely so throughout its length, is Church Street. Most of it is Georgian, including the very grand Avenue House built for a local brewer, but next door is a much older building that was once the home of Edmund Wingate, a Member of Parliament for the town who taught English to Henrietta Maria, Charles I's queen. Even more ancient are the Feoffee Almshouses by the church, which take their name from the Town Feoffees or trustees who have managed the charities that endow them since the 15th century.

St Andrew's Church was massively built of ironstone in the 14th and 15th centuries, and contains some good brasses, including an endearing one to a local 'wolman' (wool merchant), William Hicchecok, who died in 1450, and his wife. But the monument that catches the eye is the one that bears the flags of the United Kingdom and the United States. They mark

the tomb of Colonel Richard Nichols, who received the surrender of Niew Amsterdam from the Dutch in 1664, and renamed it New York in honour of Charles II's brother, James, Duke of York. He remained as governor of the new colony for three years, then returned to his native Ampthill before being summoned to fight the Dutch again in 1672. He was mortally wounded at the Battle of Sole Bay, off Southwold in Suffolk; unusually, the cannon ball that killed him is built into the monument.

The most poignant associations in Ampthill are with Catherine of Aragon, Henry VIII's rejected queen. It was in Ampthill Castle that she awaited the terms of her divorce from Henry VIII, and when the document arrived she was so incensed to read that she was now called Princess Dowager, she at once 'with penne and ynke strake out' the offensive title. The castle has long vanished, though its grounds are now a public park, where a cross marking its site was set up at the instigation of Horace Walpole, the 18th-century man of letters, who also composed the verse at its base:

> *In days of old, here Ampthill's towers were seen*
> *The mournful refuge of an injur'd Queen*
> *Here flow'd her pure but unavailing tears*
> *Here blinded Zeal sustained her sinking years.*

The town is fortunate in possessing its park, which was landscaped by Capability Brown at Lord Ossory's behest. It was Brown who created the artificial lake – The Reservoir, or 'The Rezzy', to Ampthillians – and planted the trees that are now, 200 years on, at their glorious maturity.

APPLEBY *Cumbria*

The old town, stone town, of Appleby is wrapped about by a loop of the River Eden whose defensive possibilities so appealed to the Normans that they built a castle across the mouth of the loop and let the streets grow up about it. Not that the defences, natural and Norman, did much good, for the town was raided three times by the Scots in the 14th century.

But long before the Scots and Normans, the Norsemen came to Appleby, and farmed in what is now the part of the town across the river that is called Bongate, the district of the bondsmen. Little evidence remains of their passing, save perhaps an ancient gravestone built into the lintel of St Michael's Church, some street names, such as Shaw's Wiend, Doomgate and Scattergate, and the name of the town itself, which may or may not mean 'the place of the apple tree'.

The river has made what is in effect two towns, joined by a Victorian bridge. A good deal of the building in Bongate is Victorian, but it also contains the 200-year-old Shire Hall with its tiny courtroom, both relics of the days when Appleby was the county town of vanished Westmorland. Near by, conveniently, is the door to the 17th-century House of Correction, and close to that the pretty little church of St Michael, part of which dates from the early 1200s. It contains the worn effigy of Lady Elizabeth Clifford, who in 1394 was appointed Sheriffess of Westmorland.

Across the bridge and into the main part of the town is the Market Place and, beyond, the Boroughgate which bisects Appleby, wide and straight as a Norman sword. It is a delightful thoroughfare, closed at one end by St Lawrence's Church, and at the other by the bastion of the castle keep, thrusting above an avenue of lime trees. It is flanked by shops with bright awnings, and by good-looking buildings of all periods, Jacobean, Georgian and Victorian. On an island in the middle is the black-and-white Moot Hall; built in 1596.

Before looking more closely at the street, it is necessary to know something of the life and works of Lady Anne Clifford, Dowager Countess of Dorset, Pembroke and Montgomery, High Sheriffess of Westmorland, who died in 1675 aged 86. The owner of vast estates, she lived like a queen and built like a pharaoh; even to this generation, we owe her a debt of gratitude for her restoration work on castles and churches throughout the north of England. But for Appleby, she seems to have had a particular affection. Not only did she rebuild the castle and restore the parish churches of St Michael and St Lawrence – in which she is buried – but she built and endowed the almshouses of St Anne's Hospital off the Boroughgate as well. To this day they fulfil their original function of providing a home for poor widows.

Not too surprisingly, Lady Anne was a fervent Royalist who defied Cromwell and, due to her example, when the Commonwealth's Charter was presented to the town, no one could be found who would read it. Until, that is, the commissioners unearthed 'an unclean bird, hatched in Kirkby Lonsdale, the nest of all traitors, who proclaimed it aloud'. She lived to see the Restoration of Charles II when she built two great platforms, draped with cloth of gold, at either end of the Boroughgate, and on them, the Countess 'seeming young again', the Mayor and Corporation, and the local gentry, all upon their knees, proclaimed King

Charles and drank his health. Where she built her platforms, the High Cross and Low Cross now stand. The High Cross bears the motto: Retain your Loyalty, Preserve your Rights.

Lady Anne lies beneath a black marble altar tomb in St Lawrence's Church, beside the much grander monument to her mother, Margaret, Countess of Cumberland. But Lady Anne's true memorial is the church itself, which she so beautifully restored in 1655. Some rebuilding of the 14th-century structure had already been carried out after the Scots fired it in 1388, but much of the interior is her work. It contains what is perhaps the oldest working organ in Britain, a Bible of 1617 and a 17th-century copy of *Foxe's Book of Martyrs*. Among the monuments is one to Richard Yates, headmaster of Appleby Grammar School from 1723 to 1781. During his half-century reign he taught the father and half-brothers of George Washington, first President of the United States. Washington himself would have attended the school, except that his recently widowed mother was reluctant to let him leave Virginia.

For most of the year, Appleby is a quiet enough place, until the first week in June when there converges upon it, from all quarters of Britain, a mighty cavalcade of horses, dealers, trailers trimmed with glittering chrome and traditional bright-painted caravans. For 300 years Appleby Fair has been the great occasion in the gipsy calendar, and anyone who thinks that Romany folk are now interested only in second-hand cars, should attend too. Horse coping is alive and well, a noisy and expert business in which bargains are clinched by the slap of the seller's palm against that of the buyer; a bill of sale is unnecessary. Then the children of the new owners leap on the horses and ride them in riotous bareback charge to the river and plunge in, the hooves kicking up a bright rainbow of spray.

FAIR DEAL *At Appleby Fair, gipsies and horse traders gather in an atmosphere of robust hard bargaining that has changed little since the fair was given its charter by James II in 1685. Hundreds of caravans make their way to Fair Hill for the event, many being the traditional gipsy vans, or* vardos, *such as the bow-topped wagon with its richly carved and painted bodywork. They, as well as horses, often change hands during the week of the fair.*

ARUNDEL *West Sussex*

Supposing the visitor had missed it, the crowding together of antique shops, tea shops, chintz-furnished restaurants, pubs, and a stately coaching inn bearing a vast coat of arms would tell him that he was in the neighbourhood of some major piece of English military architecture, and one of venerable and distinguished history at that. So it is in Arundel, where the inn bears the arms of the Duke of Norfolk, Hereditary Marshal of England and its premier Duke and Earl. The fairy-tale castle, whose battlements, towers and turrets peep over every rooftop in the town, is his principal address.

Nowhere could be more English than Arundel, for it was created out of English wars, English trade and English compromise. Also, it is not quite what it seems, and that is fairly English too. To begin with the castle, and it is difficult to begin anywhere else, it is true that the first fortification on the site was built a year after the Norman Conquest and was added to throughout the Middle Ages by the Fitzalan Earls of Arundel. But it was smashed into ruin by Parliamentarian guns in 1643, and most of what can be seen now – apart from the original, massive gatehouse – is 18th and 19th-century restoration.

Across the way and half buried in a cascade of laburnum is St Nicholas's Church, Arundel's most civilised compromise, for it is both Roman Catholic and Church of England, which was built of squared split flints and sandstone in 1380. In its early days, canons of the nearby priory used the chancel as a chapel which was separated from the rest of the church by an iron grille running from floor to ceiling. At the Reformation, the priory was suppressed, and the chancel was sold to the Earl of Arundel – while the rest of the church continued to serve the parish under the new faith. The grille still stands and is backed by a glass screen through which may be seen the splendid tombs of the Earls of Arundel and the Dukes of Norfolk and their families.

The Roman Catholic cathedral, standing on its hill like some Notre Dame or Chartres in miniature, has been a cathedral – the Cathedral of Our Lady and St Philip Howard – only since 1965, when the Roman Catholic diocese of Arundel and Brighton was created; before that, it was the Church of St Philip Neri. It was built by J. A. Hansom, the inventor of the hansom cab, and largely at the expense of the 15th Duke of Norfolk, in 1868–73. But with its Gothic pinnacles and great rose window, it could easily be 400 years older. Saint Philip Howard was sentenced to death in Elizabeth I's reign for his adherence to the Roman faith. Since he was the 13th Earl of Arundel, he was buried in the Fitzalan Chapel in St Nicholas's Church. But his bones were moved to the cathedral in 1971.

From castle, church and cathedral the streets fall steeply away, mostly lined by 18th and 19th-century buildings superimposed upon a medieval plan, and sometimes upon medieval buildings; for the town, too, suffered under the Parliamentarian bombardment. High Street – literally – climbs up to the

battlemented walls of the castle, over which stately chestnuts lean. The buildings are mostly rose-red brick, enclosing about a dozen antique shops, tea-rooms and pubs, including the flat-fronted, vast-windowed Norfolk Arms; this was an officers' mess during the Napoleonic Wars, and it still carries something of that air. Maltravers Street, Tarrant Street and the rest look pleasantly Victorian or Georgian, but not infrequently this aspect is a later shell fronting Tudor buildings. At the bottom of the town the swift, muddy River Arun swirls beneath a modern bridge. Close by are the ruins of Maison Dieu, almshouses built by an Earl of Arundel in 1396.

At several points in the town, visitors will discover memorial plaques to Bernard, 16th Duke of Norfolk, who died in 1975. In his capacity of Hereditary Earl Marshal, he was responsible for stage-managing all great state occasions, including the coronations of King George VI and the present Queen, and the funerals of George V and VI, and of Sir Winston Churchill. He was also a keen cricketer, and the lovely cricket ground in the castle park has been maintained in his name. A pleasant memorial.

NOBLE CREST *Arundel Castle sits like a ducal crown on a beech-clad crest of the Sussex Downs, dominating the Arun Valley that it was built to guard 800 years ago. Below, Arundel's wood-carved town crest – its motto means 'Steadfast in Ancient Virtue' – stands on the Town Quay.*

ASHBOURNE *Derbyshire*

It was not by chance that some of the country's greatest houses – Chatsworth, Haddon Hall, Kedleston Hall, Bolsover Castle, Hardwick Hall and Melbourne Hall among them – were built in this area. Good brick-making clay available to the south and mellow stone to the north influenced their siting, and the proximity of some of the loveliest of English landscapes, Dovedale and the Manifold Valley, clinched the matter. In the midst of it all is Ashbourne, appropriately a place of both brick and stone, with wide streets and high, broad cobbled pavements.

Ashbourne's business is time. For hundreds of years it was famous for its clocks, and to some extent still is, but nowadays its chief preoccupation seems to be in preserving the best of the things its many centuries have given to it, whether it be an ancient game of football, memories of great men and women, or entire, handsome thoroughfares.

The finest of these is Church Street, given splendid emphasis at its end by the slender 212 ft spire of the parish church, dedicated to St Oswald, King of Northumbria, in 1241. The wrought-iron gates, with their spirited design of skulls and flames, date from about 1700, while beyond, in the churchyard, there is a patch of ground where the many townspeople who died of the plague at the end of the 16th century are buried.

The interior is every bit as grand as the spire promises. There is a great deal of stained glass. Some of it, like the font, medieval, but most of it is more recent. The monuments are so crowded as to give the impression that there can be scarcely an inch of resting space beneath. There are knights and ladies, cherubs and children, weeping angels, urns, tomb chests and lengthy epitaphs galore.

Almost opposite the church gates is a stone-gabled building with low, mullioned windows. This is the Old Grammar School, founded under a charter of Elizabeth I in 1585. The school itself has moved to more modern premises, but the old building is still used as a boarding house for pupils. So is the 17th-century house opposite, called The Mansion, where Boswell and Dr Johnson used to stay with their friend, Dr John Taylor. Close by are two groups of 17th-century almshouses, Pegg's and Owlfield's, whose mellow stone sets the keynote of Church Street as it wanders on to become St John's Street and then Cokayne Avenue. In St John's Street there is a handsome Georgian pub whose sign, spanning the road, says Green Man on one side and Black's Head on the other, the result of a long-ago take-over. Beyond, in the Memorial Gardens, there is a monument to Mrs Catherine Booth, who was born in the town and with her husband, General Booth, founded the Salvation Army.

A very different soldier is remembered at Ashbourne Hall opposite, for it was there that Prince Charles Edward, the Young Pretender, stayed one night during his advance down England in 1745. He proclaimed his father King James III of Great Britain in the town before marching on to Derby.

Ashbourne Hall is now the Public Library, a role that is more comfortably suited to two of the town's other associated figures. George Eliot, the 19th-century novelist, lived some of her wandering life at Ashley, near the Vicarage, and Izaak Walton set part of *The Compleat Angler* at the Talbot Inn, whose site has long been occupied by the Town Hall. He also loved to fish the rivers of the district.

All such associations, however, are as of yesterday when compared with the antecedents of Ashbourne's Shrovetide football game. As with a few similar games held in other parts of the country, it may well be descended from some pre-Christian rite that celebrated the coming of spring. Its survival is due to the unrivalled opportunities presented to let off steam. Membership of the two teams, the Up'ards and the Down'ards, is determined by whether one lives above or below the Henmore Brook, and numbers are unlimited. Rules are equally vague, and the match is played, or fought, between goals 3 miles apart on the afternoons and evenings of both Shrove Tuesday and Ash Wednesday.

GOLDEN HOST *Daffodils bloom in the churchyard of St Oswald's Church, Ashbourne, where plague victims were buried in the 16th century. That part of the churchyard was never used for burials again, but when the daffodils were planted in the early 1900s many people feared that the disturbed ground would release the deadly infection. But the plague remained buried and the daffodils continue to bloom.*

ASHBURTON Devon

Lapped about by the eternal wilderness of Dartmoor, Ashburton has developed a taste for things permanent. It grew up long ago, 'time out of mind' as the old phrase goes, upon the Dartmoor staples of tin and wool. As far back as 1285 it was of sufficient importance to be appointed a Stannary town under a charter of Edward I – that is, it was made the official place for assessing the quantity and quality of all tin mined in the area. However, the award of the charter was but yesterday, when compared with its system of municipal government. This, under the Lord of the Manor, consists of a Portreeve, a Bailiff, a Court Leet and a Court Baron. The Court Leet elects a chairman, or Portreeve, annually – so far there have been 1,160-odd of them. The Court Baron appoints officials such as the Viewers of the Market and of the Watercourses, and the Scavengers and Pig Drovers, whose responsibility it was to impound straying swine. Sadly, these fascinating occupations have now largely fallen into abeyance and, in fact, many more of the powers of the Portreeve and the Courts were stripped from them by an Act of 1894. Nevertheless, they adhered firmly to their right of Ale-tasting, which they exercise in all licensed premises during carnival week.

Ashburton is a place of higgledy-piggledy roofs, slate-hung fronts and buildings of all ages. A walk about the town should begin at King's Bridge, which crosses the little River Ashburn leaving room for a water-sprite named Cutty Dyer to shelter beneath the left-hand arch; in a less sophisticated age she was a useful threat to hang over the heads of recalcitrant children. To the left is North Street with the United Reform Church which, dating from 1665, is one of the oldest Nonconformist establishments in the country. Also in North Street is an ironmonger's shop that was once the Mermaid Inn where Sir Thomas Fairfax, the

BARONIAL GIFT The 19th Baron Clinton, Ashburton's Lord of the Manor, built the Town Hall in 1850 and showed good taste in both style and choice of material. The Italianate building combines pale limestone with the dark grey granite from the nearby Haytor quarry on Dartmoor, and is fronted by massive granite paving slabs.

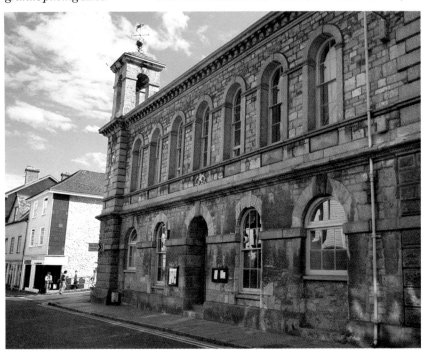

Parliamentarian general, stayed in 1646. Also in the 17th century, the International Stores had a giddier existence as a gaming house; card patterns are still picked out in slate on its white front. East Street has the early 18th-century Golden Lion Hotel, the Conduit, which is a public water supply provided by a local benefactor in 1797, and a number of fine two and three-hundred-year-old buildings, mostly wearing frontages of more recent date.

In St Lawrence's Lane there is a 14th-century tower which is all that remains of St Lawrence's Chapel where Ashburton Grammar School was founded as a Chantry in 1314; the Tower Room is still preserved and is said to be the oldest schoolroom in England.

There are some dignified houses in West Street to give suitable support to the opulent wrought-iron gates of St Andrew's Church, beyond which is the 15th-century building itself with its slim spire soaring 92 ft into the air above the town. Among its treasures is an oak chest, made for the church in 1483 and still locked with its original keys, and the magnificent carved oak reredos, placed in the church in 1928.

One of the saints represented in the reredos is St Gudula, a Belgian saint who has a holy well just outside the town, marked by a Saxon cross. Its waters are said to be efficacious in treating eye complaints.

AXMINSTER Devon

The name is a household word, but the town that produced and still produces the famous Axminster carpets remains much more a market place than a manufacturing centre. It is not surprising, since in Axminster's long history the founding of the carpet works in 1755 was but yesterday, and its importance as a market had been established long before by its siting in the Axe Valley, at the junction of the two ancient roads, Icknield Street and the Foss Way.

The course of the main east-west road through the town has forced the principal streets into a slow, graceful curve of mostly Georgian and early Victorian houses and shops. These periods have formed Axminster's present character and have produced some fine buildings, such as the George Hotel with its Adam assembly room and musicians' gallery, and Oak House, which used to be an Academy for Young Gentlemen, and is now council offices. In Chard Street there are some Regency shop fronts and a prim Congregational chapel of the mid-18th century. Altogether, it is a busy and bustling little town, especially on Thursdays when its three markets – including one for cattle – are in full swing, and the pubs are open all day long.

The hub is Trinity Square, where St Mary's Church stands. The church belongs to all periods, with the 13th century predominating, though it has a fine Norman doorway and a 16th-century porch; some of the furnishings are Jacobean. The church was quite badly damaged during the Civil War after the Royalists had fortified the building, which was then besieged by the Roundheads. St Mary's also has a fine peal of bells, some of which date from the reign of Edward VI, though they have been re-cast since. In the early days of the Axminster factory, they would ring out whenever a carpet was completed, and everyone within earshot would hasten in to celebrate the joyous occasion.

The old factory still stands close by the church, looking like a cross between an elderly prison and a satanic mill. It was founded by Thomas Whitty, a local weaver who, having seen a large Turkey carpet in London's Cheapside, decided to make them himself. He erected his first huge, upright loom in 1755, and began making his first carpet, using a process called hand-knotting – best carried out, it was said, by 'the pliant fingers of little children'. His first team consisted of his own five daughters, supervised by his sister Elizabeth. Some of the original carpets survive including one made for the Throne Room in the Prince Regent's Carlton House and now in the Victoria and Albert Museum, London. Despite the demand, however, the firm was eventually defeated by machine-made carpets and was declared bankrupt in 1835. But this was not the end of carpet manufacture in Axminster, for in 1937 a new factory was opened there and continues to make carpets to the present day.

BAKEWELL *Derbyshire*

It must be very pleasant to live in a town like this – on Fly Hill perhaps – in a pinky-brown stone house with a tight slate roof. Never a leak or a draught, no problems about the house growing old on you, or visitors raising an eyebrow at aggressive newness. Given a decade of weathering, a recent building constructed in the local square-cut style will look just like its ancient neighbours. While the only sign of old age, after a couple of centuries or so, is a little wearing on the cornerstones and on the mullions of the windows. Even the garden walls would be decorative, with stonecrop and thrift growing in the cracks, while on summer mornings you could look around and beyond the dark spire of All Saints Church to the hills of the Peak District National Park, one of the loveliest sights in the Midlands.

Bakewell enters written history in 924 when King Edward the Elder went 'into Peakland to Badecanweillon and commanded a castle to be built nigh thereunto and garrisoned'. The name means 'Badeca's Well' or 'Spring', whoever Badeca may have been, and the mound on which the castle stood can still be seen on Castle Hill. A sizeable Saxon community in the vicinity at that time seems to have been centred upon the hill above the church. There is still some Saxon work to be seen in the fabric of All Saints, and in the porch there are some ancient gravestones and stone coffins that were discovered in the walls during 19th-century improvements. The gravestones, some Saxon and some early Norman, are in a remarkable state of preservation, and many are inscribed with the craft marks of the people once buried beneath them – a sword for a soldier, shears for a shepherd and so on. In those days the corpse was laid in the stone coffin,

ANTIQUE TOWN HALL *Bakewell's Old Town Hall dates from the 17th century and is now an antiques shop, as is the bow-windowed building in the foreground.*

DERBYSHIRE CUSTOM *Well-dressing is an ancient tradition in Peak District towns and villages, going back to the pagan worship of water-nymphs who had to be placated so that the local water supply would continue. The wells are decorated with pictures made from flowers, wild fruits and pebbles, and Bakewell's well-dressers rise to the occasion with considerable artistic flair, as did the local Brownies in 1982 with their butterfly picture on Gardens Well.*

and was then covered by the monumental slab which, economically, also formed part of the flooring of the church. In the churchyard there is the carved stump of a Saxon cross; legend has it that Prince Arthur, the eldest son of Henry VII, fell asleep while leaning against it and dreamed that he would marry a princess from over the sea, but she would shortly afterwards be a widow. The vision proved only too prophetic, for he married Catherine of Aragon and died four months later; his widow then married his brother, the future Henry VIII.

The church makes an excellent introduction to Bakewell, partly since from beside it the town and most of the surrounding countryside is spread out, and partly because so much of the town's story is summed up in and about it. All the great local families are represented among the monuments, of which the most charming is the one to Sir Godfrey Foljambe, who died about 1385, and his second wife, Avena. No more than 12 in. high and carved in alabaster, it is considered unique for its period.

The Vernon chapel contains the battered effigy of Sir Thomas de Wendesley – he was married to a Vernon – who was killed fighting for the Lancastrians at the Battle of Shrewsbury in 1403. The large tomb is that of Sir George Vernon, who died in 1567 and was known as 'The King of the Peak' from his extravagant and overbearing life-style. His daughter, Dorothy, married Sir John Manners and had a son, Sir George Manners, whose wife founded the Lady Manners School in the town. Their descendants became Dukes of Rutland. The exquisitely carved altar-piece looks medieval, but was in fact carved in Battersea about 1880. The misericords, or choir seats, in the chancel are supported by 14th-century angels, demons and fabulous beasts, but among them is a small plaque that was probably carved by a workman during the restorations of the 1880s. It shows three rotten teeth and a cow, and is a reference to the Chartist notion of the period that poor urban families might be given a new and independent way of life by the grant of 3 acres (achers) and a cow. The visual pun is excruciating, but it is also endearing.

Behind and above the church is The Old House, now a museum. As it stands, it is a bailiff's house of 1534, but it has been through many vicissitudes since. For more than 200 years it was the home of the Gell family, one of whom was a colonel in the Parliamentarian army. In 1795 it was sold to Richard Arkwright, who had recently built one of the world's first factories at Lumford Mill, along the Buxton Road. Arkwright's business was cotton spinning, using water-power, and he employed more than 350 people. Some of these he accommodated in the cottages he built in Arkwright Square, and others in the Old House, which he divided into six tenements. After that, the house gradually went down in the world, until in 1954 it was condemned as unfit for human habitation. The local Historical Society came to the rescue and the long work of restoration was begun. All kinds of fascinating things came to light; original fireplaces and windows, a household inventory of 1594, and even a 16th-century privy, which has a 9 ft drop beneath it into a hollow wall of the cellar below, where there is a movable stone to facilitate cleaning.

In King Street, which runs down the hill from the church, is the Old Town Hall dating from 1602. It was the Courthouse until the Napoleonic Wars, when local men faced with conscription into the Militia stormed it in the course of a riot, and Sessions were never held there again. Down the years it has been a school, a working-men's club, and is now an antiques shop. Behind it there is a small group of tree-shaded almshouses donated by the Manners family in 1709 as

A FAMOUS PUDDING

It was in 1859, or thereabouts, that Bakewell added pudding to its name, and added an essential recipe to every cookery book from Mrs Beaton onwards. The mistake made by the cook at the Rutland Arms while trying to make a strawberry tart went unnoticed by her employer, but the result was declared a 'delicious pudding' by the diners. The mistress of the inn, Mrs Greaves, was quick to cash in on her cook's mistake and instructed her to 'continue to make them in that way'. The recipe has remained unchanged to this day, though the name 'Bakewell Tart' persists.

Bakewell tarts

accommodation for six elderly, single men.

King Street opens out into Rutland Square where there are rectangular stone banks like minor palaces and the Rutland Arms Hotel which is like a major one, filling most of one end of the square. Most of the other buildings are impressive too, and all date from the beginning of the 19th century when the Duke of Rutland, inspired by the presence of chalybeate springs, had visions of turning Bakewell into a spa that would rival the one created by the Duke of Devonshire at Buxton. There was already a Bath House, built by an ancestor in 1697 in Bath Street, and for a time the signs were propitious. But the spa never really developed, and though the spring still pumps out its healing waters at a steady 59°F all the year round, the Bath House itself has for many years been the home of the local branch of the British Legion.

Nevertheless, out of the waters there emerged two

glowing moments of immortality. Jane Austen stayed in the Rutland Arms when she was writing *Pride and Prejudice* in 1811. She calls Bakewell 'Lambton' in the novel, and sets one or two episodes in the hotel; the settings are still quite recognisable. The other brush with divinity was in 1859, when the cook in the hotel misunderstood her instructions and poured an egg mixture on top of the jam in a tart she was making, instead of the other way round. The result was Bakewell Pudding (*not* tart) which is still made in the town and can be purchased at the pudding shop in the square.

Bakewell is the heart of the Peak District National Park, and the elderly Market Hall is its tourist and information centre. Built in the 17th century, the open arches in the ground floor where the market was held have long been filled in, and since those days the building has been town hall, courtroom, wash house,

rates office and library. Now its walls are covered with pictures of the wondrous country that can be seen by the trails through the high peaks and by posters bearing the wise exhortation: 'Take nothing but photographs, Leave nothing but footprints.'

From there, Bridge Street leads down to the River Wye, and to the 13th-century bridge with its pointed arches and sharp cutwaters. It was widened a bit in the 19th century, and with this addition it copes just as well with modern traffic as it did with that of the Middle Ages. Farther along the river is Holme Bridge, built in 1664 with a parapet deliberately low so as not to interfere with the loads of packhorses; near by is the attractive Holme Hall, some 40 years older than the bridge. Pause anywhere and drink in the peace of the worn stone houses, of the flowers piled along the banks, and of the green islets breaking the swift, clear stream below the high rim of the hills.

TRADE ROUTE *Bakewell's Holme Bridge over the River Wye was part of a busy thoroughfare when packhorses were used for transporting goods. An important merchandise was Derbyshire Chert, a stone cut from local quarries and taken to Stoke-on-Trent where Josiah Wedgwood used it to improve the glaze on his pottery.*

STYLE AND GRACE *St Mary's Church makes a perfect introduction to Banff's High Street, its elegant tower and graceful steeple giving a foretaste of the town's Georgian character. Overlooked by it, but by no means overshadowed, is Collie Lodge, a delightful 19th-century example of the Greek Doric style whose columned portico makes a rather grand entrance to the Tourist Information Office.*

BANFF *Grampian*

It has that look, not uncommon in the coastal towns of north-east Scotland, which seems to indicate that the inhabitants get up early each morning, before the tourists are about, and scrub the whole place, streets, buildings and all. But probably this bright, sparkling appearance is really due to good lines and good stone, and to the clean, salt-laden wind that blows endlessly, sprightly in summer and savagely in winter, from the North Sea.

Banff, at the mouth of the River Deveron, was a busy port in the 12th century, and as a mark of its steadily increasing prosperity was created a Royal Burgh by Robert II in 1372. In the religious wars of the 17th century, Banff was harried and pillaged by Royalists and Covenanters in turn, and in the aftermath of the Jacobite Rising of 1745 it had the misfortune to be garrisoned by the Duke of Cumberland's dragoons.

Yet it was at about this time, the middle and late 18th century, that Banff was coming to the zenith of its prosperity. Trade with the Continent had never been better, the fisheries flourished, Smeaton, the designer of the Eddystone Lighthouse, threw his splendid seven-arched bridge over the River Deveron, and Lord Braco awarded the supreme accolade by building his lovely Duff House at the town's edge. Designed in Georgian baroque style by William Adam, it belongs to the town now, and both it and its park are open to the public.

Encouraged by Lord Braco's example, rich merchants and minor local gentry began to build town houses, and it is these buildings, big, clean-lined and plain, but by no means dour, that give Banff much of its present character.

The raised, paved area called Plainstones is the heart of the town. Here stands the Town House with its soaring spire built by Adam in the 1760s, and the ancient Mercat Cross. Plainstones is also the site of the town gallows whereon the notorious outlaw James MacPherson was hanged in 1700. Robbery and murder apart, James's chief passion was his fiddle, on which, according to an old ballad, 'he played a tune and danced it roon, beneath the gallows tree'.

Low Street, despite the name, is the high street of Banff, in which the 18th-century theme continues with some fine buildings such as Carmelite House, which stands on the site of a Carmelite monastery, the Dunvegan Hotel with its central Venetian window, and No. 15, built by a Mr Robinson in 1745. This unfortunate man was run through by a drunken officer who had been pursuing one of Mr Robinson's maids; the killer was never apprehended.

Scotstown of Banff begins at the far end of Castle Street. Until the 1750s this was a separate village, the place where the fisherfolk lived. The architecture there is very different; terraced, single-storeyed cottages, with deep net-lofts beneath their roofs. The harbour, close by, is one of those lovely Scottish harbours, composed of great square blocks of dark stone, with the whole town, seemingly, piled above the quayside. At one time, Banff harbour was crowded

with coasters and small merchantmen, and the town's own fleet of drifters. But alas, no longer. At the beginning of this century, the River Deveron changed its course and the harbour gradually silted up. It was very nearly the end of 800 years of history, but in 1974 sufficient dredging was carried out to permit the passage of small craft. Now the bright sails and gleaming hulls of dinghies and yachts preserve at least an illusion of busyness in the old harbour.

BARNARD CASTLE *Durham*

Almost too good to be true, the castle ruins brood most satisfyingly from their crags over the town, the bridge and the lovely Tees. The town takes its name from the castle, and the castle acquired its name from Barnard, or Bernard, Baliol, the tough soldier who built it at the beginning of the 12th century. That Barnard was more than a mere warrior is apparent from the splendid siting of the great castle on its precipitous rocks above the river, sealing and com-

manding one of the major routes between Durham and Yorkshire. And since castles are expensive things to run, he encouraged local people to settle about his gates and to start a market, offering them protection in exchange for service, rents and market dues.

For almost 200 years the castle was held by Barnard's descendants, one of whom, John Baliol, founded Balliol College at Oxford. Later, the castle came into the possession of the Beauchamp and Neville Earls of Warwick, and then into that of Richard III. Whatever the truth of the stories about the little princes in the Tower of London, Richard seems to have been popular with the townsfolk, and he did a considerable amount of building in the castle; his boar emblem can still be seen, carved on the walls. After Richard's death on Bosworth Field in 1485 the castle was seized by Henry VII, and thereafter remained Crown property.

In all its long years, the castle was besieged only once, during the Northern Rising of 1569 when the Earls of Northumberland and Westmorland rebelled on behalf of Mary, Queen of Scots. Elizabeth I's Steward, Sir George Bowes, held out for 11 days and was then forced to surrender because, according to one account, some townsmen had poisoned the water supply. However, the 11 days delay granted time for the Earls of Warwick and Surrey to march north and crush the rebellion. After this, the castle fell gently into decay until, in 1630, it was sold to Sir Henry Vane, who stripped the roof, timbers, and anything else that was movable and carted them off to his other seat at Raby Castle.

The life of the town had, of course, long diverged from that of the castle. For centuries it had a thriving woollen industry, and its site ensured its success as a market town. Its centre is the Market Cross, an octagonal building erected in 1747 and intended to serve as a town hall, lock-up and covered market. It was not thought much of architecturally at the time, but it has grown on people since, and there was considerable outcry when its demolition was suggested a few years ago. The two holes in the weather-

ROMANTIC RUIN *Few castles, even those that have better withstood the ravages of time, are as fair or as romantically set as Barnard Castle. Its crumbling walls seem a natural part of the limestone crag on which they stand, high above the stone banks of the Tees, and the graceful bridge seems to spring from the solid rock.*

CENTRE POINT *The Market Cross in Barnard Castle's town centre has also served as town hall, lock-up and court. It now serves as a roundabout at a busy road junction.*

BLAGRAVES HOUSE *Oliver Cromwell is said to have stayed here in 1648, when the house was an inn. Dating from pre-Tudor times the house has had one or two additions, notably the magnificent 17th-century bay front extending to four storeys. The doorway and steps date from the 18th century, the original door being still at street level.*

vane are bullet holes – put there in 1804 by a militiaman and a gamekeeper to settle which of them was the better marksman. Considering that they were firing from outside the Turk's Head, more than 100 yds away, and considering too the weapons of the time, they must both have been excellent shots.

The steep street that runs down from the Market Place to the river is The Bank, and it contains several fine buildings with heavy, stone-flagged roofs, and the magnificent Blagraves House. The Tudor shell, with its mullioned, diamond-paned windows and figures of musicians fixed to the wall, masks a medieval core. A legend of doubtful authenticity says that the house was given by Richard III to one Miles Forest for his part in the murder of the little princes in the Tower; he was later executed on Henry VII's orders. Blagraves, too, since it was once an inn, may well be the place where Cromwell stayed when he visited the town in 1648. A contemporary diarist recorded how he was greeted by the townspeople who 'conducted him to his lodgings and presented him with burnt (mulled) wine and shortcake'. Not everyone felt the same way, however, for there is a record of Francis Walker, Gent., of Barnard Castle, being put on trial for saying: 'The Parliament are rogues, rebels and traitors; God confound them and the Devil confound them.'

A little further down and The Bank becomes Thorngate, which in the 18th century was Barnard Castle's most desirable address, as Thorngate House, a most elegant Georgian edifice, bears witness. It must have lowered the tone a little when the mills were built in the street a few years later, but perhaps the inhabitants could be philosophical as they reflected upon the prosperity that stockings, cloth and carpets brought to the town. Almost at the bottom of Thorngate are a number of old weavers' cottages, distinguished by their long windows, built to give the workers the maximum amount of light.

Past the cottages there is a footbridge over the river and, beyond, a view north to the tremendous bulk of the castle towering 80 ft above the Tees. On the opposite bank there is another structure almost as imposing but not perhaps so inspiring. This is the Ullathorne Mill, which, between 1760 and its closure in 1932, was the largest manufactory of shoe thread in the country. The Victorian Society was of the opinion that there are 'few more dramatic combinations in Britain' than the high-chimneyed mill and the castle. Dramatic does not necessarily mean attractive, of course.

Between the two is the bridge which until fairly recently bore the date 1569, but this is worn away now. Almost certainly 1569 was the date of rebuilding after damage caused during the siege, rather than the first building, which is thought to have been in the 13th century. At one time a Bible clerk named Cuthbert Hilton used to make a living by conducting illicit marriage ceremonies in the middle of the bridge. Apparently he used to bid the betrothed couple to jump over a broomstick and then recite:

*My blessing on your pates and your groats
  in my purse
You are never the better and I am never the worse.*

Over the bridge and past the castle is Galgate, which follows the line of the Roman road from Binchester to Bowes. The name of the street used to be Gallowgate, for it was there, until the reign of Henry VIII when capital trials were moved to Durham, that the condemned were executed. They were not always hanged, it would seem, for in the last century a stone platform with steps leading up to it was excavated which, it was surmised, was the base for a 'machine for the decapitation of felons'.

From Galgate, the scene opens out to the busy Horse Market – busy with shoppers nowadays, rather than with horses – and thence to Market Place. There are some good, old pubs hereabouts, such as The Three Horseshoes, the Golden Lion of 1770, and the King's Head, where Charles Dickens stayed in 1838 while investigating the north country schools he caricatured as 'Dotheboys Hall' in *Nicholas Nickleby*. The nearby parish church of St Mary is mostly Norman, though the west tower is late 19th century. There are some fine monuments, and the portrait heads on the 15th-century chancel pillars are said to be those of Edward IV and Richard III. Richard's boar crest appears again in the exterior moulding of the east window of the south transept. In the churchyard a cross stands as the memorial to 143 people of Barnard Castle who died of cholera in 1849. The cause was appalling sanitation and polluted water.

The most astonishing building in Barnard Castle, the castle not excepted, is the Bowes Museum. It has been described as 'gloriously inappropriate' and the 'Taj Mahal of the North-East', though the great stone confection, with its towers and rows of windows, is much more reminiscent of Versailles. It was designed in 1869 by Jules Pellechet for John Bowes, the son of the mine-owning 10th Earl of Strathmore, and his French actress wife, Josephine. It was intended as a museum from the start, a receptacle for their fabulous collections of beautiful objects, but by the time it was opened in 1892 the couple were dead. The museum now belongs to Durham County Council, and in its 30 galleries may be seen a wonderful array of furniture, ceramics, textiles, antiquities and paintings including works by El Greco, Goya, Tiepolo, Boucher and Courbet. There is a collection of dolls and dolls' houses, and in the landscaped gardens there are sports facilities and walks overlooking the lovely Teesdale countryside.

BATTLE *East Sussex*

England began at the top of the High Street, behind the great gatehouse that commands its entire length and therefore most of Battle. This is the gatehouse of the Abbey of St Martin de Bello, built at the command of William the Conqueror in thanksgiving for his famous victory of 1066. It was built on the very key point of the battle which the Saxons called Hastings, since in those days the name meant the entire district as well as the town. The Normans, however, called it Senlac, which means 'Lake of Blood', and for a long time it was believed that, after rain, the ground continued to ooze the blood spilled upon it. Perhaps the iron content of the soil helped to promote the story.

Entrance to the abbey is not via the gatehouse, which leads to a girls' public school, but by a humbler door around the corner. Once through this, and you are standing on the western end of the Saxon defences, which then made a slight curve around the back of what is now the abbey ruins. In the centre stood the king, Harold, with his 2,000-odd thegns and House carles – knights and elite professional soldiers – grouped about him, while the flanks were occupied by the Fyrd, some 6,000 men of the Saxon militia. Their position was a strong one, the crest of a hill looking down a grassy, wooded slope – much the same as it is today – upon Duke William's army of about 7,000 Normans, Bretons, French and Flemings.

The battle began not long after sunrise on October 14, as William discovered the Saxons blocking his advance. All morning it raged, the Saxon line proving unbreakable, and it was not until the afternoon, when everyone was tiring, that William was able to seize an advantage. The Bretons attacking on Harold's western flank broke on the Fyrd's defences and fled down the

CHÂTEAU OF ART *When John and Josephine Bowes sold their Paris home in 1862 they needed somewhere to house their priceless collection of works of art. The Bowes Museum was the result. Barnard Castle was chosen as the site because John Bowes owned the nearby Streatlam Castle, and in 1869 work began on this astonishing building – a 17th-century-style French palace in the heart of England's Teesdale.*

hill, closely followed by the exultant Saxon militia, contrary to Harold's strictest orders. William flung his heavy Norman cavalry into the mêlée, who cut the Saxons to pieces. After that it was a slogging match, which only the heavily armed Normans could win. They pressed ever harder on the diminishing Saxon army who, nevertheless, yielded not an inch. Contrary to legend, Harold died not by an arrow in the eye, but in fighting to the end among his House carles. His hacked body was discovered after the battle and was buried, so it is said, above the shore at Hastings that he had struggled so valiantly to defend. William went to Westminster to be crowned, and though there were centuries of bitterness to come, it was the first step in the creation of the modern English nation from the Saxons and the Normans.

It is not surprising that the town is a little pre-occupied by the battle that gave it its name. There is a pub called The 1066, and a brand of elderflower wine marketed under the same title. The museum, housed within the 16th-century Langton House (now the Memorial Hall), contains a locally produced full-size replica of the Bayeux Tapestry and a diorama that shows the battle at its turning point. The staff are extremely knowledgeable and helpful, and if they tend frankly to favour the Saxon cause it is under-standable; after all, that was the local team.

There are houses and buildings of all kinds of periods along the High Street, though some of them conceal their ages behind modern shop fronts. Probably the most elderly is the Pilgrim's Rest near the great gates. It was an abbey guest-house in the 12th century, largely rebuilt in 1420, and is now a res-taurant. So it is still fulfilling much the same function as it did 900 years ago. The Clock Shop was built in the 15th century, and the Old Pharmacy in 1500. No. 19 is thought to be the oldest ironmonger's in the country, having opened its doors to business in 1680. Startling in a mainly brick street is the stone Nonsuch Hotel. It was built in 1688 from the stone blocks of the abbey kitchens, demolished and sold by a needy Lord Montagu. The George, near by, is about a century younger and has a famous Regency staircase.

Near the Church of St Mary the Virgin is the 12th-century Prior's Lodge, to which the last abbot retired after the Dissolution. There, too, is the rather grand Tudor Deanery. Battle has neither a vicarage nor a vicar, but a dean instead, because that was the title given to the monk from the abbey who conducted the services in the parish church. This was built about 1200 and underwent some fairly strenuous restoration in the 19th century. There are some good brasses to medieval deans. In this place, too, the great battle is remembered in special services and prayers for those who fell in it, just as William the Conqueror vowed there would be when he won the battle in 1066.

BATTLEGROUND *Battle Abbey stands on the site of the most famous battle in English history. Here in the rolling Sussex countryside William the Conqueror defeated King Harold in the year that every schoolboy knows, and after his victory ordered an abbey to be built with its high altar placed on the spot where Harold died. Only a stone slab marks the spot now, among the ruins of William's abbey that went the way of most abbeys during Henry VIII's Dissolution of the Monasteries in 1538.*

BEAUMARIS *(Anglesey) Guynedd*

A gallows, a condemned cell, a punishment room and a treadmill – these are some of the unusual attractions with which Beaumaris tempts tourists. All are contained within the gruesomely fascinating gaol, which was opened in 1829 and closed in 1874, thereafter being used as a police station and lock-up. Lately it has been restored to its original condition, as a museum and monument to the Victorian penal system.

During the days of the Welsh princes, Beaumaris was known as Llanfaes, but in 1295, following a major uprising in North Wales, Edward I determined to build a castle there, partly to tighten his grip upon Anglesey and North Wales in general and partly to cut off the rebels from their supplies of Anglesey grain. He expelled the entire Welsh population of Llanfaes, and selected for the site of his castle a 'fair marsh' – a *beau marais*, in Norman French – where wild flowers and rushes grew.

It was the last Welsh castle undertaken by Edward's great architect, Master James of St George, and is therefore the last word in Britain on medieval castle building, even though shortage of money prevented the defences from being raised to their intended full height. Despite this, they incorporated some 300 firing positions, and so many turns, portcullises, drawbridges, ambush points and the like, that it is estimated that any attacker would have to overcome 14 separate obstacles before gaining the vast inner ward where the domestic buildings and state apartments once stood. The southern end of the moat no longer exists, but from there at one time a short channel controlled by sluice gates led to the sea. This permitted the entrance and docking of ships up to 40 tons burden, which tied up at the iron ring that can still be seen and unloaded supplies straight into the castle's outer ward; the dock itself was overlooked and defended by the Gunners' Walk above.

Having expelled the Welsh from Llanfaes, Edward I filled the vacuum about his new castle with English immigrants, offering them several kinds of tax and trading inducements to settle there, to the intense irritation of the Welsh. Even after all this time, Beaumaris still has an English air, with its sedate Georgian terraces round The Green – the site of the 'fair marsh' – the many town houses built by Anglesey's Regency and early Victorian gentry, and its old inns, whose names, the George and Dragon, the Bull's Head, the Liverpool Arms, are hardly reminiscent of Wales. These were built between the 16th and early 19th centuries, when Beaumaris was a major stopping place on the route from London to Dublin.

The parish church of St Mary and St Nicholas predates everything in the town except the castle, which is precisely one year older, since the church was founded in 1296. Most of the present structure still belongs to the early 14th century, though there are also some 16th and 19th-century changes and alterations. Among the monuments is the fine alabaster tomb of William Bulkeley, who died in 1490.

BECCLES *Suffolk*

Sunburned children on the quay, the rattle and clatter of dinghy sails, cabin cruisers coming dead slow down the River Waveney, their crews savouring the last minutes of their holiday on Oulton Broad, a drink at the Loaves and Fishes through the arch in the converted Maltings – these are the memories of Beccles. And over all, like some guardian totem, the 92 ft bell-tower of St Michael's Church standing so massively against the paling evening sky that you feel that it must be visible in Holland.

Traditionally, and by long tradition too, Beccles is a market town that more than a century before the Norman Conquest belonged to the Collegiate Church of St Edmund at Bury; part of the rents that Beccles paid were 60,000 herring a year, which could be delivered straight into the town by way of the arm of the sea that stretched inland before the fens were drained. In fact, and most unusually for a small country town, Beccles has two markets – the Old Market that dates from Saxon times, and the New Market which dates from the mere Middle Ages. The reason may have been that the Old Market, at the bottom of the town, was subject to periodic flooding,

DEATH'S DOOR *Through a door in the wall of Beaumaris Gaol, condemned men stepped on to the scaffold for public execution, high above the waiting crowds. In fact, only two executions took place, in 1830 and 1862. The second man to die is said to have put a curse on the church clock that struck the hour of his death. The clock never showed the right time again, until it was overhauled in 1980.*

ROYAL FAVOUR *In 1584 Beccles received its Town Charter, and its lively town sign at the end of Ballygate depicts Elizabeth I handing the charter to the Portreeve, Sir John Bass.*

but more likely it was simply due to the sheer pressures of medieval prosperity.

Fire seems to have been a particular hazard in Beccles, since it was ravaged by four major conflagrations between the late 16th and late 17th centuries. These account for the town's present appearance, which is mostly Georgian, despite its great age. The old street plan remains, however, and the old street names too, such as Saltgate, Ballygate, Northgate and Puddingmoor.

Ballygate is generally accounted the most attractive street in Beccles, partly for its views over the Waveney Valley, but mainly for its fine Georgian houses. The Rectory, with its grandly pillared doorway, is particularly impressive, though some of the other buildings are not quite what they seem, in possessing Georgian façades fronting much older structures.

Northgate, sweeping narrowly and crowdedly down to the Quay, has a different charm, in that it is composed of all kinds of buildings from cottages to near-mansions. The houses of rich, 18th-century merchants predominate. A good example is Northgate House, whose elegant but deceptively narrow front masks a grandly spacious interior.

Below the Old Market is Smallgate, and just off it, the famous Caxton Printing Works that has been the town's chief employer for more than a century. Near by are the Town Museum and the little 17th-century Meeting House of the Society of Friends. Nonconformism was always strong in Beccles, but its chief monument is not the Meeting House, but the more prosaic Baptist Church, built in 1860. This is a memorial to three Protestant martyrs who were burned to death on the site during the Marian persecutions of 1556. *Foxe's Book of Martyrs* says that 'they all went joyfullie to the stake, and being bound thereto, and the fire burning about them, they praised God in such an audible voice, that it was wonderful to all those who stood by...'

BERWICK-UPON-TWEED
Northumberland

It has been said that to stand with a foot in both camps is to invite someone to build the fence straight through you. Something along those lines was Berwick's fate, and that the experience was a memorable one is apparent still in the town's watchful, embattled look, even after centuries of peace. It was not Berwick's fault. Long, long ago, perhaps 1,000 years ago, it was more or less settled – though not by any formal treaty – that the natural division between England and Scotland lay along the line between where 'the tide rins tae the Solway Sands and Tweed rins tae the ocean'. And since Berwick stands on the north bank of the Tweed, this would seem to place it solidly and forever in Scotland. In fact, sometimes it was, and sometimes it wasn't, usually depending on the whims and relative strengths of the kings to the north and those to the south. Berwick, always a place of strategic and commercial importance, bounced uneasily between them.

In 1097, King Edgar of Scotland gave it to the Bishop of Durham, but less than 30 years later David I made Berwick one of the first of the Scottish Royal Burghs. Between then and 1482 it changed hands no less than 13 times, as a rule to the detriment of the populace, though with occasional periods of bright prosperity. The brightest of these was during the reign of Alexander III (1247–86), when Berwick developed into one of the most important international seaports in Britain. Alexander left no direct heirs, however, and in the dispute as to who should succeed him, Robert Bruce or John Baliol, Edward I of England appointed himself arbitrator. Edward chose Baliol, and enthroned him in the Great Hall of Berwick Castle; then, seemingly under the impression that this made Scotland a vassal state, demanded a Scottish levy to serve under him against the French. The Scots refused, and Edward promptly invaded. His first act on crossing the Border was to slaughter 7,000 of Berwick's inhabitants. Then, as had been his custom in Wales, he resettled the town with English merchants, but allowed a few of the remaining Scots to stay on, provided that they promised him fealty. By way of public entertainment, he suspended the Countess of Buchan in a cage upon the castle walls, and left her imprisoned there for six years for crowning Robert Bruce King of Scotland at Scone.

The Border Wars and the War of Scottish Independence went on and on in a spirit of curious and everescalating savagery. Berwick was the bone to be gnawed by every passing army, and why the townsfolk did not abandon the place would be a mystery, if they had not been as tough as anything that was sent against them. On one occasion, the Governor, Sir Alexander Seton, and his wife stood on the castle wall and watched their two sons being hanged on the knoll still called Hang-a-Neuk Hill, rather than surrender the keys of the town to Edward III. As was usual along the Border, the event was celebrated in a ballad. The last time that Berwick was in Scottish hands was during the Wars of the Roses when the Lancastrians gave it to Scotland in return for help against the House of York. Twenty years later, in 1482, it was besieged by an English army, and this time, heartily tired no doubt of the whole business, the garrison surrendered without firing a shot. It has been English ever since.

Well, not quite. Berwick and the 8 sq. miles about it was for much of its later history a kind of semi-independent buffer state, with a certain amount of autonomy – like Wales – and some laws of its own. Runaway couples could get married there, for example, as at Gretna Green. It is said, too, that Berwick has been at war with Russia ever since the Crimean War was declared it would seem, in the name of England, Ireland, Scotland, Wales and Berwick, and Berwick alone never signed the peace treaty. Even if the story were untrue, it still illustrates the sturdy independence of the Berwicker who invented it.

Independent or English, Berwick was not finished with the military. In the early years of Elizabeth I's reign, there was a very real fear of a Scots-French invasion in support of the claims of Mary, Queen of

CLERICAL ERROR *With its lofty steeple rising above an imposing portico, the elegant building on the corner of Church Street, Berwick-upon-Tweed, matches the common image of a Georgian church. So much so, that in the days when Berwick had a garrison, more than one regiment new to the town fell in outside for church parade. A vain exercise. The building is the Town Hall.*

MARKET PLAQUE *Berwick has two weekly markets which date back to the early 14th century, but the cattle market, held on the appropriately named Hide Hill, was moved to a larger site outside the Scotch Gate in 1886.*

Scots to the English throne. The town's medieval walls, built to withstand medieval armies, were no longer adequate, and new defences, built to carry and withstand guns, were constructed. The last word of the period on military engineering, they consisted of a 12 ft thick wall backed by a 30 ft thick mound of earth, from which protruded huge stone bastions shaped like flat arrowheads. From each angle of the arrowheads, guns sprouted, covering the wall and each other, and the whole thing was fronted by a ditch 200 ft wide. The invasion never came and the defences were never put to the test, but they remain still, pierced only by the town gates, and are probably the most formidable fortifications in Britain. Nowadays, they make a perfect walkway from which to view, on one side, the old town, all pinkish-brownish-grey stone topped by red pantiles, running down to the river, and on the other, the still substantial remains of the earlier defences begun and added to by Edward I, Edward II and Robert Bruce.

What made Berwick so well worth defending was its position as the lowest possible bridging point on the Tweed, yet until 1624 the river was crossed only by a rough wooden structure. The inspiration for the first stone one is said to have come from James VI of Scotland, on his way to London to be crowned as James I of England. 'Is there no' a man in Berwick,' he queried in his sour way, 'wha can wark stanes tae mak a brig ower Tweed?' Twenty-three years later his request was granted, and the Old Bridge stands yet, supported on 15 fine arches, still capable of carrying considerable weight.

The Royal Border Bridge, which carries the east coast railway line to Edinburgh, built by Robert Stephenson in 1847–50, was considered one of the wonders of the Railway Age. It soars on 28 arches from Tweedmouth on the southern shore to the approach to Berwick Station, which stands on the site once occupied by the castle. Only a few battered walls remain of this, and it is believed that the Great Hall, where Baliol was enthroned, is now covered by the down platform. The third bridge, the Royal Tweed, which carries the main burden of the road traffic, was opened by the then Prince of Wales in 1928. It is a glum, hefty concrete structure, and if it is not so ugly as some critics say, it certainly suffers by comparison with the other two.

Soldiers and Berwick are practically inseparable, since the town has housed a garrison for almost all of its existence. It is therefore not surprising that it contains Britain's earliest barracks, built in 1717 to accommodate 600 troops because the townspeople refused to have them billeted upon them any longer. As barracks go, it is a handsome building, stone-faced and stepped-gabled, and with an imposing entrance that may well have been designed by Vanbrugh. It was continuously occupied until quite recently, and now houses the Regimental Museum of the King's Own Scottish Borderers. The garrison commander lived in the Governor's House, a fine 18th-century building in Palace Green. Near by is the Main Guard, a porticoed, lodge-like building. As an active guardhouse, it used

to stand in Marygate where it caused an almost permanent traffic jam, even in the days of the horse and cart. It was moved to its present site in 1816.

On the corner of Marygate and Church Street, there is a splendid example of Georgian ecclesiastical architecture which bears a 150 ft spire containing a peal of eight bells. In fact, it is the Town Hall, which incorporated not only the council offices, but the court room and a police station as well. On the top floor there was a prison, whose cells, including one for those condemned to death, can still be visited. The parish church, dedicated to the Holy Trinity, is much less imposing, and has no spire at all. It is one of only two churches in England – the other is at Staunton Harold in Lincolnshire – built during Cromwell's

Commonwealth, which probably accounts for its rather austere interior. Like the barracks, it is constructed of stone quarried from the castle ruins, and the lack of spire is believed to be due to Cromwell's personal intervention. He disliked church bells, and found time to forbid the building of the steeple, despite his preoccupation with the Battle of Dunbar at the time. The church contains some 17th-century Flemish glass and a panelled oak pulpit from which John Knox is said to have preached.

Berwick is a good strolling town, with handsome streets still keeping a firm hold on a fair remaining share of solid, square-cut Georgian houses. Quay Walls with its old Custom House, Wellington Terrace and Palace Street are all cases in point, while Marygate

is the busy shopping thoroughfare. There at the end of May is held the six-day long annual fair, opened with great pomp and ceremony and based upon a charter dating back to at least the beginning of the 14th century. The town's other great ceremony is the Riding of the Bounds which takes place on May 1. Several other Border parishes have similar ceremonies, in which horse riders, followed by a large number of people on foot, ride the town boundaries. In centuries when maps did not exist, it was a means of impressing ancient rights upon succeeding generations, and modern surveys notwithstanding, no one sees any reason why the practice should be discontinued. Berwick's Riding is particularly interesting, in that part of its bounds is the Border with Scotland.

SLENDER LINK *Towering 126 ft above the pewter-grey waters of the Tweed, the slender arches of the Royal Border Railway Bridge carry the line linking London and Edinburgh. When the bridge was opened by Queen Victoria in 1850 it was considered a marvel of railway engineering – a view undiminished by the passing years.*

BEVERLEY *Humberside*

As you approach the town over the Pastures – common land for 1,000 years and more – and see the west front of the minster lift ethereally into the sky, it is at once apparent that Beverley is a very special place. Long ago, it was even made legally so, and in a rather curious way. About 937, King Athelstan, the first ruler of all England, marched north to fight the Scots and paused for spiritual refreshment at the minster. He laid his dagger on the tomb of its founder, John of Beverley, and vowed that if he were successful in the coming battle, he would grant all kinds of favours to the church. John's intercession seems to have tipped the balance, for the Scots were soundly defeated at Brunanburh, which may or may not have been near Dumfries. At any event, true to his word, the king gave the minster a handsome endowment, and certain rights, which included that of sanctuary. Any fugitive who got within 2 miles of the church – the boundaries are still marked by stone crosses – was safe from justice, though the closer he got, the safer he was. Ecclesiastical penalties against anyone who seized him became progressively more severe as he approached the minster until, when he reached the High Altar he was, or should have been, inviolable. Equal safety could be attained by sitting on the Frith-stool, or Chair of Peace, a Saxon stone seat that still stands beside the altar; this gave the fugitive 30 days to settle his differences, to flee the country or to serve the church within the town's confines. Despite the town's protests about its steady population of villains down the years, the right was not finally repealed until 1624.

The present minster is the fourth on the site since Bishop John of Beverley founded his church there in 706 and dedicated it to St John the Evangelist. The bishop was canonised in 1037 as St John of Beverley and it is often assumed that the minster bears his name. But though he is buried in the Choir, and the sense of his presence is everywhere in the minster, it is not dedicated to him. John's building and its two successors were either destroyed by the Danes, ravaged by fire, or simply fell down. Tragic though these occurrences were, later generations had cause to be grateful, for it meant that the present minster did not begin to rise until the middle of the 13th century, the high moment of English Gothic.

From the great West Door with its splendid carvings, the nave sweeps, tall-columned and sunlit, to the circular altar. Between the altar and the west door is the font, made of fossil-studded marble from the banks of the River Wear in about 1140; St John of Beverley and King Athelstan are justly celebrated by metal statues near by. Other monuments to the great include the magnificent tomb of Gilbert de Grimsby, Precentor of the minster in the 14th century, and a number of tombs of the Percy family, who for centuries were virtually monarchs of the North Country. Most remarkable for its carvings is the tomb of the Lady Idonea, wife of the 2nd Lord Percy, and there are helmets and banners said to have belonged to Shakespeare's Harry Hotspur (Henry Percy) and to the 5th Earl of Northumberland, known to his 15th-century contemporaries as Percy the Magnificent. Good carving is one of the major joys of the minster; see especially the 16th-century misericords – choir seats – carved with any kind of subject that took the craftsman's fancy, from illustrations of Biblical texts to a wife beating her husband.

For a town of Beverley's size, one would have thought that a single possession so grand as the minster would have been sufficient, and indeed it is the dominating note not only of the town but of the entire surrounding landscape. But at the other end of Beverley is St Mary's, an independent parish church that has nothing to do with the minster, and so lovely that it seems unfair it should have been built within the greater church's shadow. In the Middle Ages it was the church of the local craft guilds, and was supported and enriched by them.

Most of the old town lies between the minster and St Mary's, and the meandering lines of the streets were determined long ago by the courses of the streams that used to flow through them. Many of the names end in 'gate' – Highgate, Lairgate, Eastgate and so on which, as in other northern towns, is derived from a Norse word meaning street or thoroughfare. Walkergate, again as in other towns, was the place where woollen cloth was 'walked' or trodden in a stream to clean it.

After the Reformation, when the minster became a parish church, the fortunes of the town went into a slow decline, accelerated by two Civil War sackings, and did not begin to recover until the 18th century. In that Golden Age for the well-to-do it became, like so many of the prettier country towns, a social centre for the local gentry, and it is to this period that the racecourse and a large number of the most handsome buildings belong. The Guildhall, for example, was built in 1763 and contains what must be the prettiest magistrates' courtroom in Britain, with plaster mouldings of Justice, unblindfolded and floating upon clouds, and a vast and colourful Royal coat of arms. The figure of Justice on the portico of the Sessions House is more conventional, and the entire building, with its tall columns, has an altogether more serious air. All about it in New Walk and North Bar Without is a fine array of Georgian houses, a theme that is continued in Walkergate, Highgate, Newbegin and many other streets. There are literally hundreds of buildings in Beverley that have been listed as being of special architectural or historical interest, but particular highlights for a brief visit are Norwood House, immensely regal and now part of a girls' school, Lairgate Hall, now council offices but still retaining its famous Chinese room and two almshouses, both clean-cut and gracious. Those at 62 Walkergate were built in 1723, while Anne Routh's Almshouses in Keldgate belong to a quarter of a century later.

The Saturday Market and the Wednesday Market should also be visited; the first traditionally served the people of St Mary's parish, while the other catered for the parishioners of the minster. The two are joined by Toll Gavel and Butcher Row, which contains the East Yorkshire Regimental Museum.

In the middle of the Saturday Market there is a charming wood and stone Market Cross which bears the arms of Queen Anne, the Borough, and of local dignitaries. It was built in 1714 to replace an older cross, after the Corporation of the time launched an appeal for funds 'towards the building of a new cross in Saturday Market where the present cross, lately demolished, now stands'. Presumably Yorkshire's reputation for direct speech dates from a later period.

BEWDLEY *Hereford & Worcester*

Beaulieu, the Normans called it, 'the beautiful place', and a rash of prosperous suburbia on the outskirts notwithstanding, it remains a fairly accurate description still. Mostly, it's a matter of siting; Bewdley slides down a steep wooded hillside to the lovely Severn, but there are some handsome buildings of the 17th and 18th centuries, and it also possesses an attractive air of antique and fading graciousness.

Bewdley began as a clearing in the Wyre Forest at a point where a prehistoric trackway forded the Severn and wandered on westwards. Until 1544, when a special Act of Parliament was passed, it was uncertain whether it lay in Worcestershire or Shropshire, making it something of a haven for fugitives and criminals, 'for if any were indicted in Worcester, they said their town and franchise were in Shropshire and vice versa'. All the same, by the Middle Ages, it had built a bridge, was holding a weekly market and enjoyed growing prosperity as an inland port. This was its chief role for centuries, and as late as 1800 it was reported that from the bridge it was sometimes impossible to see the water, so closely were the barges packed together. This must have been the port's swan-song, however, for already James Brindley's Staffordshire and Worcestershire Canal was taking effect. Built in the 1770s and terminating at Stourminster further downstream, it gradually took Bewdley's trade, making the town quite literally a backwater, a place of minor craftsmen and a dormitory for Kidderminster carpet workers.

Depressing as this must have been at the time, it did at least permit the pleasant little market town to be preserved practically unscathed, for posterity. It is approached by Thomas Telford's fine sandstone bridge, built in the dry summer of 1798 when the water was so low that it enabled the engineer to raise the structure in a single season 'as if by enchantment'. It replaced a much older bridge, washed away in a

QUALITY STREET *Bows and bays, fluted columns and neat dormer windows give Beverley's Saturday Market a touch of Georgian elegance that blends happily with the Tudor nobility of St Mary's Church tower.*

flood. Telford's bridge, built a little upstream from the old one, springs lightly over from the outlying parish of Wribbenhall and enters Bewdley proper at Load Street, a wide, sedate, Georgianish thoroughfare leaned over by the square tower of St Anne's Church; the tower, re-erected in 1695, predates the present church by half a century. The Post Office, in Load Street, occupies a 17th-century timber-framed building, and the chances are that the George Hotel opposite was once very similar, though it now wears a dignified 18th-century mask.

Round the corner, in High Street, is the Bailiff's House and the Manor House, both built in the early 1600s, and the Cooke Almshouses, bequeathed by Thomas Cooke, who died in 1693, aged 19. Stanley Baldwin, three times Prime Minister between the wars, was born in the big Georgian house at the corner of Lax Lane.

Perhaps the prettiest street is Severnside, whose old quays gently embrace the curve of the river, making it a wonderful place for a stroll. Here, too, the keynote is Georgian, though River House and the Thurston Hotel are both 17th century. Tickenhill Manor, above the High Street, occupies the site of an earlier house in which Prince Arthur married Catherine of Aragon by proxy in 1499; after his death three years later, the unfortunate princess was married to Arthur's younger brother, the future Henry VIII.

Bewdley Museum is housed in the 18th-century Shambles, or butchers' market, which consists of a cobbled street with arched arcades that contained the butchers' stalls; at its end are three stone cells with exercise yards that were the town lock-up. The museum concentrates upon local crafts of the past – hornwork, saddlery, ropemaking, metalwork, coopering, tanning, basketry, charcoal-burning and the wheelwright's craft.

Wribbenhall, across the river, is an attractive place with a history at least as old as that of Bewdley, of which it is now a suburb. It contains one of the area's great tourist draws, the Severn Valley Railway, whose gleaming steam locomotives and rolling stock make the 25 mile round trip to Bridgnorth every weekend of the year and daily in the high season.

BIDEFORD *Devon*

The thing that appealed to Charles Kingsley about the place was its being a true seaport, with none of the annoyances of 'a resort of fashion'. 'The little white town,' he enthused, 'slopes upward from its broad tide-river, paved with yellow sands, and many arched old bridge …' Thus he saw Bideford in 1854, when he made it the starting point of his novel *Westward Ho!* and so, though a little shabbier, it remains to this day.

The novel, based upon the exploits of Elizabethan seafarers, drew upon a rich vein of fact. Bideford men fought the Armada, and Sir Richard Grenville's *Revenge*, whose crew was drawn entirely from Bideford, challenged an entire Spanish treasure fleet off the Azores in 1591. Grenville's epic has thrilled the hearts of young England ever since, but to Bideford he

bequeathed a more concrete legacy – an ascendancy in the importing of tobacco and other products of the New World that was to assure the town's prosperity for well nigh a couple of centuries.

A notion of the affluent years can be grasped by looking along Bridgeland Street, built about 1690, but the heart of the town is still the tree-lined quay where coasters and small vessels from the Continent tie up. That, and the bridge that hop-scotches upon 24 unevenly spaced arches over the Torridge. Built of timber at some time in the dim past, it was clad with stone in the 1460s, and with numerous later widenings and strengthenings continues to connect Bideford with 'East-the-Water'. There stands the 17th-century Royal Hotel where Kingsley stayed, and which also contains some glorious original plasterwork. The popularity of *Westward Ho!* led, in the 1860s, to the development of a seaside resort of the same name, some 2 miles to the north. Its wide, sandy beach is one of the finest in Devon.

BIGGAR *Strathclyde*

London's big, but Biggar's Biggar – so runs an antique joke still enjoyed by the young of this ancient Scottish town where tradition and an absorption with the past is almost a passion. At Hogmanay, the townspeople bid the old year farewell and welcome the new round a great bonfire by the old Mercat Cross. That the old Mercat Cross ceased to exist a century and a half ago does not really matter; it crumbled in the intense heat of a bonfire lit in 1820, but its spirit lives on in a fragment buried in the wall of the Corn Exchange close by the original site. The cross was given to the town at the same time as its charter in 1451; they were granted by James II at the request of Lord Robert Fleming, whose family held Biggar for centuries.

The name of Fleming occurs again and again in Scottish history, patriots and soldiers, supporters of Scottish Independence, loyal friends of the Stuarts. Mary Fleming was one of Mary, Queen of Scots 'Four Marys', the queen's ladies-in-waiting. In the course of a game in the tragic queen's happier days at Holyroodhouse in Edinburgh, Mary Fleming was made 'Queen for a Day', and the event is still celebrated each summer at Biggar on Gala Day, when a local girl is crowned Fleming Queen.

Another memento of the heroic days is the little bridge over the Biggar Burn called Cadger's Brig. Legend has it that the Scottish patriot William Wallace crossed over it disguised as a pedlar or cadger on his way to spy out the dispositions of an English army commanded by Edward I; next day, Wallace and his men fell upon Edward's army and annihilated it.

Biggar is determined to let no moment of its past slip away unrecorded. The 19th century is commemorated in the Gladstone Court Street Museum, in which a number of Victorian shops have been delightfully re-created, goods, furniture, advertisements and all; together with a bank, a library, a telephone exchange and a schoolroom. Even the old gasworks of 1839 is preserved and open to the public.

NOVEL APPEAL *The writer Charles Kingsley began his novel* Westward Ho! *while visiting Bideford. Published in 1855 it popularised the appeal of Bideford which had caught Kingsley's imagination, and led to the building of the seaside resort named after the novel.*

BLANDFORD FORUM *Dorset*

One of the nice things about living in Blandford Forum – if you are a civilian – would be to listen to distant bugles piercing the stilly morning air, then to turn over and go back to sleep. The town has been the centre of a military training area since Wellington's day, and was so in 1914 when Rupert Brooke, in camp there, composed the sonnet that begins:

> *'If I should die, think only this of me:*
> *That there's some corner of a foreign field*
> *That is forever England…'*

Brooke's poem moved the hearts of 1914 youth to tears and their feet towards the recruiting office. Later, as casualties mounted, it struck a sour note. But by then, Brooke himself was dead.

However, in Brooke's hymn of praise to his native land there might have been lurking somewhere an image of Blandford which is, without doubt, one of the most handsome Georgian country towns in England. It is due to a set of circumstances that began on a summer afternoon in June, 1731, when a tallow-chandler's premises in the centre of the town caught fire. So furious was the ensuing blaze that it soon engulfed the town's three man-powered fire engines, and whirled burning thatch through the air to descend upon neighbouring hamlets, and ignite those too. At the church, according to the vicar of the time '… the lead melted, the stones split and flew, nay, so fervent and irresistible was the heat that the bells dissolved and ran down in streams'.

As it happened, the Archbishop of Canterbury of the day was a Blandford man who not only made a generous contribution to the town's rebuilding, but so publicised its plight that the sympathy of the nation was aroused. Benefit performances were held at Drury Lane and donations poured in from every side, enabling the work of rebuilding to begin without delay. The task was entrusted to two local builders, John and William Bastard, and it was their devotion and their industry over the next 30 years that were mainly responsible for the present gracious and superbly civilised town. The chief materials are red brick and Wiltshire sandstone, and the scheme includes church, town hall, market terraces and such fine town houses as Coupar House in Church Lane, now occupied by the British Legion. A little Doric temple covering a drinking fountain by the church commemorates 'God's dreadful visitation by fire', and reminds posterity that John Bastard suffered considerably in the great calamity.

Very few buildings survived the fire, but among them is the Old House of the 16th century that was occupied by the local physician at the time of the fire, the Ryves Almshouses, founded in 1682 by Charles II's chaplain, and Dale House, also late 17th century, that has in its garden an ancient tulip tree whose magnificence equals that of the one in Kew Gardens. The oldest building is St Leonard's Chapel, a medieval leper-house whose sorry remains may be seen near the Railway Arches.

INSPIRED RESURRECTION *The Old Red Lion in Blandford Forum's Market Place is typical of the good taste shown by John and William Bastard when they rebuilt the town after the fire of 1731. They followed the example set by Sir Christopher Wren when he rebuilt the City of London.*

BOSTON *Lincolnshire*

Those who live on the east coast say that once you have become accustomed to the sense of freedom imparted by the enormous skyscape, you can live nowhere else. Others, less used to it, feel a little intimidated, like a very small ladybird crawling across a very big grand piano. In such a countryside, it seems pointless to walk any distance to view anything, since even if the objective is 5 miles off, it can be seen quite clearly before setting out. In any case, in all that great fertile plain, so flat that it curves, there is only one object to catch the eye, and that is the Gothic stone lantern of St Botolph's Church, known as the Boston Stump. Reaching up as though it were the control tower of nature's airfield, it is something of a surprise to learn that the Stump is a mere 272 ft high.

Boston is a seaport on the River Witham and a market town, as it has been since the days of the Normans, and though it is both aware and proud of its past, it has little time for prettifying. But there is so much of significance to see, that a lack of cosmetics is forgivable.

So far as is known, it all began when a monk named Botolph, who was later canonised, founded a monastery on an island in the Fens in about 650. The community that grew up about the monastery eventually became known as Botolph's Town or Botolph's Stone; the present name could be a contraction of either. Boston's commerical importance began in the early Middle Ages and flowered so rapidly that by 1289 it was collecting a third more in customs dues than London. Continental merchants settled in the town, including those of the German Hanseatic League, but in the mid-15th century, as ships got larger and the River Witham began to silt up, Boston slid into a slow decline. This continued for about 150 years and more, until the Fens were drained presenting Boston with an enormously fertile hinterland.

In 1763, Boston was inundated, not for the first time, and to prevent it happening again, the Witham was straightened and deepened, and a canal, the Grand Sluice, built to create a non-tidal basin that permitted seagoing cargo vessels to come to the heart of the town via The Wash. After numerous improvements, the port can now accommodate ships of up to 3,000 tons.

Nevertheless, Boston's best-known exports are not commodities, but people. The Puritan sect later known as the Pilgrim Fathers came mostly from East Anglia, and attempted to sail to the New World from Boston in 1607. They were betrayed by their Dutch captain and arrested, but later allowed to depart for Holland; they did not reach New England until some 12 years later. Another, and more successful expedition quit Boston in 1630 and landed in Massachusetts where its members, together with some of the Pilgrim Fathers, founded a settlement at Trimountain. A few years later, the name of the place was changed to 'Boston', and the long transatlantic association was begun. Boston names, too, appear on the maps and in the histories of Australia and New Zealand; the explorers George Bass and Matthew Flinders and the scientist Sir Joseph Banks were all natives of the town.

The climax of Boston is St Botolph's, one of the largest parish churches in England. The interior of the church is vast and airy, 282 ft long and 65 ft to the panelled ceiling. It contains a number of medieval features, including misericords – choir seats – of 1390 that illustrate the savage humour of the period. Bagpipers are satirised by jesters torturing cats, a choirboy is flogged, and a friar preaches to geese. The monuments are unusually varied. They include memorials to John Cotton, the dissenting vicar who took a large part of his congregation to the other Boston in 1633; five local men who became Governors of Massachusetts; the explorers of Australasia; and a merchant of the German Hanse who died in Boston in 1340.

In the shadow of the Stump is the spacious Market Place which is fronted by some good-looking buildings, particularly the Assembly Rooms of 1826 and the Exchange buildings dating from half a century earlier; together with the church, they make a grouping that would bring dignity and grace to any town. There are many other good buildings in the centre of the town, but they are scattered and often hidden away in a mass of Victorian nondescript. Shodfriars Hall in South Street, originally a 15th-century timber-framed building, was so restored in 1874 as to be almost reconstructed, but has some fine decorative plasterwork. Not far off is the business-like Customs House built in 1725, and off South Street is the Unitarian Chapel, a handsome building in Georgian red brick. Just round the corner in Spain Lane is Blackfriars Hall, the refectory of a 13th-century Dominican Priory which has been lovingly converted into an Arts Centre.

The Guildhall was built in 1450 as the hall of the Guild of St Mary, the richest of the 15 medieval religious guilds in the town. After the Reformation, it became the Town Hall and Courtroom, with a couple of cells below for prisoners awaiting trial. It was there that the Pilgrim Fathers were imprisoned and tried, making the place something of a shrine for visiting New Englanders. The Guildhall is now a museum that gives an insight into domestic arrangements of 300 years ago, including a spit worked ingeniously by smoke-fans, and exhibits portraits, paintings and relics of local interest. One of these is a copy of an early edition of the *Book of Martyrs*, published in 1576 by John Foxe, who was born in a house in the Market Place. It describes, in gruesome detail, the sufferings of the Protestant martyrs in the reign of Queen Mary I, and was required Sunday reading for the faithful for many generations.

Cheek by jowl with the Guildhall is Fydell House, one of the most distinguished small houses in the Queen Anne style in England. It was built in 1726 by William Fydell who was three times Mayor of Boston. It has some fine panelling and a glorious carved staircase, and its American Room is dedicated to the use of visitors from Boston, Massachusetts, and members of the English Speaking Union. The building is open every weekend to the public.

BRADFORD-ON-AVON *Wiltshire*

Stone, wool and rubber have given Bradford its style, its longevity and its living. The stone is limestone, the foundation of the steep escarpment on which the town is terraced above a noble curve of the Avon, it is also the material from which walls and roofs were constructed, giving a unity to the buildings, whether they were built one, two or three centuries ago. Wool and the cloth trade brought wealth to Bradford from the Middle Ages to the 19th century and paid for the astonishing number of very grand town houses, and for the weavers' cottages ranged along the hillside. Rubber ensured continuing prosperity when the cloth business began to falter in the 1840s. The innovator was Stephen Moulton who introduced the material to Britain, first as a means of waterproofing the capes of the troops bound for the Crimea and later as a material for the manufacture of tyres and other products. The Moulton family took over and restored mills and Georgian houses with equally happy results. Their finest effort, in this context, was the restoration of The Hall, an Elizabethan extravaganza built in about 1600, and architecturally the most important house in the town.

There are good things to see everywhere in Bradford, but as good a place as any to begin is high up on the path called Conigre, which means rabbit warren. This follows the line of the prehistoric track that ran past the Iron Age fort where the town began, and down the hill to the broad ford that gave it its name. A little way down the path is a street with the delightful name of Top Rank Tory, which has nothing to do with politics, but is derived instead from 'tor', a high place, as in Glastonbury Tor. It is a row of mainly 16th-century weavers' cottages, as is Middle Rank, the terrace below.

The lowest terrace is Newtown, whose buildings range in period from Queen Anne to Victoria, but Barton Orchard near by is all 18th-century weavers' cottages. The Chantry, a little to the west, was owned by a succession of rich clothiers from the late 16th century onwards, though it wears a Georgian façade. From there, a walk goes over the fields and the railway to Barton Bridge, beyond which lies Barton Farm and an abrupt step back across six centuries. The massive bridge was designed to carry the farm wagons of the 1300s. Barton Farm, which belonged to Shaftesbury Abbey until the Dissolution of the Monasteries in 1539, was a working farm until 1974. But it still has its medieval chapel and its dove loft, whose inhabitants provided fresh meat for the household during the bleak months of winter.

One thing that has changed not at all is the Tithe Barn in which was gathered the tenth of the farm's annual product that was the Abbess of Shaftesbury's

QUIET WATERS *In a wooded valley the gentle Avon flows through the mellowed limestone heart of Bradford, and under a bridge that has spanned the untroubled waters for seven centuries.*

due. Most of the tenth, or tithe, was in fleeces, and a glance at the interior of the barn will give a shrewd idea of the prodigious number of sheep that grazed upon the surrounding grasslands during the Middle Ages. Bigger than many churches, the barn is 168 ft long, buttressed, walled and roofed in the local stone. It is the interior supports of the roof, however, that take the breath away – great baulks of timber in three tiers, arching and intermeshing like the upside-down skeleton of a man-o'-war. On the other side of the river, up the hill, there is another large barn, Priory Barn, that belonged to a long-vanished estate. Some 200 years younger than the Tithe Barn, it has been restored as a public meeting place by the Bradford Preservation Society.

SAXON GLORY *Inside the Saxon Church of St Lawrence there is a simple grandeur in the ancient walls of rough-hewn stone and the tall chancel arch.*

ABBESS'S BARN *The Tithe Barn on Barton Farm dates from the 14th century and was built to store the tithes, a tenth of the farm's annual product, due to the Abbess of Shaftesbury. Its cavernous roof consists of trussed timbers spanning a width of 33 ft and bearing the massive weight of thousands of stone slates.*

From Barton Farm, a path leads to the Frome Road, and so to the Town Bridge. Two of its arches have been carrying traffic since the 13th century, but most of it belongs to the 17th, including the little chapel that stands upon it. For a large part of its career the chapel was in fact the local lock-up, and it still has two cells with iron beds fixed to the wall. On top of the chapel there is a weather-vane with a gilt fish, so that anyone who was jailed in Bradford was said to be under the fish and over the water.

The bridge leads to the town centre, to Market Street and Silver Street, both handsome thoroughfares with buildings of all periods, and with pretty shopping streets, such as the Shambles, running off. To the west, at the end of Church Street, is the parish church of Holy Trinity, which has grown up, almost casually, over 700 years, and is the embodiment of the town's history over that period. In the plague year of 1348–9, it had five vicars, indicating the fearful death-toll in the area; a later vicar was indicted for high treason after accusing Henry VIII of heresy, while two others were royal chaplains, and another a close friend of Dr Johnson. Among the monuments is one to the early 16th-century wool merchant, Thomas Horton and his wife, who lived in Old Church House which still

stands in Church Street. Beneath the carpet in the chancel there is a brass to Anne Longe, who died in 1601. The protection by the carpet is necessary, since the monument is one of the finest portrayals of Elizabethan dress in existence; nevertheless, a reproduction on the wall shows her in every detail, from her tiny feathered hat and lace-edged ruff to the rich embroidery of her dress.

Across the way from Holy Trinity is the chief treasure of this remarkable town, and a treasure for all England. It is the Saxon Church of St Lawrence, built about 700 by Aldhelm, Abbot of Malmesbury, with some additions of a century or so later. It is very small, no more than 38 ft long though tall in relation to its length. That such a building should have survived for so long is extraordinary, but what is even more extraordinary is that from about the 12th century until 1857, it disappeared. What may have happened was that when Holy Trinity was built St Lawrence's ceased to be used as a church, and gradually other buildings grew up around it and were even attached to it. A floor was put into the nave, converting it into a two-storey building that was used first as a dwelling-house and then as a schoolroom with a kitchen below. A rich layer of ivy completed the disguise, and its original purpose was long forgotten until 1857; during some internal repairs, a carving of a pair of angels was revealed. The vicar of Holy Trinity, William Jones, was a keen amateur archaeologist and recognised the carvings as Saxon. This was the first clue, but another 14 years were to pass before the surrounding buildings could be bought out and cleared away and the church restored to its ancient form. Now once again it is a place of worship, very stark and simple, and high on the chancel arch there can still be seen the two angels that gave Canon Jones the first inkling of what the place might be.

BRECHIN *Tayside*

For many visitors, this is an unexpected face of Scotland, one that has little to do with tartans and heather and wild roaring floods. Though the dark Grampians fill its northern horizon, Brechin's own situation is gentle enough – a hillside above the pretty South Esk River in the rich and fertile Vale of Strathmore. As its centre is approached up the steep High Street from the ancient bridge, it has a huddled, medieval air, with its grey-brown, closely packed buildings, narrow, unexpected closes and flights of outside stairs. The steep, crow-stepped gables carry more than a hint, too, of Flanders and Holland. Like many another of Scotland's east-coast burghs, it looked not south to England for trade and inspiration, but over the sea.

Brechin can trace its beginnings back 1,000 years, to the Celtic monastery whose Round Tower still stands, 106 ft tall and pencil slim. To judge by the elevated doorway and the high windows pointing to all four quarters of the compass, it was a place of refuge for the monks in troublous times. Such towers occur in many places in Ireland, but there is only one other example in Scotland, at Abernethy. Brechin's Round Tower is now attached to the largely medieval cathedral; 'largely', because it fell into part-ruin after the Reformation, and suffered even more horribly during a robust rebuilding in 1807. Almost a century later, however, a more thoughtful restoration returned the cathedral to almost its original appearance.

The town itself grew up around the market which the bishop established in the 11th century at the top of what is now the High Street; even though it has changed its site, Brechin Mart, dealing in livestock and general produce, is still an integral part of the life of the town, surviving the later occupations of weaving and distilling. Nineteenth-century prosperity is apparent in St Ninian's Square, and at the station, which has recently been most admirably restored by the Brechin Railway Preservation Society. But even among more recent building, an older Brechin breaks through in street names. Maisondieu Lane recalls a medieval chapel and almshouse, while Witchden marks the place where witches were burned in the 17th and 18th centuries. The last unfortunate to perish there was Janat Couper, whose crime was that a dog jumped up and licked her face as she crossed Brechin Bridge. The dog was judged to be her familiar, her contact with Satan, and poor Janat was consigned to the flames.

Just outside the town, upon a high rock, are the remains of Brechin Castle. Here, Edward I of England stayed in 1296 when he publicly stripped John Balliol, the gentle but inadequate King of Scots, of his royal regalia, and made him swear to 'resign his kingdom, its people, and their homage into the hands of his liege lord, Edward'. This humiliation gave rise to the fervour of patriotism that gripped the Scottish nation and led to the resounding defeat of the English at Bannockburn 18 years later. Long before that, however, in 1303, a small blow for freedom was struck at

Brechin Castle when its garrison held out for three weeks against Edward's entire army, and did not surrender until its commander, Sir John Maule, was killed by a missile from a siege engine. Sir John's descendant, the Earl of Dalhousie, still lives in the early 18th-century house on the site.

BRECON *Powys*

If Brecon's buildings and even street plan seem a little haphazard and confused, then a glance at the town's story will not make all plain exactly, but at least induce a degree of understanding. Known equally legitimately as Brecknock and Aberhonddu, Brecon was first a Celtic stronghold then a Roman fort garrisoned by Spanish auxiliaries; the remains of both structures can still be seen near by. It was named after Brychan, a semi-legendary Irish adventurer, but its founder was a

TOWER OF REFUGE In troubled times, and there were many in this corner of Scotland, the monks of Brechin could keep an eye on the surrounding countryside from the windows high in the Round Tower. Only 15 ft across at the base the tower is an outstanding piece of 10th-century architecture, and was probably built by Irish masons.

Norman baron, Bernard de Neufmarch (or Newmarch) who, having annihilated the forces of Rhys ap Tewdwr, the ruler of South Wales, consolidated his position, temporal and spiritual, by building the castle and the Priory of St John. The town that grew up between them has been in its time a market, a centre for the clothing and shoemaking trades, a county town, a railhead, a regimental headquarters and, since 1923, a cathedral town. All these roles Brecon wears easily, changing its character almost at every turn, from medieval to Jacobean to Georgian or Victorian. So perhaps it is not entirely coincidental that the town produced some striking originals of Shakespearian villains and heroes, and two of the greatest actors of the 18th-century theatre.

No doubt when Bernard de Neufmarch built his castle on the hill above the confluence of the rivers Honddu, Tarell and Usk, he did so for strategic rather than scenic reasons. Yet later and less-militaristic generations have reason to be grateful to him, for what remains of the old defences offers one of the finest views in Wales – the southern horizon filled with mountains, above which soars Pen y Fan (2,906 ft), the summit of the Brecon Beacons. Different families held the castle at different times – the de Breos, the de Bohuns, the Stafford Dukes of Buckingham, one of whom was the original of the smoothly

villainous crony of Shakespeare's *Richard III*.

During the wars of Welsh independence, town and castle suffered the usual sieges and raids, but in the days of the Tudors at least, Brecon was left relatively in peace. In the Civil War, the castle was earmarked as a Royalist stronghold, but the townsfolk cried a plague on both sides and dismantled its defences, knocking down their own town walls at the same time. This made Brecon untenable to both King and Parliament, who were then forced to go off and fight in the towns of less far-sighted people.

The swords into ploughshares theme was continued a century or so later, when a Georgian inn – now a hotel – was woven into the fabric of the castle, creating an unusual, and most attractive, blending of medieval and 18th-century materials and styles. This part of the castle, the part occupied by the hotel, dates from the reign of Edward I. Bernard de Neufmarch's original mound and tower are next door, in the grounds of the Bishop's Palace.

To understand Brecon, the best course is to begin at the old Shire Hall. It stands on the corner of a lane called Captain's Walk, said to be so named because it was a 'favourite lounge' of French officer prisoners-of-war in the early 19th century. The hall is a honey-coloured Grecian temple built in Queen Victoria's reign, and though it no longer has any executive function, it houses one of the liveliest and most evocative local museums in Britain. Particular highlights are the exhibition of Brecon Beacons' wildlife, and the clear exposition of the Roman occupation of the area. The tombstone of one of the garrison, a 20 year old named Candidus, adds poignancy to the display. There is also a dug-out canoe from the 8th-century AD lake-dwellers' village at Llan-gors. The exhibit that most provokes the imagination, however, is the Assize Court, in what really was the courtroom from 1843 to 1970. There it all is, varnished benches, spike-railed dock and lofty judge's seat surmounted by a royal coat of arms.

Beyond the Shire Hall is The Bulwark, which is not quite a street and certainly not a square. It is lined by colour-washed Georgian-esque buildings on one side and by shops on the other, and is filled at the top by the massive, purple-red bulk of St Mary's Church. It is a medieval foundation, but the 100 ft tower dates from the 16th century. Beside the church there is a statue of the Duke of Wellington, who in his lifetime had little to do with Brecon. The reason for the statue's presence, according to the inscription, is that it was 'carved from life' by a local JP.

The Bulwark, about this point, becomes a branch of the High Street, where there are some houses and shops of the 16th and 17th centuries, though many must have had face-lifts since. One of them is a pub called the Sarah Siddons, and it was there that the Divine Sarah, the darling of the 18th-century stage, was born in 1755, though the inn was then known as the Shoulder of Mutton. Mrs Siddons's brother, the equally celebrated actor Charles Kemble, was also born there, and, in a sad continuance of the theatrical motif, the actor-manager and matinée idol Owen Nares died at the inn in 1943.

The High Street, or rather, High Street Inferior, wanders on until it becomes Ship Street, whereupon it divides into two bridges, the Watergate over the brawling Honddu, and the many-arched crossing of the more stately Usk. There is a tree-shaded Promenade along the bank of the Usk at this point, a pleasant place to stroll on a summer evening, or to sit and watch the light change on the Brecon Beacons.

The ancient farmhouse on the opposite shore was the home of the family of Davy Gam, who was killed at Agincourt, and was probably the inspiration for Fluellen, the Welsh professional soldier in Shakespeare's *Henry V*. Not far off is Christ's College, one of the few Welsh Public Schools. Its crest shows a crowned H, for it was founded by Henry VIII in 1541 in buildings that were formerly a Dominican Friary.

Lion Street was meant to be Brecon's main street, it seems, but though it is filled with shops, it somehow failed to achieve its intended status. To compensate, the town has two High Streets instead, High Street Superior as well as the Inferior one. These, and the other streets that make up the mesh of Brecon's centre, are composed of a charming jumble of buildings of all kinds of colours, shapes, ages and sizes, that tilt gently up to the quaintly named thoroughfare of Struet. This climbs to Priory Hill and

the lovely stone close that was put together out of ancient ecclesiastical buildings when the Church – formerly the Priory – of St John, became the Cathedral of the Diocese of Swansea and Brecon in 1923.

Though small and intimate as cathedrals go, it is hard to believe that a building of Brecon Cathedral's size and majesty could ever have been a parish church. In the nave, tall, soaring arches in stone of the softest grey lead the eye to the golden flood of light that pours through deep, narrow, lancet windows on to the chancel floor, illuminating the deeply carved reredos. But grand as it is, there are still touches that bind the cathedral very firmly to the town. The stone, for instance, on which bowmen sharpened their arrowheads before departing for the French wars, or the wooden effigy of a young girl, a descendant of Davy Gam's, or the chapel that has been a place of pilgrimage for the Guild of Cordwainers (shoemakers) since the Middle Ages.

The closest tie, however, is that forged by the Havard Chapel, the regimental chapel of the South Wales Borderers, the old 24th Foot. From its founding in 1689 until its amalgamation into the Royal Regiment of Wales in 1969, the regiment's name appears with distinction in all the annals of Britain's wars. Its hardest, though in some ways, most glorious hour was on January 22, 1879, when the 1st Battalion, and most of the 2nd, were slaughtered almost to a man by the Zulu impi of King Cetewayo at Isandhlwana in southern Africa. The troops stood and fought as a disciplined force to the last, gaining time for B Company of the 2nd Battalion to prepare for its gallant and successful defence of Rorke's Drift later the same day. Nine Victoria Crosses were won in the two engagements. The full story, and that of the South Wales Borderers' long history, is told in the Regimental Museum in the town.

DIVINE SARAH *The Sarah Siddons pub in Brecon's High Street was the birthplace of the 18th-century actress who is reputed to be the finest tragic actress this country has known. At the height of her career she was the idol of the London stage. One of her greatest roles was Lady Macbeth, which she played in her final appearance in 1812.*

BRIDPORT *Dorset*

Back in the days when gallows humour was fashionable, a Bridport dagger meant a hangman's noose, a rather grisly advertisement of the town's chief occupation, that of ropemaking. Perhaps it did make ropes for hangmen; it certainly has made them for every other purpose since 'time out of mind', as an Act of Henry VIII's reign put it. Certainly, the business was well established by the beginning of the 13th century, for there still exists a letter from King John to the Sheriff of Dorset, written during an invasion scare of 1213, demanding that he should 'cause to be made night and day as many ropes for ships, both large and small and as many cables as you can and twisted yarns for cordage and ballistae'.

The reason for the town's paramount position in the craft was that hemp grew abundantly in the district, which is something of a curiosity in itself; hemp is a native of southern Europe and how it reached Dorset would be a mystery, if it had not been firmly ascribed to the Romans. Whoever brought it, Bridport had reason to be grateful. Even when the Royal Navy and the merchant service ceased to use as many ropes as they did, the town was able to slip naturally into the manufacture of nets and twine, using flax as well as hemp, and latterly, man-made fibres too. They are made now in small factories rather than in cottages as was the practice for centuries. But it is by no means uncommon to find people working in them bearing exactly the same names as their ancestors who made rope for the navy 150 years ago.

To some extent, rope shaped the town – its long alleys and gardens are the former ropewalks where hemp was twisted into rope by hand. And its sturdy cottages once housed the net looms. Rope brought the prosperity, too, that laid the foundations of the handsome, exceptionally broad, three main streets. These, mostly Georgian in aspect now, meet at a T-junction by the Town Hall which was built in 1728. This, like many another of its kind, had arches below forming a covered market, while the rooms above were the magistrates' court and the council chamber. The arches are bricked up now, but the market continues as busily as ever, its bright stalls flowing along the pavements which are quite broad enough to

BAY OF BLUE WATER *West Bay, Bridport's harbour, was once a busy shipbuilding centre where vessels of up to 1,000 tons were launched. The last ship built there, the* Lilian *of 80 tons, was launched in 1879, and the site of the old shipyard is now covered by holiday flats and a shopping precinct. West Bay, however, has managed to retain its charm – a quiet haven where inshore fishing boats mingle with the pleasure craft of holidaymakers.*

take them without impeding the traffic. Wednesday and Saturday are the market days, as they have been since they were established in the reign of Elizabeth I. On market days the cheerful, bustling air of the town can best be savoured – enhanced by the quiet contrast of the green hills at the ends of the long streets.

On the whole, the years have been fairly kind to Bridport. Like many West Country towns it suffered dreadfully during the Black Death of the 14th century; the disease was brought to England by a ship that docked at Weymouth just 15 miles to the east. However, the Civil War largely passed it by, apart from a brief visit by Charles II on his flight from the Battle of Worcester in 1651. He stopped at the George Inn, now a shop near the Town Hall, but moved on rapidly when he excited the suspicions of an Ironside regiment about to embark for Jersey. Later in the century, a few young townsmen were hanged by Judge Jeffreys for their part in the Monmouth Rebellion, and there was a setback when the Royal Dockyards at Portsmouth and Chatham began making their own ropes.

By the beginning of the Georgian era, however, the even tenor of life had reasserted itself, as can be sensed from the serene array of Georgian buildings, especially those in East and South Streets. Those in South Street are interrupted by the parish church of St Mary, mostly 14th century with later additions; it has a fine effigy of a cross-legged knight, dating from the late 1200s. On the other side of the street are the Friends' Meeting House and Almshouses of the 17th century, while further along is an extraordinary building called The Chantry. It seems to have been a priest's house in about 1400, but to judge from the cresset, or fire-basket, high on the south wall it was built about a century earlier as a lighthouse. Along South Street is a restored Tudor house containing the town museum and art gallery. There are displays of the net and ropemaking crafts, rural bygones and a splendid collection of dolls from all over the world that were given to Dr Donald Omand, the international padre of circus folk, who was rector of the neighbouring parish of Chideock.

BUCKINGHAM *Buckinghamshire*

The Loyal and Ancient Borough is Buckingham's proudly worn title, the first part of it gained by a generally unswerving devotion to the throne down the years. Certainly, Mary Tudor and Charles I both had cause to be grateful to the town during their troublesome reigns, and later monarchs also had an affection for it.

The Ancient part of Buckingham's title is also true. Standing on a tight bend of the Ouse, it was already the chief town of the shire when Edward the Elder fortified it in the 10th century as part of his defensive system against the Danes. It was also a famous place of pilgrimage, since the relics of St Rumbold, or Ronald, were kept there. A scion of the royal house of Mercia, he was born in November 623, and died three days later. In the interval, this infant prodigy demanded baptism, and preached a sermon on the Holy Trinity

to those about him, citing Scripture, so it is said, and the Athanasian Creed.

Since the Norman Conquest, however, Buckingham's role has been that of a market town of local, rather than wide, importance, and this is the image it presents still. The Town Hall facing on to the wide Market Square is Georgian, and is topped by the chained Swan of Buckingham, adopted from the crest of the Staffords. The Church of St Peter and St Paul is also of the 18th century, with Victorian additions by Sir George Gilbert Scott, who was born at nearby Gawcott.

West Street has the most imposing building, Castle House, whose Georgian front masks a much older house where Catherine of Aragon stayed in 1514. The Manor House, once a priest's house, in Church Street, is also early Tudor and has a renowned curly chimney, the like of which appears elsewhere only at Hampton Court, and that is considered inferior. The oldest building in the town, at least in parts, is the Latin School, once a chapel, which has a zigzag-patterned Norman door-arch. The grimmest building, a mock fortress on Market Hill that was once the gaol, is happily now an antique shop.

In the last few years, the town has developed a new facet in becoming the home of the University of Buckingham, which offers two-year courses of four terms each, instead of the usual three years of three terms each. The university has already a patina of age, since its nucleus is the early Georgian barracks in Hunter Street, once the home of the Buckinghamshire Imperial Yeomanry.

BUNGAY *Suffolk*

A stormy past lies behind Bungay's tranquil present. Take, for example, the occurrence in St Mary's Church in August 1577 when, at the height of a tempest, a terrible Black Dog appeared, 'or the Divel in such a likeness' and in the midst of fire, flew down the aisle, leaving behind it two worshippers strangled at their prayers and another 'as shrunken as a piece of leather scorched in a fire'.

Black Dogs, Shucks, Padfoots and the like are fairly common in the eastern counties where they may have descended from the Hounds of Odin, left behind by the Danes together with a large number of place names. But the chief scourge of early Bungay was human, its Norman overlord in fact, named Hugh Bigod. He built Bungay Castle in 1165, and from this base pillaged his way through East Anglia. The twin-towered castle beside the scant remains of Hugh's fortress was the work of Roger Bigod and dates from a century later; the damage to this structure was caused not by wars, but by an 18th-century building contractor, who used the place as a quarry.

Actually, the castle is not the oldest building in Bungay, since it is predated by the round tower of Holy Trinity Church which was built well before 1100. The remainder of the church is composed of rebuildings, restorations and patchings carried out between the 15th century and 1926, which gives the place

PENALTY POINT *In Bungay's market place the 17th-century Butter Cross also served as a place where justice was done – and was seen to be done as the figure of Justice on the domed roof is not blindfolded. The cross contained a cage, stocks and a cell beneath the floor, all of which were removed during the 19th century. But some wrist irons attached to a pillar remain.*

marvellous character if not architectural cohesion. It has a fine Tudor pulpit, a beautiful modern window in the Lady Chapel and a group of monuments to people whose lives counted for much in the town.

Holy Trinity is now the only parish church in Bungay, since in 1977, St Mary's was sadly made redundant. Founded in the 12th century as the church of a Benedictine priory – whose ruins can be seen at the eastern end of the churchyard – it is a marvellous building with a soaring square tower that can be seen for miles around. The church is still consecrated and is used for occasional services of civic importance, and for concerts. It remains as beautiful as ever, and is generally open to the public. Both churches bear inscriptions that refer to the great fire of 1688 that devastated Bungay from end to end. Out of the ashes grew a handsome Georgian town with a theatre, club, and even a small spa to serve the gentry of the surrounding countryside.

YESTERDAY TODAY *The most modern building in Burford's High Street dates from the 18th century, for the 19th century with its hard-faced commercialism passed the town by, and the 20th century has had the good sense to keep Burford as the 18th century left it.*

BURFORD *Oxfordshire*

It sells the best lemon curd in the world, and antique furniture with the deepest, waxiest shine. Best of all, for the traveller going west from London, it provides the first proof positive that small English towns can be just as pretty, quaint and olde worlde as they seem in the calendars and the Christmas supplements. Burford's charm is derived from the happy sum of a number of components; the lovely, greenweed-swaying River Windrush, Cotswold stone, whose colour and texture are particularly suited to buildings that were intended to live for ever, to some good architects and builders down the years; and long ago, the medieval wool merchants who made the town rich.

The buildings left by generations of prosperous merchants and tradesmen are a cavalcade of England's social history. The almshouses built by Warwick the Kingmaker near the church, the Lamb Inn, some houses at the top of the High Street and on The Hill are all of the 15th century, while The Tolsey, on the corner of Sheep Street, is only a little younger. This was where the council met and conducted the town's business, including the collection of market tolls; it is now the museum. Burford's great benefactor, the Elizabethan textile merchant Simon Wisdom, founded the Grammar School and paid for a number of other buildings, including the Weavers' Cottages by the pretty bridge whose arches are so low they seem hardly able to rise above the river. The 17th century is also well represented, most notably by The Great House, built by Christopher Kempster, one of Wren's master masons during the rebuilding of London after the Great Fire of 1666.

The Church of St John Baptist mirrors the history of the town from the church's foundation in the 12th century to the present. Even the gravestones in the churchyard tell a story, for the round-topped ones are modelled upon wool bales and mark the graves of people who were engaged in the wool trade. There is a profusion of more ornamental carving, ancient and modern, throughout the building, and inscriptions and coats of arms tell of the close involvement of the old Craft Guilds with the church.

BUXTON *Derbyshire*

The Romans were great hypochondriacs, or at least the ones who were exiled to this chilly outpost of empire, and it was they who first experimented with the therapeutic qualities of the waters at Buxton, just as they did at Bath, Cheltenham and other spas. They called the place Aquae Arnemetiae – the watering place of the goddess of the grove – and they built two baths there. One of these survived until 1709, when a Sir Thomas Delves built an arch of thanksgiving over a spring that he believed had cured him of some malady or other, and destroyed the Roman bath in the process.

The Saxons had little use for water in general nor spas in particular, and for 1,000 years Buxton was abandoned. Then in the early Middle Ages the curative

properties of the waters were rediscovered, and a small chapel was built beside what had come to be known as St Ann's Well. Its walls were festooned with the crutches of those who had experienced beneficial results, but at the time of the Dissolution of the Monasteries, Henry VIII denounced the whole thing as an idle superstition, and ordered the chapel to be closed and the medieval bath sealed.

His subjects thought otherwise, however, and continued to patronise the well. Elizabeth I's courtiers came to take the waters, and Mary, Queen of Scots' gaoler, the Earl of Shrewsbury, took his unfortunate charge there on several occasions in an effort to cure her of rheumatism. She stayed in a house on a site now occupied by the Old Hall Hotel, where she scratched on a window-pane a Latin verse expressing her disquieting suspicion that she might never again

sample the 'milk-warm waters' of Buxton. The pane can still be seen in the Poole's Cavern Museum.

But it was the late 18th century that witnessed the most glorious days of the English spas. As is apparent from the novels of Jane Austen, it was an age when a certain delicacy of health was considered genteel, and it could be enjoyed all the more in the convivial atmosphere of the Pump Rooms, Assembly Rooms and Ballrooms of the spas. The 5th Duke of Devonshire, on whose land Buxton stood, saw his opportunity, and determined to build a spa to rival Bath itself. The plan had every chance of success. Buxton, standing 1,000 ft up in the High Peak, was already renowned for the purity of its air. More important, its slightly saline water, rising from a natural reservoir about a mile down through the limestone, arrives in an attractive pale blue shade at an unvarying 82°F, and is con-

SPA OF THE HIGH PEAK *In a landscape of rolling moorlands the elegant façades of Buxton's spa stand in panoramic splendour. Most notable are the sweeping curve of the Crescent and behind it the Great Stable, which later became the Devonshire Royal Hospital, while set back from the town is the Palace Hotel, built when the nearby railway arrived in 1868.*

GRAND MANNER *Buxton's Opera House was built in 1903, with all the opulence and grandeur of the new Edwardian era. For many years it served as a cinema, but in 1979 it was restored to its original purpose and is now the home of an annual festival of opera, music and drama.*

siderably more palatable than the sulphurous concoctions offered by many other spas.

In 1780, the Duke of Devonshire engaged John Carr of York, the leading Palladian architect of the day, and beside the little medieval market town of Buxton there swiftly arose the breathtaking, pale brown stone Crescent, whose massive pillars support the beautifully curving arcade, the 70 ft long Grand Assembly Room and an array of shopping and hotel facilities. The Duke's scheme also included the Great Stables, containing stalls for 110 horses and a circular exercise court that was later roofed with an enormous, slate-covered dome. The Square, the Quadrant, and a precinct of fashionable shops were added to the plan, and later, with the coming of the railways, the gigantic Palace Hotel, and a number of only slightly smaller ones, and the iron-framed glass Pavilion in its 23 acres of gardens. The present Pump Room, still containing St Ann's Well in an oval, marble basin, was completed in 1894.

Even if spas in general have lost some of their old appeal, present-day Buxton has responded to the challenge by adapting its old facilities and adding others to attract a new generation of visitors. People still flock to the Pump Room, and if no longer in search of a cure, nevertheless sample the waters out of curiosity. The Assembly Room has been superbly restored, and is now the reference library, while the Great Stable was long ago given a new role as the Devonshire Royal Hospital, which specialises in hydrotherapy treatment for rheumatic complaints. The water for this is supplied by the spring, which also feeds the new swimming pool and provides for the town's thriving bottled-water plant.

CAERNARFON *Gwynedd*

The lofty walls and towers of Caernarfon Castle, one of the finest examples of medieval military architecture in Europe, are relatively recent arrivals on the scene in this fascinating little 'royal town' on the Menai Strait which has flourished in one form or another for nearly 2,000 years. Its colourful history is embellished with such names as Edward I, Owain Glyndwr and David Lloyd George.

Caernarfon's story starts in about AD 78 when a Roman fort, known as Segontium, was established alongside what is now the main road to Beddgelert. Controlled by the 20th Legion, based in Chester, Segontium became a key outpost whose responsibilities extended from Snowdonia to the Menai Strait and Anglesey. The original garrison is believed to have totalled 1,000 men from a regiment raised by the Romans in northern Spain.

Segontium was excavated by Sir Mortimer Wheeler in the 1920s. A museum on the site tells the story of the fort itself and of the native community of shops, taverns and dwellings that developed outside its walls. Segontium was held until the end of the 4th century when its troops, like their comrades elsewhere in Britain, were recalled to defend the hub of the crumbling Roman Empire.

Caernarfon's 'modern' period dates from the end of the 12th century and the death of Llewelyn the Last. Edward I, determined to solve the Welsh problem, decided to build a ring of great castles around the mountains that had been the native princes' natural fortress for hundreds of years. Caernarfon, first mentioned as such in 1188, was to be the centre of English rule in North Wales.

The existing settlement and its people were moved to make way for a castle and a new town, protected by a wall, whose man-made defences were supplemented by the River Seiont, the Menai Strait and the River Cadnant. Like the rest of Edward's strongholds, Caernarfon could be supplied from the sea whereas most native fortresses were inland, guarding passes through the mountains.

Work started in 1283 and involved craftsmen from as far afield as Yorkshire and France. Progress was slow. The town was burned in 1294, during the revolt led by Madog ap Llewelyn, and by the end of the 13th century its population was probably no more than about 400.

The future Edward II was born in Caernarfon in 1284 and became the first English Prince of Wales. His birthplace was almost certainly one of the timber-framed buildings erected by Edward I and Queen Eleanor while work on the castle itself was still in the early stages. Tradition tells how Edward offered his baby son to the people of Wales as a Welsh-born prince who could speak no English. He was, of course, too young to speak anything.

The castle cost about £20 million in today's money and saw action for the last time during the Civil War, when it changed hands three times. Parliament ordered its demolition in 1660, but the majestic fortress

survived, together with its town walls, and is now one of Britain's greatest tourist attractions. In 1969 it echoed to the pomp of a royal investiture when Prince Charles became Prince of Wales.

The Queen's Tower houses the museum of the Royal Welch Fusiliers, a regiment whose roots go back to 1689. Exhibits include a Russian cannon captured during the Crimean War.

A statue of David Lloyd George, fist raised in an oratorical pose, stands in Castle Square. He was Member of Parliament for the Caernarfon Boroughs from 1890 until 1945 and rose from a humble village background to become President of the Board of Trade, Chancellor of the Exchequer, Minister of Munitions, Secretary of State for War and Prime Minister. Sir Winston Churchill hailed him as the greatest Welshman since the Tudors. Lloyd George was also Constable of Caernarfon Castle.

The town walls, punctuated by eight towers and two twin-towered gateways, extend for almost half a mile and enclose a gridiron of streets whose basic layout has not changed since the end of the 13th century. The north-west corner of the walls embraces St Mary's Church, built at the same time as the castle and also known as the Garrison Chapel. Other buildings of interest include the Market Hall of 1832 and the impressive County Hall, completed 31 years later, which has all the grandeur of a Roman temple.

The booming slate industry was one reason for Caernarfon's population increasing by more than 100 per cent during the first half of the 19th century. The road beside the River Seiont is still known as the Slate Quay, while the Harbour Office, built in 1840, is another reminder of the days when sailing ships from this historic town carried the 'grey gold' of Snowdonia to ports in many distant lands.

ROYAL TOWN *Edward I's formidable castle stands guard over the Menai Strait, with the old town of Caernarfon clustered beneath its ramparts. The town has its own walls, which extend from those of the castle and enclose a maze of narrow streets, unchanged in layout for 700 years.*

CALLANDER *Central*

It often says of itself – and other authorities are of the same opinion – that it is the gateway to the Highlands. If so, then it is the outer gateway, for though the hills of Perthshire and the immensely picturesque Trossachs girt it half about, Callander itself is unquestionably a Lowland town. It stands among green fields and by the sedate River Teith in as gentle a setting, if the horizon is ignored, as any in southern England. The town too, with its rectangular stone houses, wide walks and streets and its airy square, looks planned and orderly, as if consciously shunning any temptations from the wild Highlands.

Perhaps this was half-deliberate, for Callander was created by the Commissioners for the Forfeited Estates in the aftermath of the Jacobite Rising of 1745. The estates were those of the chiefs who had been 'out' for Prince Charlie, and Callander was part of the scheme to pacify the Highlands and introduce its inhabitants to such benefits of the modern world as industry and commerce. A major part of the town, therefore, is late 18th century, as can be seen in the splendid symmetry of Ancaster Square, whose focal

HIGHLAND PRELUDE *On a misty horizon the purple-clad Trossachs give a hint of the Highlands beyond Callander, and the town itself gently ushers in the scenic grandeur with the wooded Callander Crags climbing steeply above the waters of the River Teith.*

point is the tall, slim spire of St Kessog's Church. Kessog was a 6th-century Irish monk who brought the Gospel to the Callander area and is traditionally believed to have preached from Tomnachessaig, the grassy knoll named after him, by the river.

If the visitor experiences the curious feeling that he has seen Callander before, he is very probably right, for the town represented 'Tannochbrae' in the long-running TV series, *Dr Finlay's Casebook.* The streets, the surrounding countryside and even the inhabitants appeared weekly on the nation's screens over a period of several years. Obligatory viewing for enthusiasts is, of course, Arden House, the hero's home. In Callander, it is called Auchengower, and may be found above Ancaster Gardens. It was an admirable choice, since the stone villa is as straightforward and slightly quirky as Dr Cameron, its fictional owner.

CARMARTHEN *Dyfed*

For one of the most ancient centres of population in Britain, Carmarthen reveals little of its age to the casual glance. A lot of Victorian, a fair amount of Georgian, a great deal of supermarketry; but then, to a town that has been busy for the best part of 2,000 years, what matters is the present and the future.

It all began with the Celtic hill-fort that watched over the River Towy (Afon Tywi) from Castle Hill, above and behind Nott Square. This was superseded by the Roman town of Maridunum – fortress of the sea – but as with the Celtic stronghold, little of it remains to be seen. The Quay is the site of the Roman harbour, and the remains of a thriving commercial centre have been discovered recently beneath St Peter's car park. But the most important Roman site is the amphitheatre in Priory Street. It offered seating for 5,000 spectators at gladiatorial combats and wild-beast shows; now it is a turf bowl, which, in spring and summer, smells sweetly of new-mown grass.

After the Romans left, there followed the so-called Dark Ages, the period of Celtic dream-time and Arthurian legend, when the wizard Merlin may or may not have been born in the town. Tradition firmly asserts that he was and, until recently, there was at the corner of Priory Street and Oak Lane the shattered and buttressed stump of an ancient oak to prove it. Of this it was said:

When Merlin's tree shall tumble down
Then shall fall Carmarthen Town.

But it no longer has a chance to tumble since it resides safely in a glass case in St Peter's Civic Hall, having been poisoned early in the 19th century by a local shopkeeper who objected to his neighbours meeting and chattering under its shade.

This being Wales, there is no shortage of churches and chapels in Carmarthen – Welsh Baptist, English Baptist, Calvinistic Methodist, Congregationalist, Independent Methodist and a number of others – but to the visitor in search of Carmarthen's story, it is St Peter's that beckons. It is at least 800 years old – the first-known vicar was appointed in 1278 – but owing to the lack of decorative detail, it is almost impossible to date precisely.

The interior of the church is graceful and austere, brightened here and there by fading, laid-up Colours of The Welch Regiment and the Royal Welch Fusiliers. The monuments are fascinating. They include the tomb of Sir Rhys ap Thomas, who fought for Henry Tudor at Bosworth Field, and is said to have cut down Richard III with his battleaxe.

The centre of Carmarthen is really the Guildhall, a classical, stone-porticoed building of 1767 fronted by a monument to townsmen who served in the Boer War. From there, a web of streets runs out, mostly composed of brick or coloured-washed houses and big, busy shops, for Carmarthen is, and has been for centuries, the marketing centre of West Wales. The market pavilion is a magnet for the entire surrounding countryside on Wednesdays and Saturdays.

CHEPSTOW *Gwent*

Seen through the romance-tinted spectacles of the 18th century, the place was perfection indeed: 'Uncommonly excellent', enthused an 18th-century traveller, '... in the assemblage of wood, cliffs, ruins and water', while local cleric and bard, Edward Davies, fancied that '... through this town must be the road to Heav'n, whose gate is straight, streets narrow and uneven'. Taken together, these sentiments add up to a very fair picture of present-day Chepstow, especially when Edward Davies's more prosaic thought is included:

> *Strange to tell, there cannot here be found*
> *One single inch of horizontal ground.*

Old Chepstow is a compact town – enforcedly so, since it is crammed down a steep slope into a great oxbow bend in the River Wye, which here separates Wales from England. The Portwall, the town wall built in 1275, runs in a 1,200 yd curve round the top of the town to rest each end on the river. This compacts Chepstow still more, but it is no disadvantage, for few towns present such a cohesive image to the world, a picture in which all the elements and stories of streets, church and castle are interlocked to a quite astonishing degree.

The town proper begins at the dark, medieval tunnel of the Town Gate; the part without the wall is known as Hardwick, or Garden City, and was built to house the workers in the National Shipyard that was constructed on the Wye during the First World War. Immediately beyond the Town Gate, which was intended more as a collecting point for market dues than as a defensive feature, is the steep and busy High Street, with No. 1 immediately to the right. Known also as the Gate House, it was rebuilt in 1609 for Mrs Margaret Cleyton, a rich and merry widow and local benefactress. Her initials are inscribed on the wall and her elaborate tomb may be seen in the church. The High Street plunges on down, an unselfconscious mixture of supermarkets, pubs, hotels, yellow and minareted Coronation Buildings of 1902, and much older houses – until it reaches Beaufort Square.

This spacious, steeply sloping quadrangle was the market place for the surrounding countryside for 650 years and more, and though it is no longer so, it is still unquestionably the hub of the town. There, some pretty Georgian and Regency buildings are mingled with good modern stone; Barclays Bank is particularly handsome. Lord Nelson stayed in what was an inn at the bottom end of the square, and no doubt would have been interested in the deck gun taken from a captured U-boat during the First World War.

Below Beaufort Square, the town breaks up into the tangle of smaller streets that are its principal charm. Bridge Street, for example, with a block of 1716 almshouses at the corner, is a ski-run of bow-

BORDER LINK *The River Wye forms the border between England and Wales at Chepstow, and is spanned by the delicate tracery of a cast-iron bridge which has been a gateway to South Wales for more than 160 years. It was built by John Raistrick of Bridgnorth in 1816 and still carries road traffic on the main road south from Gloucester.*

windowed cottages dropping down to the river, beyond which rise the magnificent wooded cliffs on the English side of the Wye. Cobbled Hawker Hill Street is something of a problem, since on one side it is labelled Hocker Hill Street and on the other Hawker Hill Street, perhaps the result of some ancient and unsettled council dispute.

Perhaps the prettiest of the small thoroughfares is St Mary Street, a steep, narrow climb lined with colour-washed buildings bearing turrets, wrought-iron Regency balconies and dormer windows. Such a street is the natural habitat of antique shops, book shops and small restaurants, and they are present in droves.

St Mary's Church, from which the street takes its name, is not best served by a glum surrounding of factory backs and a car park, but there is a merry avenue of young chestnuts through the churchyard and in any event, all is forgiven when the front door is reached. It takes no great knowledge of ecclesiastical architecture to realise that this is a rarity, a magnificent early Norman doorway consisting of five concentric arches on receding columns and flanked by two smaller arches; and since its recent cleaning, the old stonework positively glows.

Such grandeur in a parish church is not usual, and in fact St Mary's is the nave of a priory that was the gift of William FitzOsbern, Earl of Hereford and builder of Chepstow's castle, to the Abbey of Cormeilles in Normandy in about 1071. The remainder of the priory was dismantled after the Dissolution of the Monasteries, and of its mother-house in Normandy, very

little is left either. But by a pleasant touch, Chepstow is now twinned with the town of Cormeilles, whose citizens have presented a fragment of the abbey ruins to St Mary's. The interior of Chepstow's church is every bit as splendid as the entrance – lofty walls of worn stone leading the eye along the nave to the, literally, high altar on top of its three graceful steps. The chancel, and the entire nave, are lit by the soft colours of the great east window, which depicts the Ascension and was given to the church in 1896.

There are some lively, if that is the right term, monuments; see especially the life-sized effigies of the second Earl of Worcester, who died in 1549, and his wife. Both are golden-coroneted, ruffed and in full colour. Then there is the large monument to Mrs Cleyton, the lady of the Gate House, who is shown with her two husbands kneeling beside her, and her 12 children underneath.

Behind the church, a couple of streets with 17th and 18th-century houses run down to the Wye and to the cast-iron road bridge, which was built in 1816 and, with a little strengthening, copes perfectly well with modern traffic. Close by are the old warehouses of The Back, really all that remains of the great port that flourished from the time of Domesday Book until the early years of the 19th century.

Chepstow's other contribution to the good life is its racecourse, surely the scenic wonder of the British turf. One end undulates gently to a vast upland meadow where cattle and sheep graze against a background of the Wyndcliffe heights, while at the other, the slim towers of the Severn Bridge lift over an assembly of venerable trees. This is also a fine way to come to the town – from the Welsh side, that is – for in a short time the road affords a spectacular view of Chepstow's great theatrical set-piece, its castle.

The first fortification was built on the spur above the Wye by William the Conqueror's henchman, William FitzOsbern, Earl of Hereford and Lord of Striguil, as the place was called then. Defended on one side by a gully, and on the other by cliffs falling sheer into the Wye, the site could easily be supplied by river, and at the same time overlooked all movement on the route into South Wales. FitzOsbern built straight away in stone, unusually for the Normans, whose earliest, hastily raised fortifications were normally of wood. Much of his Great Tower still stands.

Despite, or perhaps because of, its defences, the castle saw very little action until the Civil Wars of the 17th century. Then it was besieged twice; on the second occasion, four Parliamentarian guns blew a hole in the walls and the Royalist governor, Sir Nicholas Kenneys, deserted by his men, died in a last, lonely stand.

After the war, the big round tower, known as Marten's Tower, in the middle of the bailey was used as a political prison. One of the prisoners was the regicide Henry Marten, who for some reason escaped the usual hanging and quartering suffered by the other signatories of Charles I's death warrant, and spent a not too rigorous 20 years instead in the tower named after him.

SATIRICAL SIGN *In Georgian times John Bull was a symbolic figure representing the British people, and present-day drinkers at the Five Alls pub in Chepstow will have much sympathy with the sentiment expressed by him in the pub's sign. Even the name of the brewer seems ironically appropriate.*

CHIPPING CAMPDEN *Gloucestershire*

Whether raised by a knight that helped to rid Henry II of the troublesome Thomas Becket, or in the decade that America was discovered, or the day before yesterday, almost all of Chipping Campden comes out of a single quarry at the top of Westinghouse Hill. The pale brown stone, dabbled with golden lichen, gives a unity and a mingling of the centuries that must be very pleasant to live with.

In fact, the town was old long before the slaying of Becket. Five hundred years earlier it was sufficiently well known for a council of Saxon kings to be held there. By 1100, it was a prosperous market; the Chipping, or Chepe-ing part of the name indicates this, for it is derived from the Anglo-Saxon word for market. Its speciality was wool, raw wool collected from as far away as the Welsh Marches, and exported much farther, to the Low Countries and even to Florence.

Like London Bridge, Campden's Church of St James was built upon sacks of wool – not literally in either case, but rather upon the wealth of England's wool merchants. There was almost certainly a church on the same site in Saxon times, but most of the present cathedral-like building dates from the 15th century, and was paid for by the woolmen, several of whose memorial brasses can be seen in the chancel. One of

them, William Grevel, is described as 'the flower of the wool merchants of all England', though it has been suggested that most of the work in the church was completed before he came to live in Campden. There are a hundred things to see in the church, bright with the light pouring through its delicately columned clerestory windows, but its greatest treasure is its needlework, kept in glass cases beneath the tower. There is a cope of 1380, and a perfect and unique set of 15th-century altar hangings that were copied, at Queen Mary's order, as a thank-offering to Westminster Abbey after the coronation of George V in 1911.

Close by the church are the Jacobean lodges and gateway of the great house that the first Lord Campden built. Of the house itself, only fragments remain, since it was fired by Royalist troops during the Civil War, either in the course of a drunken spree, or more creditably, to prevent it falling into the hands of the enemy.

A good deal of the stone from the house was used to patch, fill and build in the High Street and, sad though the loss of the house was, it could not have been put to a better use, for this is one of the loveliest small town main streets in England. The buildings are of all periods, but they mingle happily together, from Woolstapler's Hall, now a museum, and William Grevel's House, both of the 14th century, to the very grand Bedfont House, built by the master mason

MEDIEVAL MARKET *In the cool shade of the Market Hall, Chipping Campden's townsfolk once set up their stalls to sell butter, eggs and poultry. Built in 1627 by Sir Baptist Hicks, a wealthy merchant and benefactor, the hall's cobbled floor is time-worn by the passage of many feet, but its ancient arches still look out on a scene little changed from medieval times.*

Thomas Woodward in 1740. Also in the High Street is the arched Market Hall and the elegant almshouses, all the gift of the first Lord Campden, a large number of 17th and 18th-century houses, and some immensely aged pubs. Spare a particular glance for Dover's House, for it recalls a true innovator, Robert Dover, who founded his 'Olympick' Games in the town in the 17th century. They were stopped by the Puritans, and by later killjoys too, but they survive to this day, and are held in early summer each year on Dover's Hill.

Another, and very different, innovation took place at the Silk Mill at the beginning of this century, when C. R. Ashbee took over the derelict building and made it the home of his Guild of Craftsmen. This Utopian experiment involved the importing of 40 or 50 London craftsmen of different trades, with the double object of forming a workers' co-operative and improving the standard of British craftsmanship. The Guild itself did not last very long, but Ashbee carried out some splendid restorations on the old buildings in the town, and short-lived though the society was, its work gained an international reputation. Some of the descendants of the Guildsmen still work in the Silk Mill, producing goods of equally high standard.

CIRENCESTER *Gloucestershire*

A few years after the invasion, the Romans built a fort at this place in the Cotswolds, no doubt to keep an eye on the Dobunni, the principal tribe of the area, whose capital was at Bagendon, some 4 miles to the north. The fort was garrisoned by probably about 500 auxiliary cavalry recruited from far distant parts of the Empire, and now put down upon this benighted spot with nothing to do in their off-duty hours and nothing to spend their pay upon. Enterprising tribespeople swiftly remedied both wants, and within a short time, a small settlement grew up about the gates of the fort to supply food, drink and other necessaries to the soldiery. From this modest beginning there grew Corinium, the largest town in Roman Britain after Londinium.

It was a walled town with wide streets and a public baths, with a vast forum – market place – dominated by a most imposing basilica, which was more or less the town hall. One end of its outline is marked out in a cul-de-sac opposite modern Tower Street, and traces of the Roman town walls can be seen in Beeches Road, in Watermoor Gardens and in the Abbey Grounds. Apart from a grassy hollow that was once its amphitheatre, the remainder of Corinium lies a few feet beneath present-day Cirencester, which long ago abandoned the Roman rectangular street pattern, and went its own random Saxon and medieval way. However, for those who would wish to glimpse the glory that was Corinium, and understand the development of the town afterwards, there is the Cirencester Museum, one of the best small town museums in the country.

Following upon the Romans and the Saxons, the Normans built a castle, and, in 1117, Henry I founded an abbey there. No one knows quite what happened

RETIRED CROSS *Like an elderly retainer whose work is done, Cirencester's Market Cross now stands in the quieter environs of West Market Place, a few yards from where it had stood for centuries as a focal point and meeting place.*

to the castle, but the abbey's fate was that at the Reformation it was decreed that not one of its stones should be left standing, and indeed they were not. They were distributed instead as building materials about the town.

During the wool boom of the Middle Ages, Cirencester rose again to greatness, and to a prosperity that surpassed even that of the days of the Roman occupation. Cotswold cloth and wool were in demand throughout northern Europe, and the wealth they brought to Cirencester's merchants is reflected in the almshouses that are squeezed among the Tudor, Georgian and Victorian buildings along the old streets.

The church of St John the Baptist that overshadows

COTSWOLD GLORY *Built of honey-coloured stone in the Perpendicular Gothic style, Cirencester's parish church dominates the ancient Cotswold town.*

the Market Place and the entire town, might almost be said to be a hymn to wool. It was founded, probably on the site of Romano-British and Saxon churches, in 1117, the same year as the abbey, but most of the present glorious structure was paid for by the merchants of the 15th and early 16th centuries. All except the tower, that is, which was inadvertently suscribed to by the rebellious Earls of Kent and Salisbury in 1399. They were seized and beheaded by the townsmen of Cirencester, and the delighted Henry IV graciously permitted them to retain the earls' treasure as a contribution towards the church tower. Apart from this, the most remarkable, and in fact unique, exterior feature is the south porch; a lovely pinnacled, three-storey stone wedding cake that was built about 1490 as a suite of offices in which the abbot conducted his business with the town. Another survival from abbey days is the exquisite fan tracery in St Catherine's Chapel, so delicate that it looks as though it had been moulded from some plastic substance, rather than carved from solid stone. This was the gift of John Hakebourne, the last abbot but one before the Dissolution. Despite these connections, St John's was always a separate entity and always the parish church, serving the community rather than the abbey. Though grander than most, it might easily be demonstrated as everyone's ideal of a parish church, from the fascinating detail of its monuments and its venerable fonts and pulpit, to the richness of its medieval wall paintings. Like all good parish churches, it has its touch of eccentricity, in this case a curious effigy of a Bluecoat boy standing on a plinth. It used to stand in the porch as a reminder to the congregation to give alms to the church school.

Visitors who collect superlatives should, before they leave, stroll into Cirencester Park, whose Broad Avenue, 5 miles in length, is the longest in England. The entire park is criss-crossed by rides and dotted with follies, monuments and conceits, and was the creation of the first Lord Bathurst at the beginning of the 18th century. His friend, the poet Alexander Pope who had a hand in the planning, wrote admiringly:

Who then shall grace or who improve the soil
Who plants like Bathurst or who builds like Boyle.

Now, in maturity, the park has reached perfection, and its pleasures have been enhanced by what is said to be the finest polo ground in the country. The present Lord Bathurst lives in The Mansion, tucked away behind an enormous, semi-circular yew hedge at the edge of the town. The house is not open to the public, but everyone is very welcome to wander in the park.

But perhaps the best place from which to view it is the top of the church tower – 150 ft up – from which town, park and a large stretch of the Cotswolds can be seen.

CLITHEROE *Lancashire*

Clitheroe stands athwart the only place in the lower Ribble Valley where the river flows between two high fells, the dark and rather sinister masses of Easington Fell and Pendle Hill. The 3 mile gap between them is the passage through which all traffic, military and mercantile, must travel, and it is conveniently overlooked by two limestone knolls. On one of these, shortly after the Norman Conquest, Rodger de Poictou, the lord of half of Lancashire, built a small castle. The other, a few years later, was capped by the Church of St Mary Magdalene. Clitheroe grew up between them.

Roger's keep, the smallest in England, is only a shell now. It has a great hole in one wall that was caused either by the Devil hurling a boulder at it from a spot near Pendle Hill, or by a roundshot from Cromwell's artillery; in this Royalist area, it meant much the same thing. All the same, the castle is still the keynote of the town and the main street, Castle Hill, curving nobly down to the Town Hall, would yet make a believable backdrop for a clattering expedition of knights and men-at-arms. That most of the architecture is Geor-

gian or Victorian would not detract from the scene, since the sombre limestone, of which much of it is composed, is timeless. The castle now belongs to the town, and is surrounded by a splendid public park, while the view from the top of the curtain wall stretches over Clitheroe to the majestic folds of the Bowland fells and the lovely Ribble Valley.

The Town Hall, at the corner of Church Street, dates only from 1822, but it is the citadel of a borough founded in 1147. It incorporates some fine heraldic carving, and the Corporation plate is picturesque and venerable, reflecting the town's ancient traditions and civic pride. So too does the Royal Grammar School in York Street, founded in 1554 by Mary Tudor.

St Mary Magdalene, the parish church, has also undergone considerable change, and little can be seen now of the original Norman structure. Most of the building dates from 1829, but some medieval fragments are incorporated in the fabric.

LORDLY MANSION *Behind a 40 ft high yew hedge, planted in 1818, the mansion built by the first Lord Bathurst sits on the edge of one of the largest parks in England. In the 3,000 acre grounds, vast avenues stretch into seemingly limitless space with glimpses of the Cotswolds beyond.*

BRIDGE IN TRUST *The National Trust now owns the suspension bridge which carried the Chester-Holyhead road across the River Conwy for 130 years. Built in 1826, it is preserved as a memorial to its designer, Thomas Telford, who tastefully and conscientiously suspended his graceful chains from turreted archways that blended with the ancient walls and towers of Conwy Castle.*

CONWY *Gwynedd*

Looked at from the castle battlements, Conwy seems not a town, but the crowded foredeck of a great ship, whose bows rise to a high-towered peak to the north-west and whose massive bulwarks are defended by turrets incongruously sprouting deep yellow wall-flowers. From this viewpoint too the ship appears to be joined to the shore – actually the opposite bank of the River Conwy – by three mighty gangplanks: a modern road bridge, Thomas Telford's suspension bridge of 1826, and Robert Stephenson's tubular construction, built 20 years later to carry the railway. All three make their entrance beneath the towering superstructure of the fortress that Edward I threw up in the 1280s as part of his strategy to contain, and then to crush, Welsh resistance. But see the town in a softer light, at evening say, when the castle's eight towers are umbered by the lowering sun, and the edges of the woods on the low hills beyond the Conwy glow golden. Then it becomes a city of the troubadours, a

place that belongs more to Languedoc perhaps, or to the banks of the Loire, than to homely Wales.

Conwy people say that their town was founded by Llywelyn the Great (1175–1249), and have erected his statue in Lancaster Square to prove it. But there would seem to be a certain amount of patriotic wistfulness in the idea, since all that the Welsh prince did was to found a Cistercian abbey on the spot where the parish church now stands. When Edward I arrived, he moved the monks to Maenan, some 8 miles up the river, and built the castle and town walls. His architect was Master James of St George, the greatest military engineer of the time, and what he built at Conwy can be seen today almost in its entirety. The roofs and floors have gone from the castle, but the town wall, three-quarters of a mile around, and its 22 guard towers and three gates are still complete. Though a good deal of building, and much character too, has been created outside the wall, this great encircling arm has tended to confine the town, so that down the centuries, each generation has built upon foundations laid by its predecessors, so amassing an astonishing array of styles.

At first, the steeply sloping area within the walls was divided into building lots, each with its own garden-space, and let to English merchants whose rents and market-dues were intended to go towards the castle's maintenance. It was never Edward's intention that the place should be held by a large, permanent garrison. Like battleships in later wars, it was not necessary that the mighty fortress should fight, but merely exist as an ever-present threat.

Only occasionally did the castle appear in history's headlines. Edward I himself was briefly besieged in it by Prince Madog in 1294; it was the scene of Richard II's betrayal and capture by the Earl of Northumberland in 1399, and it was taken and held by followers of Owain Glyndwr for a few weeks in 1401. Its last battle was during the Civil War, when it was held for the king by John Williams, Archbishop of York, but it surrendered after a three-month siege.

For much of Conwy's history, therefore, the castle was little more than a backdrop to the lives and affairs of its townspeople. As well as a trading centre, the town was an important ferry point on the road to Holyhead and Dublin, and even after Telford built his bridge, travellers continued to break their journey there. Fishing was, and is, important; Conwy mussels have been raked from their estuary beds since Roman times, traditionally for their pearls, but now simply for dispatch to fishmongers all over the country. Shellfish and the trawling fleet have between them made Conwy the busiest fishing port in Wales. Yachts and dinghies dance at anchor in the harbour, and there is often a fishing boat unloading, attended by seagulls and jackdaws – which nest in holes in the castle's walls – picking their way among the 12 ft handles of the mussel rakes that lie about the Quay. By the Lower Gate the visitor may buy fresh Dover sole, plaice, whiting, or whatever else the Irish Sea yields on the day. These creatures, together with octopuses, lobsters and the like, all fished from Conwy's home

Edward I's castle at Conwy and the town within its walls were built as a unit; the town supplied the castle which in turn protected the town behind walls 35 ft high with towers set every 50 yds. It was a tight squeeze, especially along the Quay where one dwelling claims to be the smallest house in Britain (above). At 10 ft high by 6 ft wide few would argue with the claim, particularly its last occupant who stood 6 ft 3 in. tall. More spacious is Aberconwy House (below left), of uncertain age but probably almost as old as the castle. It is now a National Trust museum with rooms furnished in 15th-century style.

waters, may also be seen in the quayside aquarium.

Much of Conwy's story, and particularly that of the life of its people, is told in the fine National Trust Museum in Aberconwy House, which itself is a contemporary of the castle. In its time, it has been merchant's house, coffee shop, Temperance Hotel, and many other things.

Aberconwy House stands on the site once occupied by the abbey, and shares it with the Vicarage Gardens Car Park, on which are held the ancient Seed Fair in the spring, and Honey Fair in the autumn. It also shares it with St Mary's Church, which dates mainly from the late 13th century, though its west door is older, and is very likely that of the chapter house of the long-vanished abbey. The church has one of the finest rood screens in Wales, a 15th-century font, and the grave of Nicholas Hookes who, the 41st child of his father, himself sired 27 children. He expired in 1637.

The grandest house in Conwy, and perhaps the finest town house in all Wales, is Plas Mawr, which fronts on to the High Street, but is so hemmed in that in order to appreciate its vastness and noble lines, it is better to walk round the corner and look on the side that faces into Crown Lane. It was built by the Elizabethan soldier and adventurer Robert Wynne of Gwydir in 1577–80, and is a handsome conglomeration of courtyards, crow-stepped gables, stone-mullioned windows and a watch-tower. The interior features some amazing plasterwork, especially in the

Banqueting Hall and in the Queen's Parlour, where the initials of Elizabeth I can be seen above the fireplace, together with her coat of arms supported by the lion and the Tudor dragon. It belongs to the Royal Cambrian Academy of Art, who open it to the public and hold exhibitions there. Naturally, it has a ghost, that of a Dr Dick, a physician who at some unspecified period, failed to save the life of a young woman, and climbed up the chimney to escape the wrath of her husband. He still clumps about among the flues, seeking a way out.

BACKWARD LOOK *The view south over Crieff is one of broad farming land in the Lowland vale of Strathearn. The town stands on the southern slopes of the 911 ft high Knock, a foothill of the towering Grampian mountains to the north which form the granite heart of the Highlands.*

CRIEFF *Tayside*

The name Crieff probably means 'tree', or rather, '*the* tree', a reference to the 'Kind Gallows' of Crieff on which so many Highlanders were hanged in the unruly old days. Gallows humour was perhaps forgivable in a town that sat so uneasily on the boundary between Lowlands and Highlands and suffered from the attentions of both. In 1715, for example, it was burned by the retreating Jacobites, who left not one house standing. During the next two decades, the town was replanned and rebuilt by James Drummond, 3rd Duke of Perth, in a scheme that included the newly laid out James Square, and a large linen factory to provide the townspeople with work. This was completed just in time for the next Jacobite Rising in 1745, when the duke, having chosen to 'come out' for Prince Charles Edward, had his estates confiscated and his linen factory destroyed.

Neither Highlands nor Lowlands could do without Crieff, however, if only for the great Trysts, or cattle markets, that were held there. At Michaelmas, 30,000 beasts might change hands, mostly the black cattle of the north, brought down by clansmen drovers to meet Lowland and English dealers who were too canny to enter the hills. It was quite a sight, apparently: 'Highland Gentlemen … mighty civil, dress'd in their slash'd short Waistcoats, a Trousing (which is Breeches and Stockings of one Piece of strip'd Stuff), with a Plaid for a Cloak and a Blue Bonnet … Their attendance were very numerous, all in belted Plaids, girt like Women's Petticoats, their Thighs and half of the Leg all bare. They had each their broad Sword and Ponyard, and spake all Irish, an unintelligible language … However, these poor Creatures hir'd themselves out for a Shilling a Day, to drive the Cattle to England …'

The traffic from north to south was not only of cattle. At Turret Fair in June, hundreds of young men and women from the under-resourced Highlands would come to Crieff, dressed in their best and mustering what English they could, to hire themselves out to Lowland employers. At the end of the 18th century, the licence for the cattle tryst was transferred to Falkirk, to Crieff's great distress; but to young Highlanders, it was a gateway to the wide world for many years afterwards.

No town in Crieff's difficult position could have survived down the centuries – and its story goes back to 1218 at least – without a good deal of corporate resilience. No sooner had the market closed than it began to build a reputation as an educational centre, with no fewer than 15 schools at the beginning of the 19th century. It was swifter, too, than most to sense the reversal of traffic as tourists trekked north to sample the romantic wilderness publicised by Scott, Byron and Queen Victoria. Now, after generations of awareness of the threat contained in the dark hills, Crieff prides itself on being 'The Gateway to the Highlands'. It is a role it performs admirably, from the 200 bedroom Strathearn House Hotel sitting in 650 acres of leisure facilities, to a myriad smaller hotels, bed-and-breakfasts and shops with tourist appeal selling locally produced knitwear, pottery, crystal and exquisite glass paperweights.

DENBIGH *Clwyd*

Denbigh lies in the broad and beautiful Vale of Clwyd where streams thread their way through a neat patchwork of fields. Its prehistoric predecessors – hillforts dating from the Iron Age – overlook the town from the Clwydian hills, away to the east, which rise to 1,817 ft at the breezy summit of Moel Fammau.

Unlike its setting, Denbigh's history *is* typical of North Wales, epitomised by the pale stonework of a ruined castle which rises above streets whose basic pattern has changed little since it was mapped by John Speed in 1610. The cartographer would also recognise the atmosphere on a Wednesday, when High Street becomes a lively outdoor market packed with stalls and bargain hunters. The colourful scene is overlooked by the County Hall built in 1572 by the Earl of Leicester, Elizabeth I's favourite, and 'modernised' 200 years later. Its neighbour, the stone-built Bull Hotel with its oak beams and panels, is another link with the 17th century.

Several other buildings go back to Tudor and Stuart times, but Victorian façades of Ruabon brick characterise Bull Lane as it climbs steeply towards the medieval town walls and castle. Walkers are rewarded with fine views across the Vale of Clwyd and pass the shell of Leicester's church. It was intended to replace St Asaph Cathedral, but building ceased after the earl's death in 1588.

The castle, like so many others in North Wales, was built during Edward I's wars with the native princes at the end of the 13th century. It saw its fair share of action before changing hands for the last time in 1646, during the Civil War, when Charles I ordered his commander to surrender.

The mighty gatehouse looks down on the site of a cottage where Denbigh's most famous son, John Rowlands, was born in 1841. Born out of wedlock, he later went to America, changed his name to Henry Morton Stanley and was sent to Africa by the *New York Herald* to find Dr David Livingstone. The quest ended with the most famous greeting in the English language – 'Doctor Livingstone, I presume' – and Stanley was later knighted by Queen Victoria. He died in 1904.

Vale Street sweeps down to the Ruthin road which runs close to St Marcella's, a church notable for its 16th-century memorials. A fine brass commemorates Richard Myddleton, a governor of Denbigh Castle, his wife and their 17 children. Even more impressive are the alabaster effigies of Sir John Salusbury, his wife, their eight sons and four daughters.

DOLGELLAU *Gwynedd*

To say that Dolgellau is a typical Welsh mountain town would be incorrect, for there is none other like it. On the other hand, it is what people see in their mind's eye when they think of a Welsh town, which is not quite the same thing. The approach from the north is by an old, seven-arched, creeper-hung bridge that leap-frogs over the Afon Wnion, a stream clean and cold and as clear as glass, that busily channels its way through and over beds of pale-grey boulders. From the far side of the bridge, the town looks as though it is composed of browny-grey crazy paving topped with dark slate. Then, above the flurries of chimney smoke, the steep fields begin immediately, dotted with sheep that get smaller and smaller with height and distance until the fields are swallowed in a belt of trees. Above them is a sweep of bracken, old gold or dark green according to the season, and above all is the noble head of Cader Idris, which, next to Snowdon, is the best-loved mountain in Wales. Even in late spring, his beard can be streaked with snow, while his great ridges, like outstretched arms, seem to enfold the town.

Dolgellau was in the wool trade once, as well as being the capital of vanished Merionethshire, but is now and for many years has been a market town. It is also a gate to Snowdonia and a gathering place for visitors who meant to take off into the wilderness, but linger because they find the old stone town so attractive. The crazy-paving effect from the other side of the river is explained when closer inspection reveals that most of the houses are made of large boulders, mostly squared but often not. It is a most pleasant material.

MAID OF THE MOUNTAINS *As prim as a maiden aunt, Dolgellau sits prettily amid green fields with the saw-toothed ridge of Cader Idris dominating the skyline. The town itself has an air of durability, its stone cottages and houses standing resolutely in tiny squares and shady alleyways.*

The town is centred upon Eldon Square and its Market Hall, all massive stone arches and huge first-floor windows. There is not an ungraceful building in the square, from the banks to the rows of little shops with two floors above. But then, given the stone and the sturdy, four-square design, they could scarcely be otherwise. Somehow, without any noticeable division, Eldon Square becomes Queen's Square and then Lion Street. Queen's Square has the big, handsome, creeper-clad Royal Ship Inn, while in tiny Lion Street there is the even larger Golden Lion Royal Hotel.

Such buildings are reminders of the prosperity of Dolgellau's marketing past and tourist present, but more endearing, perhaps, are the little streets – Lombard Street, for example, whose cottages are bright and clean as the river, their walls of massive stones enlivened by front doors gaily painted in red, blue, or leaf-green. Or there is Finsbury Square, with alleys leading off, displaying gardens with handkerchief-sized lawns surrounded by raised beds and rockeries.

St Mary's Church was rebuilt in 1716 on the site of a smaller, 13th-century place of worship. The tombstones of austere slate in the churchyard, and the brown stone and simple, straightforward lines of the building itself, are at one with the serene hills beyond. Behind the massive walls, the interior is hushed and filled with pools of coloured light from the 18th-century stained glass. Unusually, the pillars supporting the barrel roof are wooden; great rough-carved timbers sprouting from the 36 double rows of pews. The trees were specially felled at Dinas Mawddwy and hauled the 10 miles to Dolgellau by oxen. There are some good monuments in the church, including a rather flattened effigy of a Welsh nobleman, Meurig ap Ynyr Fachan, who died in 1350, and was an ancestor of the Vaughans of Nannau, a family with an incredibly long pedigree, who used to live in Nannau Park near by.

Everywhere you go in Dolgellau, Cader Idris is there also, but its familiarity, far from being oppressive, breeds affection. Its name means Chair of Idris, but whether Idris was a poet, a wizard, a giant, a Celtic chieftain who died fighting the Saxons in the 7th century, or a combination of all those things is uncertain. Neither is it certain which of the formations on its 10 mile long summit ridge is actually the chair, a lack of information that is potentially dangerous, since it is said that anyone who sleeps in it will wake up either a poet or mad. However, there is an exhilarating and not too strenuous climb to the summit up the Pony Track from Ty Nant. At a modest 2,927 ft, it is possible to look east to the far hills of the English border, and west to the even more distant mountains of Wicklow in Ireland.

Spectacular walks are a speciality of Dolgellau. The Precipice Walk (not too precipitous, really) skirts the flank of Moel Cymwch and offers grandstand views of the Mawddach estuary and Cader Idris. There is also the Torrent Walk through the valley of the Clywedog, a foaming, mostly vertical stream that races between ferns and grasses and moss-draped trees and rocks.

RARE GLASS *High in the west wall of Dolgellau's parish church are two stained-glass windows which are rare examples dating from the 18th century.*

DUNBLANE *Central*

In size, Dunblane is little more than a village, but it boasts a tall, stately cathedral and was elevated to the appropriately lofty status of a city nearly 600 years ago, in James I of Scotland's reign.

It is one of Scotland's hidden treasures, a delightful little place whose character is only glimpsed by travellers speeding by on the busy main road between Stirling and Perth. The road by-passes Dunblane's compact heart where sturdy buildings, some dating from the 17th century, line narrow streets above the rushing Allan Water. Churches' House, a row of restored homes overlooked by the cathedral, is particularly attractive in a quiet way that is typical of Scotland's traditional urban architecture. Neighbours include the house built in 1624 by Dean James Pearson. It was restored by the Friends of the Cathedral in 1959–60 and is now a museum.

The Leighton Library commemorates a 17th-century bishop and was built by a nephew who also provided £300 a year for its upkeep. Bishop Leighton spent 23 years in Dunblane and loved to stroll beside the Allan Water on a shaded path known as Bishop's Walk.

The river flows within a stone's throw of the cathedral. The lower part of its tower is all that remains of the church replaced by Bishop Clement between 1237 and his death in 1258. The nave's roof collapsed towards the end of the 16th century and services were held in the choir until it was rebuilt 300 years later.

The choir is notable for its finely carved woodwork and for stained-glass windows depicting an assortment of characters including Adam, Eve, William Blake and St Blane, the Celtic missionary who founded Dunblane in the 7th century.

It is difficult to associate the cathedral with dark deeds, but its choir also has the grave where Margaret, the eldest daughter of the first Lord Drummond, and her two sisters were buried in 1501. Margaret is said to have married James IV of Scotland in secret, then been poisoned by nobles who wished Princess Margaret of England to become the king's wife.

ELGIN *Grampian*

Elgin's greatest attraction is the majestic ruin of a 13th-century cathedral, probably the most beautiful building of its kind in the whole of Scotland when it was built. It epitomises the long and fascinating history of a royal burgh founded by a 12th-century king, burned by the infamous 'Wolf of Badenoch' and visited by Bonnie Prince Charlie shortly before his Highland army was defeated by the Duke of Cumberland at Culloden in 1746.

Elgin's roots go back to the time when David I of Scotland built a castle on a small, steep rise now known as Ladyhill. It may well have been the site of the fortress where his grandfather, King Duncan, died after falling foul of Macbeth's ambitions.

The royal castle vanished long ago, but Ladyhill – topped with a 19th-century column monument to the

NO.7 HIGH STREET *In 1694, John Duncan and Margaret Innes built this town house in Elgin. It is now known as Braco's Building, after a later owner.*

fifth and last Duke of Gordon – still dominates Elgin and rewards the walker with fine views.

Many of Elgin's oldest and most attractive buildings stand on or just off High Street, where people have strolled and shopped for more than 800 years. Its western end is ennobled by the classical façade and dome of Gray's Hospital. It recalls Dr Alexander Gray, a native of Elgin who made a fortune working for the East India Company and left £20,000 to provide shelter and medical treatment for the poor.

Near the ancient heart of Elgin stands the 14th-century Thunderton Hotel, where Scotland's medieval rulers rested and held court. It was there, too, that Bonnie Prince Charlie spent several days in 1746.

A church has stood in High Street since the 12th century, but St Giles' was built in 1827–8 after the old 'Muckle Kirk' was demolished. The architect, Archibald Simpson of Aberdeen, opted for a design inspired by the temples of ancient Greece with a lofty western portico fronted by six fluted columns. The nearby 'Muckle Cross' is a Victorian replica of one built during Charles I's reign. It stands on the site of Elgin's medieval market place.

Arcaded buildings catch the eye at the eastern end of High Street. One stands on the site of the Red Lion Inn whose cuisine failed to please Dr Samuel Johnson when he visited Elgin in 1773. Another, Braco's Building, dates from 1694 and is carved with the initials of its builders, John Duncan and his wife, Margaret Innes. In the early 18th century it became the banking house of William Duff of Dipple and Braco. The delightful old building, with stepped gables and a stone slab roof, is near Masonic Close, one of several narrow alleyways that contribute so much to Elgin's character.

The original Little Cross at the eastern end of High Street is thought to have been erected by Alexander Macdonald, Lord of the Isles, as part of a penance for raiding the cathedral in 1402. It also marks the spot where criminals were punished. Since 1842 the cross

has been overlooked by the Italianate façade of the Elgin Museum whose exhibits range from fossils to a display on the development of the North Sea oil industry.

Cooper Park with its trees and boating lake provides a tranquil setting for Grant Lodge where Elgin's public library now occupies a house built for the Earl of Seafield in 1750. Seventy years later, during a furore about a local election, 700 clansmen marched on the building to protect Lady Ann Grant. The house and its grounds were given to Elgin by Sir George Cooper in 1902.

One corner of the park embraces the ruined cathedral whose twin western towers give a dramatic impression of the great building's former grandeur and elegance. It was founded in 1224 – less than a century after King David built his castle on Ladyhill – and was considerably extended after a fire in 1270. That was tragically typical of the cathedral's turbulent history. The next disaster came in 1390 when Alexander Stewart, the 'Wolf of Badenoch', burned the cathedral and Elgin itself as a gesture of protest after he had been excommunicated. Town and cathedral

FRAGMENTS OF BEAUTY
Though only a fragmentary shadow of its former self, Elgin Cathedral still has an air of majestic elegance, and a beauty that has mellowed rather than faded. The west towers, once 90 ft tall, bear traces of French influence and were surmounted by lead-covered wooden spires.

were rebuilt. After the Reformation the cathedral fell into disuse and in 1568 lead was stripped from the roof; finally, on Easter Sunday, 1711, the great central tower collapsed. Later generations used the ruin as both a rubbish dump and a convenient source of dressed stone until a protective wall was built in 1807.

Panns Port, the last of the cathedral precinct's fortified gateways, was restored 50 years later and now provides a perfect 'frame' for views of the building's east front.

Another link with the days of monks and bishops is provided by Old Mills, on the western side of Elgin. The present building dates from the end of the 18th century, but it stands on a site granted to the monks of Pluscarden Priory, 6 miles from Elgin, by Alexander II in 1230. A restoration project started in 1978, and the corn mill is now in full working order.

FARNHAM *Surrey*

A castle has watched over Farnham since the 12th century, but the character of this Surrey town is essentially Georgian. It was during that period that farmers and merchants, flourishing in an area famous for wheat and hops, built the handsome houses of mellow brick which make Castle Street and West Street two of the most memorable townscapes in southern England.

The 18th century also produced Farnham's most famous son, William Cobbett, the radical politician and author. He founded *Hansard*, but is chiefly remembered for *Rural Rides* which describes country life in the 1820s. He was born in 1763 at the Jolly Farmer Inn, now known as the William Cobbett, in Bridge Square. The pub dates from the 16th century and is close to The Maltings, a building overlooking

HANDMADE TOWN *Bricks and tiles handmade from local clay were used in many of Farnham's buildings, including Bishop Waynflete's Tower which dates from the 15th century. Local brickwork is also much in evidence in Church Lane, where a Victorian wrought-iron lamp heralds the approach to neat terraces of cottages.*

the River Wey that was threatened with demolition before being turned into a community centre.

The town was more than 1,000 years old when Cobbett was born, having developed at a point where a prehistoric ridgeway route crossed the main road between London and Winchester, the capital of Wessex. In 688 the settlement was given to the Bishops of Winchester by King Caedwalla of Wessex.

Farnham Castle was started by Bishop Henry of Blois, King Stephen's brother, in 1138. It remained a palace of the Bishops of Winchester until 1927 and was one of the Bishop of Guildford's residences until 1955. The castle was therefore 'modernised' by many generations as domestic standards became increasingly sophisticated. One of the most striking features, Bishop Waynflete's Tower, was added towards the end of the 15th century and is a fine example of 500-year-old brickwork.

Castle Street runs southwards to where three plane trees shelter the picturesque Windsor Almshouses. They were endowed in 1619 to provide homes for 'eight poor, honest, old and impotent persons'. The Borough, at the bottom of Castle Street, is part of Farnham's essentially medieval layout. Its buildings include the Spinning Wheel which dates from about 1600 and has elaborate timber framing typical of the town's pre-Georgian architecture. Neo-Georgian workmanship from the 1930s is represented by the Town Hall on The Borough's junction with Castle Street. It is the work of Harold Falkner, the architect employed by a far-sighted local landowner who did much to preserve Farnham's character.

West Street has two of Farnham's greatest treasures – Willmer House, built in 1718, and Sandford House, its junior by just 39 years. Willmer House with its carved panels and fine oak staircase contains Farnham Museum whose exhibits include 18th-century paintings and furniture.

A short walk back along West Street and down Church Passage leads to the 15th-century parish church whose original appearance was substantially changed by Victorian restorers. William Cobbett's grave is near the porch. When he died in 1835 the London-bound stagecoach paused to let passengers attend the funeral.

FRAMLINGHAM *Suffolk*

The town, lying between church and castle, is a pretty place whose chief feature is the steep Market Hill, fringed by small and attractive shops. The appearance is vaguely Georgian, but in fact, many of the buildings date from the 16th and 17th centuries and were given their elegant frontages later. The seemingly 18th-century Crown Hotel, for example, may have housed the retinue of Mary Tudor, who held the manor of Framlingham and was declared Queen of England there before riding to London to oust Lady Jane Grey, the nine-day queen, from the throne in 1554. Then there is the so-called Regency House, whose wrought-iron balcony was brought from London in 1813 and stuck on to the front of an elderly and astonished

building. Double Street, however, is for much of its length genuinely Georgian and, so far as is known, gained its curious name from being the first street in the town to have shops and houses on both sides.

Perhaps the most attractive of the smaller buildings in Framlingham are its two groups of almshouses, each named after the benefactor who built them. Hitcham's Almshouses of 1654 owe their existence to Sir Robert Hitcham who was Attorney-General to James I's queen, Anne of Denmark, and is buried beneath a handsome tomb in the church. The other group, Mills Almshouses, were bequeathed by Thomas Mills in 1703. Mills was a wheelwright in the town who ended up owning a good deal of it and a number of properties in the surrounding parishes.

There are also a number of interesting larger buildings in the town, including the tile-hung pair of houses in Market Hill, whose tiles look like bricks at first glance, and Ancient House on Riverside with its pretty pargeting, or ornamental plasterwork. Why it is called Ancient House is not entirely clear, since, dating as it does from the late 17th century, it must be junior to several other houses in Framlingham.

It is certainly junior to the castle, whose massive cliffs of worn masonry peer over and around everything else in the town. Even when not seen face on, it

seems to stand always in the corner of the eye. The great, looming hulk with its 13 towers is a little pathetic now, the pathos enhanced, if anything, by the row of inexplicable and grotesque Tudor chimneys, few of which are connected to any fireplace, or ever were; they were just someone's idea of decoration. But in the days of King Richard the Lionheart, when the castle was first built, it was considered the last word in military engineering, with battlemented walls connecting towers whose fighting platforms covered each other. The walkway along the battlements survives, and sufficient of the defences to convey the impression of their original strength.

An earlier castle had been built on the same site by the Bigods, the first Earls of Norfolk, but the family were notable pests even by medieval baronial standards, and in 1174, Henry II ordered that the building should be cast down. It was not until the 1190s that Roger Bigod managed to get permission to begin work on the present structure, but within a short time he, too, was in trouble, for he was one of the barons who forced King John to put his seal upon Magna Carta. John's response was swift; he sacked Norfolk and Suffolk, forcing Bigod into surrender despite the strength of his castle. Both castle and lands were seized by the Crown, but were restored shortly

GEORGIAN FAÇADES *The Georgian practice of restyling the frontages of old houses is much in evidence in Framlingham. Mullioned bay windows and stuccoed walls were fashionable, but the steep sloping roofs typical of the Tudor period give away the true age of the buildings in spite of the face-lift.*

afterwards when Henry III came to the throne.

Such ups and downs were Framlingham's destiny for many a year. Bigods, Mowbrays and Howards succeeded each other, all vaguely related and most of them Earls or Dukes of Norfolk, and generally at the centre of great events. Perhaps about half of them died in their beds in the castle, the remainder in banishment, battle or under the axe, their stories greatly enriching Shakespeare's historical plays.

Most poignant was the story of Lady Anne Mowbray, who was born in Framlingham in 1472, the only child of John Mowbray, Earl of Surrey. When her father died in 1476, Lady Anne became the richest heiress in England, and was therefore married, at the age of six, to Richard, Duke of York, the younger of the two little princes who may or may not have been murdered in the Tower of London by Richard III in 1483. Anne did not long survive her husband, and at her death, the Mowbray estates passed to the Howards; but Anne's story was not quite finished. In 1964, during excavations in Stepney, London, workmen broke into a vault which was discovered to be that of the long-vanished Convent of St Clare. Within the vault was a lead coffin containing the remains of a fair-haired child. A plaque on the coffin identified the occupant, and since, by marriage, Lady Anne was a member of the Royal Family, she was re-interred in Westminster Abbey.

A considerable number of her relatives, however, lie beneath magnificent tombs in the church of St Michael at Framlingham. The grandest of these monuments covers the bones of Thomas Howard, the chilling 3rd Duke of Norfolk whose life was saved by the timely death of Henry VIII. Narrow escapes were his speciality; he promoted the causes of two of his nieces, Catherine Howard and Anne Boleyn, in becoming the consorts of Henry VIII. When they fell, he avoided involvement by utterly abandoning them.

Another splendid monument commemorates the first Howard, Duke of Norfolk who, as the Earl of Surrey, routed the Scots at the Battle of Flodden; his funeral helmet is affixed to a beam above. Effigies of two of the wives of the 4th Duke are laid on a tomb in the corner of the chancel with a space between them, presumably to make room for the effigy of the duke himself. But his beheaded remains are buried in St Peter-ad-Vincula by the Tower of London. Three times a widower, he attempted to marry for a fourth time, on this occasion to Mary, Queen of Scots. This was coldly regarded by Elizabeth I, who had him executed for high treason in 1572.

Then there are the other monuments that recount the story of Framlingham after the dukes departed, of which the most significant is the attractive tomb of the lawyer, Sir Robert Hitcham. Not only did he provide the almshouses named after him, and a school, but he purchased the entire manor, including the castle, from the Howards in 1634. He bequeathed it to Pembroke College, Cambridge, and ordered that the castle should be gutted, and the materials used to build a poorhouse within the towering outer walls. This still stands as an odd comment upon vanished pomp.

HOLY HOSTELRY *The George and Pilgrims Inn at Glastonbury was built in 1475 by Abbot Selwood, who saw the chance to swell the abbey's coffers by providing accommodation for rich pilgrims who were prepared to pay for good hospitality.*

SHOP SIGN *This delightful stone carving decorates an old shop front in Glastonbury High Street.*

GLASTONBURY *Somerset*

Glastonbury is a town where the reality of ancient buildings mingles with tantalising tales that have attracted pilgrims for more than 1,500 years. One legend tells of a visit by the boy Jesus when he travelled to England with his uncle, a merchant from the Holy Land. Stronger still is the belief that Joseph of Arimathea hid the Holy Grail – the cup used at the Last Supper – at the foot of Chalice Hill. Later visitors to this cradle of Christianity in Britain are said to have included St David, St Patrick and St Bridget of Kildare.

Another legend pin-points Glastonbury as the idyllic Isle of Avalon where King Arthur and Queen Guinevere were buried. Their grave is said to have been discovered by monks at Glastonbury Abbey in 1191. Identification was provided by a lead cross whose Latin inscription proclaimed: 'Here lies buried the famous King Arthur in the Island of Avalon.' The relic has been lost, but a 16th-century engraving suggests that it may indeed have dated from before the Norman Conquest.

The remains include St Mary's Chapel, dedicated two years after the fire, from which a galilee runs eastwards to the Abbey Church in whose choir King

Arthur's body is said to have been reburied after its discovery in 1191. The most remarkable sight in the abbey grounds is the 14th-century Abbot's Kitchen, its octagonal roof could almost be a medieval spacecraft. There are few better buildings of its type and period anywhere in Europe. St Patrick's Chapel, completed shortly before the abbey fell foul of Henry VIII, has also survived intact.

The little town is overlooked by the steep, grassy slopes of Glastonbury Tor. Rising to just over 500 ft above sea level and topped with a 13th-century tower – all that remains of St Michael's Church – it forms an impressive landmark. There are splendid views over the town and across what used to be a treacherous wilderness of bogs, lakes and waterways.

The hill was a convenient and formidable place of refuge in prehistoric times, although Iron Age people also lived on man-made islands amid the swamps. If the legends are to be believed, 'modern' Glastonbury dates from shortly after the death of Christ when Joseph of Arimathea and a small band of followers reached this part of Somerset. The sign that their travels were ended came when Joseph stuck his staff in the ground and it promptly produced flowers. They built a wattle-and-daub church on what later became the site of Glastonbury Abbey where three English kings – Edmund, Edgar and Edmund Ironside – were destined to be buried.

The abbey thrived until 1539 when Abbot Whiting refused to hand it over to Henry VIII. He and two of his monks were found guilty of treason and executed on Glastonbury Tor. The abbey itself, rebuilt after a fire in 1184, is now a substantial ruin where legends are interlaced with the hard facts of recorded history.

Years of peace and prosperity are recalled by the Abbey Barn which now houses the Somerset Rural Life Museum. It dates from towards the end of the 14th century and is notable for carved stonework and a timber roof that is a tribute to the skills of medieval carpenters.

Glastonbury's other links with the monastic era include the Tribunal, a 15th-century building in High Street where justice was dispensed by the abbot. The frontage was rebuilt in about 1500. Inside is a museum whose exhibits include relics of lake villages of the 3rd and 1st centuries BC which were built on the marshy ground below the tor.

High Street is also notable for the George and Pilgrims Hotel built during the 15th century. Its elaborate stone façade bears the arms of Glastonbury Abbey and Edward IV. A short walk down Magdalene Street leads to St Patrick's Almshouses, founded in 1517, and the 13th-century Chapel of St Margaret with its barrel roof and bellcote.

Glastonbury also has two memorable churches. St John's is 15th century and has a tower 134 ft high. A Glastonbury Thorn, the flower associated with Joseph of Arimathea, grows in the grounds and flowers in the spring and winter. Sprigs are sent to the Queen and

TOWN OF LEGEND *Standing eerily in the half-light, Glastonbury Tor (top left) is a fitting landmark for a town founded on legend. Whether Joseph of Arimathea came here or not, a great abbey grew up, and the Lady Chapel (above) marks the spot where Joseph's wooden church stood. By the 15th century the abbey was one of the most powerful in the land, and in the Abbot's Tribunal (top right) justice was meted out to a large neighbourhood.*

Queen Mother every Christmas. The 'original' bush on Wearyall Hill, where Joseph's staff flowered, was cut down by a Puritan during the 17th century.

St Benedict's Church was rebuilt by Abbot Bere at the start of the 16th century and has his initials carved over the north porch. It was originally dedicated to St Benignus, an Irish saint who is said to have followed St Patrick to Glastonbury in the 5th century.

The footpath up Glastonbury Tor passes close to Chalice Well where, according to tradition, Joseph of Arimathea buried the Holy Grail. Records of the well go back to the 12th century when William of Malmesbury in his *History of Glastonbury* told how red and blue water gushed from the ground. The well's legendary ability to cure all manner of ailments was one of many reasons for this small Somerset town becoming a place of pilgrimage.

GRANTOWN-ON-SPEY *Highland*

To the considerable gratitude of future promoters of tourism, the nobler-sounding Grantown-on-Spey replaced the ancient Castletown of Freuchie in the latter half of the 18th century. Conflicting reasons are given for the change. One version says that after a brawl between two factions of Clan Grant at Cromdale Fair, the losers fled to Castle Grant and the protection of the chieftain who then had to build some additional accommodation for them. Another story gives the cause that the laird was simply tired of the eyesore of the old Castletown at his gate, and resolved to build a new town entirely.

At any event, that is what Sir James Grant – 'Good Sir James', as posterity came to know him – did. On the wild moorland, he laid out a plan of wide streets on a square, and out of it grew the Georgian nucleus of the present handsome little town. By 1792, it had a population of 300, a water supply, a doctor of its own and a school for girls. It also had linen and woollen mills, for Sir James intended that his creation should develop as a textile centre. During the next half century, however, it became apparent that fate, the

QUEEN'S PLEASURE Like a good wine, Queen Victoria found Grantown 'very amusing', and in 120 years the town has lost none of its heady appeal. Its smart hotels include the turreted Grant Arms which can boast that 'Queen Victoria slept here'.

railway and Sir Walter Scott had decreed otherwise. Scott's novels and poems had aroused a fervent interest in all things Scottish and nowhere better reflects the images of dark hanging woods and wild, roaring floods than Strathspey.

In 1860, Queen Victoria put the stamp of royal approval on the place when she spent a night at the Grant Arms in the Square and described her visit as being 'very amusing and never to be forgotten'. True, she spoiled it a little in her *Highland Journal* with some waspish comments upon Castle Grant: 'A very plain-looking house, like a factory. We did not get out (of the carriage).' Unfortunately, Her Majesty had driven up to the north front, which is not nearly so imposing as the southern face, with its balconied battlements and raised courtyard.

A few years later, the healthful quality of the air was noted, together with the fact that 'in no other part of Scotland are there more octogenarians and nonagenarians to be met with'. Naturally, this led to a spate of hotel building that served the hill-walkers, mountaineers, naturalists and salmon fishers in the Spey at least as well as the seekers after longevity.

Fishermen, mountaineers and tourists still flock to Grantown, but in the last two or three decades it has become even better known as a ski centre for the Cairngorms and the Lecht. The town rose admirably to the challenge of an extra season and now presents skiing and *après-ski* facilities to rival any in Scotland. Certainly, anyone who wishes to sample them at the peak periods of Christmas, New Year or Easter would be well advised to book a long way in advance.

HARROGATE *North Yorkshire*

Harrogate's atmosphere is redolent of the 19th century when well-to-do Victorians, attracted by mineral springs, made it one of the most fashionable places in England. The town is now a thriving centre for conferences and exhibitions, but classical buildings, broad acres of parkland and public gardens bright with flowers perpetuate the image of an elegant inland resort. It takes little imagination to picture horse-drawn carriages clattering along the streets while gentlemen in top hats and frock coats debate the latest war news from the Crimea.

In 1837, when Queen Victoria started her long reign, what is now Harrogate amounted to nothing more impressive than two villages whose combined population of some 2,500 was swelled by summer visitors. It was not until the coming of the railway in 1848 that development really started.

But the healthy reputation that made Harrogate so popular can be traced back to 1571 when William Slingsby, riding out from his home near Knaresborough, discovered the Tewit Well a few hundred yards from what was to become the town centre. The waters tasted similar to those he had sampled on a visit to Europe, so Slingsby built a wall round the spring before announcing its medicinal value. A few years later it became the first British mineral well to be called a spa when a physician, Timothy Bright,

likened it to the waters of Spa in Belgium.

The site of the Tewit Well was described as a 'rude, barren moor' by a 17th-century visitor. It is now part of The Stray, a 200 acre expanse of tree-lined turf wrapped round three sides of the town centre. It has survived as common land thanks to an Act of Parliament, passed in 1770, which declared that it should 'for ever and hereafter remain open and unenclosed' for the benefit of people visiting the wells.

Harrogate's long-standing reputation as a town famous for flowers is epitomised by the 17.5 acre Valley Gardens where the North of England Horticultural Society stages a spectacular show in April.

Valley Gardens' main entrance is opposite the Royal Pump Room, a domed, temple-like building completed in 1842 at a cost of £2,249. Now a museum, it stands on the site of the Old Sulphur Well or 'Stinking Spaw'. Harrogate's motto – 'A citadel famous for its springs' – is carved in Latin over one of the doors.

The town's heyday as a health resort is also recalled by the Royal Baths, built in 1897, which became one of the world's biggest hydrotherapy centres with treatments that included sulphur baths, peat baths and hot-mud poultices. Turkish and sauna baths now maintain the tradition, but the stately building is also used as a social centre. A string quartet, delightfully reminiscent of the town's Victorian and Edwardian ambience, plays in the restaurant during the summer months.

The Royal Hall where Dame Clara Butt first sang *Land of Hope and Glory* in 1903 is now part of an ultra-modern exhibition and conference centre. Like similar buildings in many German spas, it was originally called the Kursaal – a name that was changed when the First World War broke out in 1914.

HASLEMERE *Surrey*

Modern Haslemere really began in 1859, when the railway pushed through the North Downs, jokingly dubbed the 'Surrey Alps', and introduced rich City men and their families to the steep meadows, wild heaths and wooded horizons of the area. Large mansions appeared among the ravines and conifers, while from the town itself, slightly more modest houses began to climb the surrounding hills.

For Haslemere it was a rescue in the nick of time, since for some years before the coming of the railway, the once-important industrial centre had been gently subsiding into village status. From early times, glass was made from local sand, bracken ash and lime. Plentiful charcoal in the area fired the furnaces, and those too of the iron foundries that drew their ore from local deposits. The streams were easily dammed to make hammer ponds, and until well into the 17th century, the town was famous for its 'ordinnance and shotte'.

By the end of the 18th century, however, the iron industry was dying, slowly strangled by competition from the coal-fired foundries of the north and by the fact that it was consuming local timber – for charcoal – faster than nature was replacing it.

Any notion of the town's becoming a backwater was dispelled half a century later, when the combination of the railway and the lovely Surrey hills began to draw not only the first commuters but, in the years that followed, a large number of writers and artists too. George Eliot lived at Shottermill and Alfred, Lord Tennyson at Blackdown, just over the Sussex border. Sir Arthur Wing Pinero, the playwright, and the poet

Christina Rossetti, both had houses in the vicinity, and Sir Arthur Conan Doyle played cricket for Haslemere. At the beginning of the century, Arnold Dolmetsch opened his workshops for the manufacture of harpsichords, viols, lutes and other period musical instruments. Out of his work, and from the enthusiastic support he received from George Bernard Shaw and the poet Robert Bridges, there emerged the Haslemere Festival of Early Music which is held each July, and is now an event of international importance. The Dolmetsch factory, which still produces exquisite reproductions of early instruments, is open to visitors by appointment.

Though there are many 19th-century houses in the town, the general impression is Georgian, due perhaps to the prevalence of plain fronts, red brick and hung tiles. The Town Hall looks Jacobean, but was, in fact, rebuilt in 1814. Farther down the High Street is the magnificent Town House of 1725. Church Hill House is of similar date and at least equal grandeur. It stands next to St Bartholomew's Church, which was completely rebuilt in 1871, apart from the tower, which probably dates from the 13th century. In the church, there is a memorial to Alfred, Lord Tennyson, who worshipped there.

Closer to the town centre is Tolle House, a group of almshouses built in 1676 and originally maintained by market tolls. They mingle very pleasantly with the occasional black and white timbered house and the colour-wash pink, beige and apple-green, among the dark-red tile. The mixture is seen at its best on Shepherd's Hill, a steeply curving street climbing up behind the Town Hall, where stone, brick and stucco of the 17th, 18th and 19th centuries harmonise in a railed terrace climbing high above the roadway. At the bottom of the hill, a large Royal Warrant on the wall of a small red cottage announces that the occupant supplies nosegays to H.M. The Queen.

HAWICK *Borders*

Like border towns in many other parts of Europe, Hawick has few obvious antiquities, and for much the same reason. For centuries, armies advancing or retreating, sacked or razed the town, and its people, over and again, had to doggedly pick up the pieces and start again. Hawick's distant history, therefore, is expressed not in ancient buildings, but in ballads, memory and tradition. As, for example, in the town song which contains Hawick's slogan, 'Teribus, ye Teri Odin'. Nobody is quite sure what it means, but it seems to be a harking back to a war-cry of the Anglo-Saxon founders, invoking the god of thunder and the god of battle: 'Thor be with us, both Thor and Odin!' At any rate, because of it, Hawick people are always known as 'Teries'.

The town began with an Anglo-Saxon settlement in the triangle formed by the joining of the Teviot and Slitrig rivers. It was called Ha-wick, the settlement of the hawthorn hedge, and on the spot where St Mary's Church now stands, Cuthbert, the missionary-saint in this part of the world, founded a small chapel. After the Conquest, the new Norman overlords, the Lovels, built a great earthwork – still the best platform from which to see the town – and put a stockade on top. A few Border winters showed the impracticality of this, so they built a stone tower instead, the Black Tower of Drumlanrig, which is now incorporated in the ancient Tower Hotel at the west end of the High Street. When the division between Scotland and England hardened, the Lovels chose to be English, and went to live on their estates in the south. Next it was the Douglasses who succeeded to the 'hous and toure of Hawick' to be followed by the Scotts. Both names are still prominent in the district, as are Armstrong, Johnston, Elliot, Turnbull and Kerr, the same names that ring in the Border ballads. They probably ring better in ballad than in reality; three weary centuries of war and feuding dulled chivalry's lustre and most of them were, as James VI sourly commented, 'even from their cradles bredd and brought up in theft, spoyle and bloode'.

Hawick is quiet enough now, for most of the year anyway, a sedate, dark stone Victorian town with new developments climbing the hills on the outskirts. Prosperity is evident in the well-stocked shops, the busy mills and in the vast livestock market, the longest established in the United Kingdom. The High Street lies long and straight, with closes – tenemented alleys – running off, and decorated by a late 19th-century towered and turreted Town Hall, almost the definitive example of the Scots Baronial or Balmoral style of architecture. No. 37 High Street was the home of Bailie John Hardie, once Provost of the town, and also its patron saint, if it went in for such things, for it was he, in 1771, who brought the first four stocking frames from Glasgow and launched the hosiery business in Hawick. From this beginning grew the town's principal occupation, the manufacture of tweed and fine knitwear of all kinds, for which it has long been famed the world over.

HELSTON *Cornwall*

The quaint old Cornish town celebrated in the song 'Cornish Floral Dance' is Helston. The song's inspiration is the town's famous annual spring festival: 'Hoorah! for the Cornish Floral Dance', it concludes enthusiastically if inaccurately, for the one thing it is not, apparently, is a Floral Dance. It may be called Flora, appertaining to the Roman goddess of spring, or Furry, probably derived from the Latin *feria* (feast day), or Faddy, whose origin is obscure. Nor does it have anything to do with the familiar tune, 'The Floral Dance'. The tune played by the Helston Town Band at the Furry Dance is far more ancient, has no words, no title and no written score; notes of the parts are passed instead from one generation of musicians to the next.

However old the tune, it is not nearly so ancient as the dance. There are various legends to account for its beginnings – how for example, St Michael the Archangel, the town's patron saint, fought the Devil high in the air over Helston and threw a huge boulder at him, causing the Devil to fall into the Loe Pool. The

GRANITE AND SLATE *In Helston's Church Street, granite buildings stand stolidly shoulder to shoulder, with the pinnacled tower of St Michael's Church soaring above the grey slate rooftops. Outside the museum a Victorian street lamp stands like a gunner's ramrod by an old cannon – a reminder that Helston once had a castle.*

71

townsfolk danced through the streets and houses in joy to see evil thus overcome, and to this day they point out the boulder that St Michael threw, still embedded in the wall of the Angel Hotel.

Helston's dance, or, rather, dances, for there are five of them, take place on May 8, unless that date happens to fall on a Sunday or Monday, in which case the ceremony is shifted to the previous Saturday. The town is decked for fête, and thousands of people attend. It is all great fun because everyone, in a minor way at least, can join in. It is also a splendid spectacle.

Its day of glory over, Helston resumes the contemplative stance it maintains for the rest of the year. It is a very attractive place, much better than the 'quaint' advertised in the song, and in a lovely setting of hills and trees. Its main street, Coinagehall Street, sweeps handsomely down in a steep curve, edged by a pair of bustling brooks in open conduits hurrying to join the River Cobar at the bottom of the hill. Helston was a market in the days of Alfred the Great, and from the Middle Ages onwards, was an important tin centre, and was made a stannary town, that is, a town where tin from the surrounding mines was assayed, weighed and taxed. This was done by clipping a corner (French *coin*) from each ingot, hence the term 'coinage'.

CORNISH KITCHEN *Home life in a Cornish cottage is displayed in the Helston Museum, with a well-scrubbed pine table laid out with utensils in front of a shining cast-iron cooking range. The long case clock was built by a Helston man, Richard Thomas.*

Architecturally, Helston is more renowned for the general pleasantness of its townscape than for any particular feature. The classical granite Market Hall of the 1830s is worth pausing for, and so is a folly of the same vintage at the bottom of Coinagehall Street. It takes the form of an elaborate, arched gateway and commemorates a townsman named H. M. Grylls.

The original church of St Michael was destroyed by lightning and rebuilt by Lord Godolphin in the early 1760s. The interior looks like a Georgian city church, with a gallery, supported on iron columns, running round three sides. A number of brass monuments from the earlier church have been assembled in the porch, and Henry Trengouse, the inventor of the rocket-fired line and the breeches buoy for saving life at sea, is buried in the churchyard.

HERTFORD *Hertfordshire*

Hertford is of great age, and of all ages, happily blended through the centuries into a busy yet easy-going market and county town. Its timelessness is neatly symbolised by Ronald Pope's sculpture of 1973 commemorating the first English Synod which was summoned in Hertford by the first Primate of England, Theodore of Tarsus, exactly 1,300 years earlier. The sculpture is fixed to the entrance of Castle Hall, a most adventurous Civic Centre dating from the 1970s. Behind lie the massive 12th-century walls of Hertford Castle, where Elizabeth I lived as a girl and some of the great power struggles of medieval England took place. Little now remains of the great fortification itself, apart from the brick gatehouse built for Edward IV in the 15th century.

But Hertford long predates its castle, and even Theodore of Tarsus. It really dates its beginnings to the years just after the Roman occupation when the bridge that carried the main Roman road to the north over the River Lea at nearby Ware collapsed.

The local Saxons had no skill at bridge-building and sought instead for a ford, which they found at Hertford; its probable site is at the end of a grassy track near the library. Later, when the River Lea came to mark the boundary between Saxon England and the Danelaw, the ford was of some importance, and two fortified burghs, grew up beside it.

In the late 18th century, the Lea was deepened and widened to bring barge traffic from London into Hertford's centre, and, as a consequence, the town swiftly developed into an important flour-milling, malting and brewing centre. The pagoda or double-mushroom shapes of the cowls on maltings, and the extraordinary cast-iron crown imperial surmounting McMullen's Brewery peep over and around the buildings about them, bringing even greater variety to the town's amazing roofline. It is a fact – or nearly so, anyway – that no two roofs in Hertford are the same; sway-backed, tiled, slated, dormered, drooping, they shoot out at all kinds of angles, creating a charming and highly individualistic confusion.

A good place to catch a glimpse of this and something of Hertford activity past and present, is by the narrow Folly Bridge, its brickwork still bearing tow-rope scars inflicted by horse-drawn barges, in the oldest part of the town. Only a few yards upstream, by a black-tarred malting, is the site of the ancient ford. The river forms a kind of basin at this point and exudes a watery tranquillity, enhanced, if anything, by the attractive Barge pub on the left bank downstream. A superb narrow boat in traditional livery is moored outside. The five-gabled house immediately to the right of the bridge, facing downstream, is the Hertford Club, whose older name is Lombard House. Like the town itself, it is of all kinds of ages from medieval onwards and was, in the 18th century, the home of Sir Henry Chauncy, a local historian and magistrate.

The Hertford Club, which wears an elegant mask of dark-red Georgian brick, looks down Bull Plain, the old cattle market. It contains a number of pretty,

plastered houses of the 17th and 18th centuries, among them the lively Hertford Museum and Dimsdale House.

Bull Plain dives into Salisbury Square and Market Street where there is an open-air market on Saturdays, and off them runs Fore Street, crammed with all sorts of good things. There is the comfortable and handsome Salisbury Arms Hotel of 1570, for example, with its overhanging bow windows, and opposite, a row of shops whose upper storeys are decorated with 17th-century pargeting – ornamental plasterwork – of huge patterns of flowers and vines in high relief. These buildings are topped by uneven, red-tiled roofs into which are tucked small, secretive dormer windows.

Just down the street is the hardly less elegant Dimsdale Arms, with Barclays Bank that was also an inn once, and before that was the house of a man called Stone, the founder of Hartford, Connecticut. The Victorian Corn Exchange and Public Hall opposite has a somewhat aggressive classical frontage, but it is by no means out of place in this delightful street. Round the corner is the gigantic Christ's Hospital School for Girls, founded in 1683 as an off-shoot of the Bluecoat School in London. Many of the original buildings survive, and also the painted lead figures of bluecoat scholars that have stood outside since 1697.

Unusually for an English town of Hertford's antiquity, the oldest place of worship is not the parish church, but a nonconformist place of worship – the Friends' Meeting House in Railway Street. It was built in 1669, and is the oldest surviving Meeting House in the world.

Both Anglican churches are Victorian, though they replace earlier buildings. All Saints, a massive confection in purple-red stone, stands forlornly on the far side of the ring road, cut off from the town centre by a torrent of traffic. The interior is opulent, all glowing pink stone supported on pillars sprouting from a lawn-like carpet. The large churchyard contains an avenue of chestnuts reputedly planted in the reign of Charles II, and by the door there are a couple of millstones recycled in the 18th century as gravestones.

Hertford St Andrew is a little older than All Saints – 1870 as against 1900 – and is therefore more mainstream Victorian. It has an ancient altar stone, and the doorway is that of the original 15th-century church.

The houses in the immediate vicinity of St Andrew's are among the most attractive in Hertford, a mixture of early Victorian, early Georgian, and a number of uncertain, but considerably greater, age. The most venerable is the Old Verger's House, whose carved black timbers and white-plastered upper storeys crouch top-heavy over a diminutive ground floor. It is an antique shop now, but it is doubtful whether any of its stock predates the building itself, which has stood there since the 1450s.

OLDEST HOUSE *The splendid timber-framed house in St Andrew's Street dates from about 1450 and is Hertford's oldest domestic building. Once the verger's house, it is now an antiques shop, but not all the antiquities are inside; on the wall above the doorway there is a snuffer, used to extinguish pitch torches carried at night during the 17th and 18th centuries, and near the small window at the far end of the building is a firemark dated 1720 which shows that the building was insured by the London Assurance Co.*

HEXHAM *Northumberland*

There can be few other English parish churches that would be likely to contain a monument like this:

> *To the Gods, the Shades of the Departed, Flavinus, Standard Bearer of the White Troop of the Cavalry Regiment of Petriana. Buried here aged 25, and in the seventh year of his service.*

But then, the Priory Church of St Andrew at Hexham is a most remarkable building. Above the inscription, which is, of course, in Latin, there is a lively representation of a senior NCO of the crack *ala Petriana*, in full regimental plumes, riding down a crouching Celtic warrior of bewhiskered and villainous appearance. Elsewhere in the church there are a number of other Roman antiquities, including an altar to Apollo, given by the second-in-command of the VI Legion, the Victorious, Pious and True. This does not mean that Hexham church was ever a pagan temple, or that it was the scene of a mass conversion of the imperial forces. In fact, Flavinus and the Prefect of the VI Legion had been dust blowing about Hadrian's Wall for three centuries at least before the church was built, and the reason for their monuments' presence is that when St Wilfrid began his great construction in 674, he used the old legionary and cavalry depot at nearby Corbridge as a quarry for building materials.

Wilfrid's church – it was a cathedral then – with its turrets, its furnishings of gold and silver and precious stones, and its even more precious relics of St Andrew, was said by one chronicler at least to be the finest building this side of the Alps. Such ostentatious wealth was a hazard in those troublous times, and in 876, the Danes swept down upon it and tore it apart, almost stone from stone. Of St Wilfrid's Church, little remains to be seen but the crypt, yet this is perhaps the most moving memorial to Christianity's early days to be seen in all of northern England. Here it was that the relics of St Andrew were kept – no one now knows what they were – and many of the stones in the walls still bear clearly incised Roman inscriptions.

After the Danes' devastating visit in the 9th century, Hexham vanished from recorded history until the Augustinian Canons began to build a priory on the site of St Wilfrid's Church in 1113. They continued to build for the next century and a half, and a good deal of what can be seen now dates from this period.

It cannot be said that the Augustinians' life was one of uninterrupted cloistered calm. The Scots were constantly raiding down into Hexham, the most desperate occasion being in 1296, when a large number of novices were burned to death and the nave was destroyed. It was not rebuilt until 1908.

SAFE SEAT *The massive stone seat in the chancel of Hexham Abbey dates from Anglo-Saxon times and was a place of sanctuary, from which a fugitive could not be taken by his pursuers, save under pain of excommunication. Known as the Frith Stool or St Wilfrid's Chair, its protection actually extended to an area of a square mile. But the church allowed pursuers to buy redemption with a scale of fines that reached a maximum within the doors of the Choir. Redemption for seizing a fugitive from the chair itself, however, could not be bought at any price.*

SOLDIER'S FAREWELL *The gravestone of a Roman soldier, buried somewhere near Hadrian's Wall, found its way to Hexham Abbey when St Wilfrid used Roman materials to build his church.*

QUIET BYWAY *At Lower Denford, east of Hungerford, the River Kennet once drove the millstones of this 18th-century corn mill; now only swans ripple the placid waters. At this point the river runs close to the Kennet and Avon Canal which, when it was built in the 18th century, relegated the river to a quiet backwater.*

Under the circumstances, it is remarkable that so many precious and ancient things have survived – for example, the stone coffin and cross of St Acca, Wilfrid's chaplain and successor, the glowing 15th-century paintings and the medieval doodlings in stone and wood, depicting almost anything from the Seven Deadly Sins to saints, Northumbrian pipers and a Border raider carting off a sheep.

Hexham town grew up around St Wilfrid's foundation, and owes a great deal to him and to his successors. The Sele, for instance, a surprising and delightful mid-town park, was probably the home farm of the priory, while the craggy-towered Moot Hall, now the library, was built in the 14th century as a stronghold and courtroom for the Archbishop of York. The Manor Offices, a remarkably grim stone rectangle was constructed as a prison at about the same period.

All about this part of the town, the street pattern, with the exception of the Victorian Beaumont Street, is of the Middle Ages, though periods of the buildings might differ so much as the Old Grammar School, chartered in 1599, and the paved shopping precinct in Fore Street, where there is a chemist's establishment whose elaborately carved front was the work of a Belgian refugee during the First World War. There are fine Georgian houses and shop fronts everywhere, among which the prettiest are the two bow windows in St Mary's Chare. Look about these, however, and it is possible to detect medieval columns, walls and doors forming part of the construction of much later shops and buildings. These are the remains of St Mary's Church, founded by St Wilfrid.

HUNGERFORD *Berkshire*

Hungerford began to thrive at the end of the 18th century when what had previously been a sleepy little Berkshire market town became an important staging post for travellers on the Great West Road between London and Bath. Many dined and rested at the 13th-century Bear Inn on the corner of Bath Road. Distinguished visitors in earlier times included John Evelyn, Samuel Pepys, Charles I and Prince William of Orange when he was marching on London in 1688 to claim the throne from James II.

The highway that brought prosperity became a menace after the advent of the motor car, but Hungerford regained much of its charm when the M4 motorway was opened north of the town in 1971.

The broad main street, spanned by a railway bridge, is overlooked by the Town Hall and Corn Exchange built in 1871 after its century-old predecessor had become unsafe. On the second Tuesday after Easter it is the setting for Hungerford's Hocktide Court which is believed to date from the 12th or 13th century.

Commoners summoned by the Town Crier meet in the Town Hall to conduct business that includes electing such officials as a Constable, Bailiff, Portreeve, Keepers of the Keys of the Common Coffer, Overseers of the Common and two official Ale-tasters. Meanwhile, two Tutti-men and the Orange-man visit commoners' homes in the old part of the town, claiming a kiss from the lady of the house and presenting her with an orange. A 'tutti' is a nosegay, and each Tutti-man carries a long, striped staff decorated with flowers and ribbons. That part of the tradition is a reminder that certain areas of medieval towns were not exactly fragrant.

The Hocktide or Tutti-Day ceremonies also include a lunch in the Corn Exchange where ale is tasted and all 'colts' or newcomers are initiated by having nails driven into their shoes by the local blacksmith.

Hungerford's day-to-day attractions include several antique shops and the Kennet and Avon Canal, a pleasant waterway completed at the end of the 18th century.

ILKLEY *West Yorkshire*

The heyday of the great English spas was, roughly, 1750-1820, an age that also bequeathed us the most elegant parts of our architectural heritage. The inhabitants of the age, or at any rate the leisured members of it, were admirably suited to their background in sensibility, dress and conversation. Today, although some of the spas are neglected, there still clings to their Assembly Rooms and Pump Rooms the graceful spirit of Miss Austen, a faint hint of pot-pourri, and a lilt of the intricate dances of the period.

Not so at Ilkley. Though its waters were discovered as early as 1760 by a Squire Middleton, who constructed a complex of rocky plunge-baths to receive them, the public did not waken to their advantages until about 80 years later. Then they were described as 'mellifluent, diaphanous, luminous waters', which, being translated, meant that though crystal-pure and icy-cold they contained no remedial chemicals whatsoever. On this basis, a hydropathic was opened in the 1840s. Its regime would have drawn adverse comment from a Spartan, since it involved a minimal diet, wrapping in cold, wet sheets, and taking cold douches and sitting in a sealed room into which bitter moorland air was pumped.

However, it must have done a lot of Victorians a lot of good, since the hydropathic throve, gathering about it a pretty, Victorian stone town which encompassed the old town of Ilkley.

It may well be that Middleton was not the first to discover the waters, since beneath the very centre of Ilkley there lies the Roman fort of Olicana. Little remains now of Olicana apart from some fragments in the Elizabethan Manor House Museum and a pair of battered altars in the parish church, though the roots of both buildings are buried in the Roman fort.

All Saints' Church, heavily restored in the 19th century, retains the general appearance of the early Middle Ages, the period of its founding. The dog-tooth pattern doorway in the south porch belongs to the 13th century, and the tower and parts of the western wall to 200 years later. There is also a detailed effigy of an armoured knight, so beautifully carved that it is possible to appreciate how every part of the armour worked. All Saints' chief treasure is not in the building but in the churchyard – three Saxon crosses that were carved no later than the 8th century, when Ilkley stood on the border between Northumbria and Mercia. Since the crosses have always stood in the churchyard, their presence would seem to indicate that a major

place of worship stood on the site before All Saints' was built; but there is no sign of it now.

Ilkley likes to think of itself as the Malvern of the north and indeed there are several similarities, the waters included. There is the same sense of spaciousness all about, the same pretty Victoriana, the same long-established role as a dormitory for the well-to-do; in Ilkley's case, those of Leeds and Bradford. The grandest bit of commuterdom is a villa in King's Road called Heathcote, which was designed by Edwin Lutyens in 1906. It has pyramid roofs, huge chimneys and looks like Blenheim Palace in miniature. The rest of the town is more restrained; mostly 19th century, but here and there some Georgian and a few earlier structures such as the Old Grammar School of 1637 and the bridge over the River Wharfe, built about 30 years later.

There is marvellous walking across the moors round Ilkley – wide, airy spaces that are the setting for

HISTORIC CENTRE *The Roman fort of Olicana lies beneath the streets of Ilkley, but the town with its roots in the buried camp grew in the 17th and 18th centuries, with Church Street a charming confusion of buildings from those periods.*

the famous song *On Ilkla Moor baht 'at*, a curious ditty, which tells of the dangers of courting Mary Jane on Ilkley Moor if not wearing a hat. Death of cold will certainly follow, burial and consumption by worms, whereupon the community will be revenged by eating the ducks that ate the worms. This cheerful, practical pessimism fully entitles the song to its place as Yorkshire's County Anthem.

KELSO *Borders*

Sir Walter Scott attended the local grammar school in 1783 and later praised Kelso as 'the most beautiful if not the most romantic village in Scotland'. It is now a busy little country town whose Georgian buildings, cobbled Market Square, ruined abbey and fine bridge over the River Tweed complement the beauty of the surrounding countryside.

The abbey, believed to have been the biggest on the Border, was founded in the 12th century and flourished until 1545 when it was devastated by an English army under the Earl of Hertford. Scott's school stood on the site of the nave. There one of his school friends was James Ballantyne whose Ballantyne Press printed the 31-year-old author's *Minstrelsy of the Scottish Border* in 1802. Scott later went into partnership with Ballantyne and the Ballantyne Press published many of his later works though the venture eventually ended in financial disaster.

The Market Square is flanked by some of the town's most attractive buildings. The 18th-century Cross Keys Hotel, a famous coaching inn, shares the broad expanse of grey cobblestones with the elegant, Palladian-style Town House built in 1816. The five-arched bridge across the Tweed was built in 1803 by John Rennie, one of Scotland's greatest civil engineers, and became a model for his Waterloo Bridge in London.

Kelso Bridge is overlooked by Ednam House, a

BORDER TOWN *The fast-flowing River Tweed curls around Kelso, a town that for centuries was a strategic point in the Border wars between the Scots and the English. Today it is a strategic point for tourists – a centre for exploring the Cheviot Hills to the south or for fishing in one of the best salmon rivers in Europe.*

mansion-turned-hotel built in 1761 and notable for its Italianate ceilings and carved mahogany doors. On the opposite side of the Tweed are the grounds of Floors Castle, a huge mansion built by Sir John Vanbrugh for the first Duke of Roxburghe in 1718 and remodelled midway through the 19th century. Prisoners captured during the Napoleonic Wars earned their keep building part of the estate wall. Local tradition maintains that a holly tree in the grounds marks the spot where James II of Scotland was killed when a cannon burst during the siege of Roxburgh Castle, then held by the English, in 1460.

KESWICK *Cumbria*

Some towns owe their beginnings to Roman staging posts, others to a castle, a bridge, an ecclesiastical foundation, a market or a crossroads; Keswick, a pretty, stone Victorian town at the northern end of Derwentwater, owes it all to pencils. Partly to the manufacture of pencils, an industry based on the locally mined black lead, but even more to the wielders of pencils, the poets, writers and artists that were drawn to Keswick and the surrounding countryside. The movement began towards the end of the

18th century when a number of poets awoke to the beauty of the more rugged parts of these islands. Keswick presented them with the double advantage of sublime scenery – Skiddaw and the Saddleback lean over it like the battlements of some celestial castle – and reasonable accessibility by the not very exacting standards of the day.

Thomas Gray was in the vanguard. He spent six days in Keswick in 1767, 'lap'd in Elysium', as he put it. Among those who followed him, almost 30 years later, were William and Dorothy Wordsworth, who came to it after having walked 33 miles from Kendal, 'through some of the most delightful country that ever was seen'. William stayed on for some time after Dorothy departed, in a farmhouse called Windy Brow on Lattrigg, and at about the same time, Samuel Taylor Coleridge came to live at Greta Hall, between Bassenthwaite and Derwentwater, where he was joined by Robert Southey. Coleridge completed *Cristabel* there and wrote *Ode to Dejection*, tortured by neuralgia, which drove him to laudanum and opium. He departed for Leicestershire in 1806, but Southey remained for the rest of his life, despite his appointment as Poet Laureate; he is buried in the Crosthwaite churchyard. He was visited at the Hall by many of the great literary figures of the period – Scott, de Quincey,

Hazlitt, Walter Savage Landor, Shelley and his runaway 16-year-old bride, Harriet, and Charles and Mary Lamb. Lamb, who was no nature lover, nevertheless wrote of the scenery: 'Such an impression I never received from objects of sight before...', a sentiment echoed by Keats, who climbed up to visit the Neolithic stone circle of Castlerigg while on a walking tour in 1818. So impressed was he that he later used the memory as an image in *Hyperion*:

'... *like a dismal cirque*
Of Druid stones, upon a forlorn moor
When the chill rain begins at shut of eve
In dull November ...'

Keswick's oldest building is Crosthwaite church which was built in the 1550s, though it was founded long before that. It is dedicated to St Kentigern (also called St Mungo), patron saint of Glasgow, who is said to have set up his cross some time in the 6th century and preached from the spot where the church now stands. The building contains a 14th-century font, some 15th-century monuments and a more recent one to Robert Southey.

Canon H. D. Rawnsley, one of the founders of the National Trust, was vicar of St Kentigern's about 100 years ago, and the Trust has purchased the viewpoint of Friar's Crag as a memorial to him.

BY MOUNTAINS GREEN
Sprawling at the head of Derwentwater the little grey town of Keswick has England's highest mountains as its neighbours. The broad back of High Spy plunges down from its 2,143 ft heights to the wooded lakeside, and beyond lies a misty jumble of crags and fells with the mightiest of them all, Scafell Pikes, thrusting its 3,210 ft summit above a jagged skyline.

KING'S LYNN *Norfolk*

Henry VIII is the king remembered in the town's name; he seized the manor at the time of the Dissolution of the Monasteries and added his title to the name, presumably to silence any lingering doubts about ownership. Before that, it was called Bishop's Lynn or Lenne Episcópi, just as today it has the alternative name of Lynn Regis. No doubt, then as now, local people compromised and simply called it 'Lynn'.

Though Henry was raking in a large number of manors at the time, he must have been particularly pleased by the acquisition of Lynn, which from its very beginnings seems to have had a golden mantle thrown over it. It owes its prosperity to its location at the mouth of the Great Ouse, 'by reason of those great accommodations of merchandize, food, and necessary provisions which are constantly carried up and down it, and Lynn sits at the door of this river as it were the turnkey of it' – as one 18th-century writer put it somewhat picturesquely.

It would seem that there was a settlement on the spot before the Norman Conquest, but the town's first solid mention is in 1100, when Herbert de Losinga, the first Bishop of Norwich, built St Margaret's Church on the central island of three separated by four tributaries of the Ouse, and established a market

beside it. Sixty years later, this community had so prospered that Bishop Turbus of Norwich felt encouraged to drain the island to the north – which was called the New Lande – and create upon it a kind of suburb, with a separate market and the Chapel-of-Ease of St Nicholas to care for its spiritual needs. This duality in the town, with the old Saturday Market and the slightly newer Tuesday one, is still apparent even after 900 years.

The other aspect of Lynn that remains constant is its role as a seaport. All along the Ouse there are quays and tall medieval warehouses that still seem to carry the mingled aromas of furs, wine and timber, while almost at the corner of the eye are the shades of medieval shipmen and the ghosts of round-bottomed, clinker-built merchant vessels that brought their cargoes from Flanders and the Hanseatic League ports of the North Sea and the Baltic. There too, more solid but very attractively so, is the Customs House with its high, delicate stone lantern.

Most of the port activity has now shifted a little to the north, to Bentinck and Alexandra Docks, surrounded by towering grain silos and tall, clattering cranes, and handling between them about a million tons of cargo a year.

There are certain 'musts' even for a brief visit to Lynn and to capture them, and the flavour of the town, it is best to begin in the Saturday Market. This, and the

HOUSE OF TREASURE *Trinity Guildhall houses the municipal offices, whose magnificent public rooms, created in 1767, are hung with chandeliers, portraits and mirrors. The crypt has recently been converted into a Regalia Room in which are displayed the town's treasures – its charters, plate and regalia, including King John's sword and the richly enamelled 14th-century silver-gilt cup known as the King John Cup.*

streets about it, is where Lynn itself began, and all around are the evidences of its two overriding themes, the medieval church and medieval mercantilism. St Margaret's is the first building to seize the attention, with its awesome twin-towered front and great length. This was built in the 13th century, totally obliterating the Bishop of Norwich's earlier church, and there was further, and not too happy, rebuilding in the mid-1700s after the spire collapsed and measured its length along the nave. There are rare and wonderful things in the church, befitting the wealth of its parishioners – choir stalls beautifully carved with flowers and coats of arms, 14th-century screens, a huge organ case and an ornate Georgian pulpit. Nothing though could better symbolise the rise of medieval Lynn than the church's two brass monuments, which are among the largest and grandest in England. One portrays the merchant Adam de Walsokne, who died in 1349, and his wife, both richly dressed and surrounded by a wealth of intricate carving, while the other shows Robert Braunche and his two wives. Braunche died in 1364, and was Mayor of Lynn in 1349. During his year of office, he offered a feast of peacocks to Edward III who was on a visit to the town; a lively carving of the feast can be seen beneath Braunche's elegantly shod feet.

Beyond the west door of the church there is a long, low building with a windowless ground floor and an overhanging upper storey. This is now called St Margaret's House, but in the 1470s, when it was built, and for many years after, it was the Steelyard of the Hanseatic League of Baltic merchant towns – 'steelyard' being derived from an old German word meaning 'sample-room' or warehouse. It was purchased in 1750 by a local man, who found that he had to deal with the Burgomasters of Hamburg, Bremen and Lubeck to complete the sale.

Another attractive building of the same period near by, also composed of worn, herring-bone brick and with oversailing upper storeys, is Hampton Court. Its rather grand name seems to have occurred simply because it was owned by a master-baker named John Hampton in the 17th century, though part of it dates from at least 300 years earlier. It has recently been converted into flats by the King's Lynn Preservation Trust, who rise admirably to this kind of challenge and have made a similar conversion in the remaining wing of the Benedictine Priory built in the 12th century by Bishop de Losinga.

Back at the Saturday Market, and having emerged from the main door of St Margaret's, it is hardly possible to miss the two remarkable buildings opposite. They are the Hall of the Guild of the Holy Trinity and the Town Hall, and though they are both faced with the same startling chequerboard pattern of dark flint and pale stone, they are separated by almost 500 years, since the Town Hall was built in 1895 and the Guildhall in 1421.

All about there is a wonderful range of buildings of all kinds of periods and purposes from ancient warehouses to Thoresby College, founded in the early 16th century to house 13 Chantry priests of the Trinity

Guild. This too has been put through a metamorphosis by the Preservation Trust and is now chiefly employed as a Youth Hostel. Over the bridge and down King Street is the New Lande, though its newness is hardly obtrusive. Many of the timber-framed buildings belong to the 14th century, and Nos. 28-32 conceal a stone hall 200 years older still. A little farther on is the 15th-century Hall of the Guild of St George, the largest and most complete merchants' Guildhall in England. By an odd succession of circumstances, the old building has maintained a strong theatrical tradition throughout its long life. Mummers played there before the Dissolution of the Monasteries; Shakespeare himself might have trodden its boards when it was visited by London companies in Elizabeth I's reign: and in the 18th century it was gutted and turned into a jewel of a Georgian theatre. Later, it went through sad days as a scenery store, but since 1951, under the auspices of the National Trust and the District Council, it has returned to its former glory, not only as a theatre, but as a cinema and Arts

ARTISTS' MODEL *The Custom House, a frequent subject for water-colourists and photographers, was built in 1683 by Henry Bell, a brilliant architect who was twice mayor of Lynn. A niche in the wall contains a statue of Charles II, proudly declaring that virtually alone among East Anglian towns, Lynn remained staunchly Royalist throughout the Civil War.*

wife, traveller, visionary and writer of the first auto-biography in English; George Vancouver, who survey-ed the north-west coast of America and whose name is immortalised in that of Vancouver Island and the great Canadian city; and the many anonymous merchants, friars, seafarers and ordinary people whose ghosts cling so firmly and happily to this enchanting town.

KIRKBY LONSDALE *Cumbria*

God made the country, men the cities, but the Devil made small towns – so the sour old saying goes. It is probably not true in the case of Kirkby Lonsdale, but at least he gave it a bridge. It happened like this. One rainy afternoon, a long time ago, an old woman pastured her cow and her pony on the far side of the River Lune. Plodding homeward late with her charges, she found the river in full spate and had no means of gaining the opposite shore. But there was the Devil waiting for her: 'Don't despair,' said he. 'By morning, I shall have thrown a bridge across the stream, and you will be able to take your cow and your pony home. But there is a condition; I shall have the first living thing to cross that bridge!' The old woman agreed, and sure enough, by morning, the river was spanned by the lovely triple-arched bridge that is called the Devil's Bridge to this day. 'Now pay your price!' cried Satan – whereupon the old woman threw a bun across, and her old, mangy dog, that was desired by neither Devil nor man, chased immediately after. With a howl of chagrin, and in the obligatory cloud of sulphurous flame, the Evil One vanished, leaving his bridge to be used by Lunedale folk ever since.

It has also been said that in about 1370, a number of grants were made to the Vicar of Kirkby Lonsdale to enable the town to build a bridge, which it did, thriftily using a good deal of dressed stone from a Roman ruin near by. Whatever the truth of it, it is a very handsome structure, a bridge to linger on and watch the slow swirl of the river into the deep pool that has been a playground for local children since time immemorial.

Lingering is also made easier by heavy traffic being diverted to a more modern bridge, but either of them make a gracious introduction to the fine old town that is built almost entirely of dark grey stone. Its role is, and has always been, that of a market centre for the surrounding countryside, and on Thursdays es-pecially, the Market Place is crowded with stalls and a bustling jostle of people. There are some grand houses, notably the Manor House, which dates from 1700, and some pretty, narrow streets with peculiar names; Jingling Lane, for example, which reputedly rings when the ground is stamped, possibly because there is an ancient tunnel beneath.

Appropriately, for an old market town, there are a number of venerable inns, including the Royal Hotel, which was the Rose and Crown until Queen Adelaide, widow of William IV, stayed there in 1840. She was loudly cheered by the populace, and after her depar-ture the red cloth that had been used to line the corridors during her stay was cut up into petticoats for

SAILOR'S FRIEND *The hexagonal tower rising above Tower Gardens is all that remains of the 14th-century church of the Greyfriars which was demolished soon after the Reformation. The tower, which was an important seamark for ships using the port, was spared. The South Gates (below) were once a main entrance through the town walls. They were built in about 1440 of brick, in 1520 the outer surface was faced with stone. Under the main arch can still be seen the grooves in which a portcullis once ran.*

Centre also, and now plays a major role in the annual King's Lynn Festival.

Beyond is the big and busy Tuesday Market and the superb Duke's Head Hotel; the duke thus celebrated is the Duke of York who later became James II. Look out hereabouts for a heart carved into a brick on a wall. It may be a decoration or may mark the spot where one of the few witches burned to death in England went to the stake. It is said that her heart leaped from her body and struck the wall at that point to prove her innocence, or conversely, was too evil to submit to earthly justice and bounded off the wall to jump into the Ouse. The 15th-century St Nicholas's Chapel is close by. Its ceiling is a magnificently carved choir of angels and, not unsuitably, musicians of international repute perform beneath it during the festival.

Having glimpsed all these things, there is still so much more to see in King's Lynn. There is All Souls' Church, for example, which has a cell for an ancho-rite, a kind of pet hermit much approved of by the medieval church, and the Red Mount Chapel, lonely on the old bank surrounding the town. This is an extraordinary, red-brick octagon constructed in 1485 as a resting place for pilgrims on their way to the shrine of our Lady of Walsingham, and was later a gunpowder store and a water reservoir. Then there is the ancient Greyfriars Tower, or the Greenland Fishery House and Blubberhouse Creek that recall the days of the whaling fleet. Finally, there is the remem-brance of the people of Lynn – Fanny Burney, the diarist and novelist, Marjorie Kempe, medieval house-the poor women of the town. The Sun Inn has a pillared front that was constructed at least as long ago as the 17th century, and the King's Arms is probably even older. There, in 1658, stayed Richard Braithwaite, an amiable eccentric who wandered the north of England and wrote an account of his travels in Latin verse, under the pseudonym of 'Drunken Barnabee'. His opinion of Kirkby Lonsdale translates as: 'A poor town and a proud people, an old church and a new steeple.'

The last part must be a reference to one of the many rebuildings that the Church of St Mary has undergone during its long life. As with the bridge, no one is quite certain how old it is, but parts of it go back to the beginning of the 12th century at least, as can be seen from the arches and diamond-patterned columns in the nave, that almost precisely echo those in Durham Cathedral. Considerable alterations were made about 80 years later, and many more down the centuries. During one of these, in 1866, traces of burning were discovered, very likely a souvenir of the Scots who came marauding through this part of the country after their victory at Bannockburn in 1314. Despite this conglomeration, from Norman pillars to Georgian and later monuments, or perhaps because of it, St Mary's is a church of great charm, exactly reflecting the ageless quality of the town it serves.

The view from the churchyard is quite breathtaking, all the way down the valley of the Lune. Turner painted it, while John Ruskin, the art critic, explained his ecstasy in words: 'The valley of the Lune at Kirkby is one of the loveliest scenes in England, therefore in the world.'

KIRKCUDBRIGHT
Dumfries and Galloway

The tidal River Dee, watched over by ruined McLellan's Castle, flows down to Kirkcudbright Bay past an enchanting little town whose deep-rooted seafaring traditions are kept alive by fishing boats and a few small coasters.

Men who sailed from 'Kirkoobrie' at the end of the 18th century included John Paul Jones, the swashbuckling Scot who was one of the founders of the United States Navy. He won a dramatic victory against British ships off Flamborough Head on the Yorkshire coast in 1779 during the War of Independence. In his younger days, Jones is known to have been present when the foundation stone of the Old Bank House in High Street was laid, and he was also held prisoner in the town's Tolbooth. The building dates from the 17th century and is featured in Sir Walter Scott's novel *Guy Mannering*. It is topped with a weather-vane in the shape of a fully rigged ship.

Colourful terraced buildings, many dating from the 17th and 18th centuries, contribute greatly to Kirkcudbright's tranquil atmosphere and have helped make the town popular with artists. Among them was E. A. Hornel, the distinguished Scottish painter and collector of rare books who left his 18th-century home, Broughton House, to the people of his adopted town.

The house is now an art gallery and library, with the works of Hornel and other Scottish artists on view.

Riverside views are dominated by the lofty roofless ruin of Sir Thomas McLellan's 16th-century castle.

The Stewartry Museum with its stepped gables and jaunty little turrets was opened in 1881 and is devoted to the history of the old county of Kirkcudbrightshire. It was called the Stewartry because the area was administered by the king's stewards in medieval times. The exhibits date from prehistoric times and include a gun presented to the town by James IV of Scotland, items associated with John Paul Jones and a nautical display recalling the town's history as a port.

Horn spoons and beakers in a showcase on the ground floor were made by Billy Marshall, a tinker buried in the old St Cuthbert's graveyard. He was married 17 times and is said to have fathered four children after his 100th birthday, eventually dying in 1792, allegedly aged 120. Three Covenanters, executed in the 1680s, are buried near by. The graves are a reminder that Kirkcudbright supported the 17th-century's Solemn League and Covenant to establish Presbyterianism in Scotland.

Kirkcudbright, like many other towns in south-west Scotland, has links with Robert Burns. The 18th-century Selkirk Arms in High Street is where he wrote the famous *Selkirk Grace* dedicated to his patron, the Earl of Selkirk:

> Some hae meat and canna eat,
> And some wad eat that want it;
> But we hae meat and we can eat,
> Sae let the Lord be thankit.

Dundrennan Abbey, 6 miles from the town, was founded in 1142. It was there that Mary, Queen of Scots, spent her last night in Scotland.

PEACEFUL RETREAT *The charm of the Stewartry's most ancient burgh has long attracted painters in search of a peaceful scene. Weavers and potters were drawn there, too, and today Kirkcudbright is the centre of a lively group of artists who work in its 18th-century byways.*

KNUTSFORD *Cheshire*

So lovingly did Mrs Gaskell portray Knutsford in her novel *Cranford*, and so proud is the town of her, that it is sometimes difficult to know whether art is imitating nature, or vice versa. To Mrs Gaskell, Cranford/Knutsford was a place of lavender and lace, of steely rules for social calls that were not to exceed 15 minutes and had to be returned within three days. It was a town, she wrote, 'in possession of the Amazons; all the holders of houses above a certain rent are women. If a married couple come to settle in the town, somehow the gentleman disappears; he is either fairly frightened to death by being the only man in the Cranford evening parties, or he is accounted for by being with his regiment, his ship, or closely engaged in business all week in the great neighbouring commercial town…' Mrs Gaskell's affectionate portrait was written in the 1840s, and perhaps the rules have relaxed since then. But there is still an air of gracious primness about some parts of the little Georgian town, and it is still a dormitory for the 'great neighbouring commercial town', which is Manchester.

Like most English market towns, Knutsford is of great age. Its name is said to be derived from King Canute, or Knut, who forded the River Lily at this point when marching north to fight the Scots. As the monarch emerged from the stream, he was forced to stop to pour sand from his shoes, which is why the townspeople trace patterns of coloured sand in front of the principal buildings during the annual Royal May Day Festival. It may even be the true reason, for the festival is of immense age, and is one of the most important of its kind in the country. The 'Royal' title was gained when the festival was attended by the then Prince and Princess of Wales in 1887, and now, as then, it is held on the Heath, where a Maypole is set up. The Royal May Queen is crowned, and drives in state in a landau, surrounded by her court, and preceded by traditional local figures, such as Jack-in-the-Green and Highwayman Higgins. The real Higgins was a man of some substance who lived in the large house that is now 18–20 Gaskell Avenue, and took to the road, either from a sense of adventure, or simply from a wish to increase his substance. It was said of him that he 'Hunted with his friends in the morning, dined with them in the evening, and sought out their plate chests at night'. He was hanged in Carmarthen in 1767, but achieved a degree of immortality by being woven into *The Squire's Tale*, by Mrs Gaskell, and he appears also in de Quincey's *Reminiscences*. Two of the Higgins children are buried in Knutsford churchyard.

As is apparent, it is difficult in Knutsford to avoid Elizabeth Gaskell. She is not read so widely as she used to be, which is a pity, for she was a shrewd observer of her time, and a witty and sympathetic writer, whose works were much admired by Charles Dickens and by her close friend, Charlotte Brontë. Born Elizabeth Stevenson, she was brought up by her aunt at Heathwaite House in the later-named Gaskell

Avenue. In 1830, she married the Rev. William Gaskell, a Unitarian minister in Manchester, and took to writing, it is believed, to divert her mind from the death of their son. *Cranford*, her second novel, was a great success, and many Knutsford locations, such as Shire Lane, the George Inn and the Assembly Rooms, appear in it, as they do in some of her later works. Knutsford was not her only concern, however, and much of her writing is bitter, Dickens-like reporting upon the condition of the poor in the industrial areas.

Together with her husband and two daughters, she lies beneath a simple stone cross in the burial ground of the Knutsford Unitarian Chapel. Probably she would have considered this to have been monument enough, but in fact she has an extraordinary Memorial Tower in King Street as well. It has a bust of Mrs Gaskell in a niche, with a list of her works inscribed beneath. For good measure, it also bears the names of English sovereigns, beginning with King Egbert, and carved quotations from authors as diverse as Milton, Cromwell, King Alfred and the patriarch Job. It was built about 1900, and, together with the Coffee House and a number of other buildings in the town, is the work of Richard Harding Watt, a Manchester glove-maker with a passion for architecture.

No one knows what to make of Watt nowadays, nor really ever did. Perhaps he was an advanced student of art nouveau, with a desire to beautify the lives of the working class, or perhaps merely eccentric. At any event, he began by building a laundry, with a water tower that was a replica of a tower he had seen in Damascus, a chimney enclosed in a minaret, and boilers concealed by mosque-like domes. On the side

of the tower, in green ceramic tiles, was a quotation from Ezekiel: 'Let your garments always be white.' Near by he built a number of workers' cottages dotted with cupolas, verandas, overhanging balconies and iron scroll work, and for his employees he constructed the Ruskin Recreation Rooms where they could read, and enjoy lectures, discussions and music. Elsewhere in the town, he put up larger houses, some reminiscent of French châteaux, others with a faint touch of Tudor. It would be interesting to know what the engineer Henry Royce, who lived in Leigh Road and was about to begin his partnership with the Hon. Charles Royce, might have made of it all.

Watt's works caused a deal of unease for some years, but lately, and especially since the revival of enthusiasm for art nouveau, the town is becoming quite proud of them, or at least of those that are left, for sadly, a number have been demolished in recent years. And it must be admitted that they do add zest to the Georgian and Victorian background, and stand as proof of Knutsford's high regard for individualism.

LAMPETER *Dyfed*

Known in Welsh as Llanbedr Pont Steffan, this tiny market town lies amid steep, wooded hills in the beautiful heart of Wales. Although small and remote – many English villages have more people – it is the home of the oldest university institution in Wales or England, apart from Oxford and Cambridge, and has a delightfully unexpected 'town and gown' atmosphere when the students are in residence.

St David's College was founded by Bishop Thomas Burgess of St David's in 1822, 71 years before the University of Wales was established. Originally independent, its function was to train young men for the Anglican ministry in Wales; it did not become part of the University of Wales until 1970. The old building at its heart, opened in 1827, is the only neo-Gothic work of its kind in Wales. It was designed by C. R. Cockerell, the architect responsible for the Taylorian Buildings in Oxford, Cambridge's Fitzwilliam Museum and the old Royal Exchange in London.

In the college grounds is a steep, grassy mound – all that remains of Lampeter's motte-and-bailey castle. In 1137 it was captured by Owain Gwynedd, Prince of North Wales and the greatest Welshman of his time. In 1403, however, the castle defied Owain Glyndwr, the last great champion of Welsh independence. A footpath on the eastern side of the campus follows the River Dulas down to the point where it joins the Teifi. There, anglers fish for trout, salmon and 'sewin', as sea trout are called in Wales.

The road from Lampeter to Newcastle Emlyn passes the remains of Peterwell, a mansion built in 1641 for Sir Herbert Lloyd, a notorious Member of Parliament who ended his days in a London gambling den. The estate later became the home of John Scandrett Harford who gave Bishop Burgess the land on which St David's College was built. As well as being a seat of learning, Lampeter is the market town for the farmers of the surrounding hills and valleys.

THE IMPROVER *Whatever Richard Watt's architectural exuberance did for the appearance of Knutsford, it certainly improved the quality of life for his employees. These are the Ruskin Rooms which he built as a library and recreation centre for his laundry workers.*

LAUNCESTON *Cornwall*

In 1538, John Leland, Henry VIII's librarian and antiquarian, came this way and noticed how '... the large and auncient castelle of Launstun stondith on the knappe of the hille by south litle from the paroche church. Much of this castel yet stondith: and the moles (mound) that the kepe stonde on is large and of a terrible highth'. The description remains valid still; everywhere in Launceston is the castle, looming sternly over the market town that grew up on the slopes of its hill, peering over trees and between chimney pots, and looking like two drums, a smaller one sitting upon a larger, or a child's idea of a castle, created with a sand-bucket mould on the beach.

Despite its imposing appearance, and its commanding position over a principal route into Cornwall, the castle was regarded as obsolete even in the 13th century when it was built on the site of a wooden Norman bailey. Its chief fame, or notoriety, in the Duchy was as a prison, since until 1838 Launceston was the county town. Assizes were held within the castle, and public executions on the green outside, the last execution being in 1821.

To appreciate the full flavour of Launceston, it is best to approach it from the north or from the east. These viewpoints gloriously present the castle's silhouette on high, and only a little lower down, those of

the Wesleyan chapel's slender spire and the square tower of the parish church. The chapel was constructed in the 1870s, but the Church of St Mary Magdalene was completed in 1524, having been 13 years in the building. The reason for the delay is at once apparent from a glance at the hard granite exterior, almost every inch of which is covered with intricate carvings; these include a figure of St Mary Magdalene, her ointment box, and the plants that were used to make the ointment with which she anointed the feet of Jesus. There, too, are representations of St George and of St Martin of Tours dividing his coat with a beggar, birds and beasts, musicians, and scenes of rural life, intermingled with a Royal Coat of Arms and the arms of the Trecarrel and Kelway families.

Launceston was the only walled town in Cornwall, but little remains of the defences now apart from the square, castellated Southgate. King House close by was the birthplace of Philip King who was Governor of New South Wales in 1800 and was responsible for naming the town of Launceston and the Tamar River in Tasmania. In The Square, the heart of the town, is the White Hart, a famous old coaching inn, which has a Norman doorway; this, however, is an importation from an Augustinian priory that used to stand in the neighbouring village of St Thomas. Another house in The Square dates from 1555.

COLLEGE GREEN *Its Gothic window looking out over smooth lawns, St David's College, Lampeter, looks rather as if it had strayed there from Oxford or Cambridge – which in a sense it has. It was built in 1827 to the design of Charles Cockerell, architect of the Fitzwilliam Museum, Cambridge, and the Taylorian Buildings at Oxford.*

CASTLE TOWN *Any distant view of Launceston is a view of the castle with the town in a supporting role. And once in the town the same is true, wherever you turn the castle is there, looking down on everything that goes on – just as it has done for the last 600 years.*

The most noticeable houses in Launceston are Georgian, some of them on Castle Street, like Lawrence House – now a National Trust property and the town museum and Eagle House, now a hotel – being very grand indeed.

Generally they were the town residences of the local gentry, opened up for the social season that accompanied the Assizes.

In 1973, the Prince of Wales visited Launceston in his capacity as Duke of Cornwall. The town presented him with a pound of pepper, which is the annual rent due to him for the site of the Guildhall, as it has been due to his predecessors since the days of Henry III.

LEDBURY *Hereford & Worcester*

Tudor buildings watched over by the slender, soaring spire of a Norman church combine with a delightfully rural setting beneath the Malvern Hills to make Ledbury one of the most memorable towns in western England. Its most famous son, John Masefield, was born in 1878 and was the Poet Laureate from 1930 until his death 37 years later.

Masefield's years in the Merchant Navy inspired such famous works as *Sea Fever* and *Cargoes* while three of his long narrative poems – *The Everlasting Mercy*, *The Widow in Bye Street* and *The Daffodil*

Fields – have his home town as a background.

Ledbury's old world atmosphere is epitomised by Church Lane. Narrow, cobbled and closed to traffic since 1746, it is flanked by traditional black-and-white buildings dating from the 15th century. They frame views of St Michael's, the finest parish church in Herefordshire. There has been a church on the site since Saxon times, but the present building was started in 1140. Its detached tower, added 100 years later, supports an elegant 18th-century steeple whose top is 202 ft above the ground. The church houses an exceptional wealth of monuments spanning 700 years.

The High Street's focal point, the timber-framed Market House, has an open, six-bay ground floor and was built between 1617 and 1655. It still sports 19th-century notices warning people not to disturb the business of the corn market. St Katherine's Hospital, on the opposite side of the street, was founded in 1232 by Hugh Foliot, Bishop of Hereford, as an almshouse for 'wayfarers and the poor'. The main buildings were rebuilt in the 19th century, but the chapel and Master's House are medieval.

St Katherine's neighbour, the Barrett Browning Memorial Institute, commemorates Elizabeth Barrett Browning, who spent her childhood near Ledbury. It was officially opened in 1896 by Sir Henry Rider Haggard, author of *King Solomon's Mines*.

The High Street's eye-catching Tudor architecture includes the Feathers Hotel that was already more than 200 years old when it became a staging post for Royal Mail coaches on the road between Cheltenham and Aberystwyth. Ledbury Park, at the top of the street, was built about 1600 and looks down New Street to the 16th-century Talbot Hotel and another timber-framed house whose overhanging upper storeys are supported by stout oak pillars.

The town's long history includes a dramatic visit by Prince Rupert of the Rhine, the Civil War's most dashing commander. In April 1645, he marched his Royalists through the night from Leominster after learning that a strong Parliamentary force was on its way to Ledbury. The enemy arrived first, but were taken by surprise when the prince and his men charged towards the Market House where battle was joined. Prince Rupert's horse was killed as the Round-heads fell back to the church before fleeing towards Gloucester, leaving 120 dead and many wounded.

LERWICK *Shetland*

Ultima Thule, the Romans called Shetland: the 'Last Land', meaning that somewhere a little beyond it, the world came in some way to an end. The case of Lerwick, the islands' capital, and indeed only town, is not so desperate as that, though some of the things about it make the average Briton feel that he has been more adventurous in visiting Lerwick than, say, San Francisco. It is the northernmost town in the British

ISLAND REFUGE *Beneath the golden glow of the sun, Lerwick basks on its hill above the shore (see over). But the architecture of the town tells of another kind of climate. A forest of chimneys poking through tight slate roofs, narrow windows set in solid stone walls, the houses huddled together in narrow lanes – all speak of the need for refuge from the savage gales that lash the town in winter.*

WOODEN WALLS *Timber-framed houses of the 15th and 16th centuries peer at one another over the cobbles of Church Lane, Ledbury. The most recent addition to this view of the town is the church spire, which was added to the tower between 1727 and 1734.*

LERWICK

Isles, at 60°N which puts it level with Greenland and Siberia, and because of this has more daylight in summer and less in winter than any other British town. Though part of Scotland, the nearest large town – and railway station – is Bergen, in Norway; there is never a kilt in sight nor a word of Gaelic spoken, and the people, as a matter of course, refer to a journey to the mainland as 'going to Scotland'. It is, after all, more than 100 miles away and the Shetlanders are mostly of Norse descent.

Bressay Sound, due to the protection of Bressay Island, is also one of the great natural harbours of the world. To it, Lerwick owes its existence, but the Sound was known to sailormen long before the town was dreamed of. Maybe a Roman trireme anchored there; certainly, in the summer of 1263, a Norse fleet of 200 war galleys under the command of King Haakon rested there for two weeks before sailing south to be annihilated by the Scots at the Battle of Largs.

Lerwick itself grew out of a few bothies by the shore that some enterprising islanders established in the early 17th century as a trading post to serve the Dutchmen who were exploiting the rich herring fisheries of Shetland. A few years later, Charles II fortified the place as a naval base, a role it has fulfilled in various national emergencies ever since. At the same time, Lerwick developed its own fishing fleet, and though this is now sadly much reduced, it is still a fine sight to watch it come in on a summer morning to mingle with trawlers flying the ensigns of Norway, Russia and every other maritime nation in northern Europe. There too are the vessels serving the oil rigs, and occasionally a rig itself.

Lerwick's international look comes not only from these fairly recent introductions, but more significantly from the old stone houses that stand, like Venetian Doges' palaces, with their feet in the water. Slipways, called 'loadberries', running from them were, a century or so ago, the landing places for all kinds of cargoes, some legal and some not. Lerwick was a famous contraband port, proof of which was provided a few years ago when secret tunnels and chambers were discovered beneath Commercial Street. This, known to Lerwegians simply as 'The Street', is a twisty, flagged thoroughfare following the old coastline; the buildings in front of it are constructed on reclaimed foreshore. It is old Lerwick's main street, with the towered, Victorian town hall standing above, surrounded by steep lanes of tenements, huddled together against the shattering gales of the Shetland winter. Not a beautiful place, but brave and comforting in the face of the great ocean.

On the last Tuesday in January, however, old town, new town, fishermen, oilmen and anyone else who happens to be around gather together for the spectacular festival of Up-Helly-Aa! It is descended from the pagan Viking ceremony in which great bonfires were lit to welcome back the sun after its virtual disappearance in the dark northern midwinter. Lerwick improves on this by building, each year, a full-sized Viking longship that is dragged through the town before being burned.

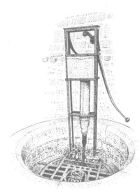

THE NEW PUMP *For centuries the well at Southover Grange, an Elizabethan house of 1572, was operated by the traditional bucket and rope method. Then, in 1889, it was modernised – a pump was installed and the shaft was covered by a wrought iron grille.*

LEWES *East Sussex*

Though one of the most glorious of southern English towns, a stroll through Lewes is not to be lightly undertaken, while on wet days an alpenstock would not look overly pessimistic. The lovely Georgian High Street, with hardly an uninteresting building in it, is manageable, but some of the smaller streets running off and the lanes or 'twittens' connecting them do not so much run downhill as plummet. One of the best of these streets, Keere Street, is positively precipitous, a series of neat houses in dark knapped flint or bright pastel colours plunging down on either side of an apparent cobbled ski-run.

It causes no particular astonishment to learn that Lewes takes its name from an Old English word meaning 'hill'. It straddles, in fact, a spur of the Downs

ROYAL ESCAPADE *George IV is said to have driven a coach down the steep cobbles of Keere Street for a bet. Possibly as a result, the street is now closed to traffic.*

that, according to a plaque in the High Street, lies precisely on the Greenwich meridian, though long before this interesting fact was noted, the Saxons had shrewdly chosen the spot as ideal for the establishment of a burgh, or fortified town. William the Conqueror's henchman and friend, William de Warrenne, also took advantage of the commanding site over the River Ouse gap and built a great castle there. Much of it still stands, burly and tough as the great Norman baron himself; but the Cluniac Priory of St Pancras that he and his wife, the Lady Gundrada, founded has all but vanished. What was not deliberately destroyed at the Dissolution in the 1530s, was ploughed through and over some three centuries later when the railway came. The remains of the noble William and his wife were discovered during this excavation, and lie at peace now in the parish church of St John the Baptist, which was the original hospice of the priory.

The Battle of Lewes, which took place within and without the town in 1264, is often cited as a proud moment in the story of English liberty, and certainly the terms which the victor, Simon de Montfort, forced upon Henry III contained the first glimmerings of parliamentary government. Whether this had anything to do with it or not, the spirit of Lewes was always staunchly independent and non-conforming, which led, during the reign of Mary Tudor, to the burning of 17 Protestant martyrs in the Market Place. The memory must still have been fresh when the Gunpowder Plot was discovered in 1605, and this victory over popery has been celebrated in Lewes ever since.

Altogether, Lewes is a town to savour, both for its history and its architecture. There are medieval churches, grand houses and modest cottages in which all kinds of materials have been employed – timbering and plaster, soft grey and red brick, hung tiles and slates, stone, and the immortal Sussex flint. One of the most fascinating buildings is Anne of Cleves House, one of the properties given to that unfortunate, or perhaps fortunate, queen after her divorce from Henry VIII. It is now a Folk Museum.

LINLITHGOW *Lothian*

When Scotland decides that the theme is Romance, she paints it with a lavish brush. So it is at Linlithgow, where, from its high promontory, the great stone shell of 'the fairest Royal House in Scotland' gazes with black and empty windows over the placid waters of its loch. The site was for centuries occupied by a royal manor, and for a time too, a fort stood there, constructed by the English Edward I when besieging Stirling. But the present Palace of Linlithgow dates from about 1425 and is perhaps, of all Scottish buildings, the one most closely associated with the tragic story of the Stuarts. James I began the building of it, and James IV brought his English Queen, Margaret Tudor, there before riding away to the Battle of Flodden. According to Scott, she climbed to a chamber in the north-west tower to await his return.

But she waited in vain, for he perished on Flodden Field along with the flower of Scottish chivalry fighting the English. Mary, Queen of Scots was born at the palace on December 8, 1542, six days before her father, James V, died in his palace at Falkland. Mary's son, James VI, who became James I of England, also visited Linlithgow, as did Charles I, for whose visit the town's middens were cleared, and its turf roofs replaced by slate. The last Stuart to stay there was Prince Charles Edward in 1745; knowing his fondness for a good party, the townsfolk entertained him royally, and made the great fountain in the courtyard run with wine. A few months later, however, some of the Duke of Cumberland's pursuing troops bivouacked about the palace and, on quitting next morning, fired their straw bedding. The blaze spread to the building and gutted it. So it stands to this day, a sad monument to the Stuarts.

Close by the palace is the parish church of St Michael, part of which dates from 1242, but most from 200 years later. It was 'cleansed' – that is, stripped of anything smacking of popery or idolatory by the Lords of the Congregation in 1559, so the interior is

TOWN WELL *The elaborately decorated covering of the Cross Well in Linlithgow was built in 1807. It is a replica of its predecessor, erected in 1628, which in turn replaced a structure of 1535. In all that time, and for centuries before, it has been the natural centre of the town. There, the weekly markets were held – and the public executions. So, when the Town House was built it had to be beside the Cross. The present house dates from 1668–70 and replaces one demolished by Oliver Cromwell.*

somewhat austere, though if anything this emphasises the beauty of the stone tracery in the windows.

In 1821, the open crown on the tower, typical of many old Scottish churches, was removed. It was eventually replaced a few years ago by an aluminium-and-timber structure symbolising Triumph rising from the Crown of Thorns.

Despite industry and the proximity of a motorway, Linlithgow remains a handsome Lowland burgh, whose centre and market place is The Cross. Next to the Cross Well is Cross House, which dates from 1700. The High Street has some fine buildings too, the most important being the crow-stepped, 16th-century tenements known as Hamilton Lands.

Throughout the town there are good examples of 18th and 19th-century Scottish architecture, the most attractive, perhaps, being the steep little Well Wynds (alleys) that run south of the High Street.

Any exploration of the place should certainly include a walk in The Peel, the public park that used to be the enclosed palace grounds and gardens.

LLANDRINDOD WELLS *Powys*

Chalybeate, magnesium, radium, sulphur and saline springs attracted as many as 80,000 visitors a year to Llandrindod Wells in its heyday as the Welsh answer to fashionable Harrogate and other English spa towns. That period of prosperity is recalled every September during a Victorian Festival, when horse-drawn vehicles take to the streets, local people dress in period clothing and entertainments include magic-lantern shows and 'old tyme' music hall.

Llandrindod's mineral springs were known to the Romans who built a fort and camps in the area, but the first attempt to develop a spa in the heart of Wales did not take place until the 18th century, when a Shrewsbury entrepreneur turned an old mansion into the Llandrindod Hall Hotel from which the town takes its name. The venture failed, mainly because local people objected to the 'fashionable gamesters and libertines' it attracted to what was then nothing more than a small, remote village.

The spa struggled into the 19th century, but the town developed only after the railway arrived in 1865. Evocative reminders of the flourishing decades that followed include the former Pump House Hotel – now the headquarters of Powys County Council – the Hotel Metropole with its art nouveau veranda, and the restored Rock Park Pavilion and Pump Room.

The Pump Room closed in 1975, but was revived in the early 1980s. Visitors can once again sip the waters taken by Victorians and Edwardians to cure or ease everything from anaemia and bronchial troubles to gout, rheumatism, kidney troubles and tuberculosis. When the future King Edward VIII sampled a glass in 1926 he diplomatically praised the scenery when asked what he thought of the taste!

Llandrindod Wells is now a popular holiday base for touring the hills and valleys of central Wales. Its attractions include a boating lake and a golf course more than 1,000 breezy feet above sea level.

LLANGOLLEN *Clwyd*

The little border town is swept about by the swift-flowing Dee and lies deeply buried among dark, pyramidal hills. From the summit of one of these, about 1,000 ft up, there hangs the shattered, fantastical ruin of Castell Dinas Bran, seemingly about to topple into the streets, and looking with particular meaning upon the blue slate roofs of the pretty Royal Hotel.

Water is a major element in Llangollen's make-up, and one of the first features to strike visitors as they approach the majestic bridge over the Dee. Black and swirling, it breaks into pale green rapids upon the rocks and dead trees dragged down by spates, and races through the arches of the bridge, whose piers were first planted in the mid-14th century. There is usually a kayak or two deftly whirling through the rocks. A toylike Victorian railway station is prettily balanced on the bank, then there are a few rows of 19th-century buildings, and high above these, though not at once apparent from the river side, is the Llangollen Canal, whose limpid waters contrast oddly with the busy torrent below. Dating from the early 1800s, it is an idyll of a canal, running through the lovely Vale of Llangollen, its quiet stream mirroring the branches that arch overhead.

From the Wharf at Llangollen you can take a trip on a horse-drawn barge, a dream-like voyage much to be recommended. In the old wharf buildings too, there is an excellent museum that tells the story of Britain's

THE SPA LOOK *Even if its name did not reveal its origins, the bold red brick and gleaming white cast iron that complement one another throughout Llandrindod Wells, proclaim the town for what it is – or was – a comfortable Victorian spa.*

inland waterways, and shows the life and art of the highly individualistic people who worked upon them. Those interested in folk-life should not fail to visit the European Centre for Folk Studies in the town.

A little to the south of the town is Plas Newydd (The New Place), an extraordinary confection of white-washed stone and carved oak surrounded by topiary work. It may be admired or not, but it is impossible to ignore. At any rate, from 1780 until their deaths in 1829 and 1831, it was the home of the celebrated 'Ladies of Llangollen'. Lady Eleanor Butler and the Hon. Sarah Ponsonby were Anglo-Irish gentlewomen who, shunning the fashionable marriage market of the day, moved to the town with their servant and friend, Mary Carryl. Llangollen was a stopping place on the coach road from London to Holyhead, and since the ladies were as reputed for their intelligence and wit as for their unconventional views upon matrimony, dis-tinguished travellers to Dublin broke their journeys at this point to visit them. Sir Walter Scott, the Duke of Wellington, Wordsworth, the Irish patriot Daniel O'Connell and most of the great political figures of the day became their firm friends (though Wordsworth was later barred for describing their house as a cottage in a poem), and it became the custom among these and other visitors to bring some small gift as a mark of appreciation for the ladies' hospitality. The Duke of Wellington, for example, brought Cordovan leather panelling acquired on his Peninsula campaign, and this and many other treasures can be seen in the

house, which is open to the public. The ladies and their servant lie, all three together, beneath a simple triangular monument in Llangollen churchyard.

A little over a mile from the town are the lovely and austere remains of Valle Crucis Abbey – austere because it still reflects the way of life of the Cistercians who lived in it, and lovely because despite the frugality of their own existence, the monks believed that to create beauty was to serve God. The abbey was founded about 1200 by Prince Madoc ap Gruffydd, the father of the man who built Castell Dinas Bran, and its name, which means Valley of the Cross, is derived from a monument of immense age which stands close by. It commemorates Eliseg, a Welsh hero who died fighting the Saxons at the Battle of Chester in the early 7th century, and its present truncated appearance is due to an over-zealous Parliamentarian soldier.

However, the attraction that really brings the crowds is not architectural but musical – the Interna-tional Musical Eisteddfod that is held in the town each July. Arising from tremulous beginnings in 1947, this festival of choral music and folk-song and dance now attracts some 10,000 competitors from all over the world, and audiences that total over 120,000. Where they all stay is a mystery, but Llangollen squeezes them in somehow. Llangollen's contribution to inter-national amity is truly remarkable for a town so small, and it wears its motto with pride – *Byd gwyn fydd byd a gano, gwaraidd fydd ei gerddi fo* – Blessed is a world that sings, gentle are its songs.

THE LADIES' HOME *An extraordinary confection of whitewashed stone and carved oak, hedged about with ancient topiary work, Plas Newydd was the home of the 'Ladies of Llangollen' for 50 years. Now it belongs to the local council and is open to the public during the summer.*

LOUTH *Lincolnshire*

No one can be long in the Fens without coming to the conclusion that the great spires and towers pricking the horizon – Boston, Ely and the rest – are local man's shouts of defiance against the idea of living on a billiard table beneath an upturned pudding bowl. The tallest – 295 ft – and loveliest of these spires is that of the Church of St James at Louth, which can be seen from miles off. The 19th-century artist and designer William Morris said, with justice, that it 'claims homage from the intellect as well as the imagination of Man'.

The late medieval spire is a harmonious pointer not only to the sternly handsome church, but to Louth which is, and has been since long before the Norman Conquest, a thriving market town. Market days are good times to visit Louth, to hear the quick-fire patter of the auctioneers cutting across the lowing and stamping of cattle in Newmarket or, farther into town, to wander through the stalls and shops in Market Place.

Many of the streets about the centre have names ending in 'gate' which, as in other northern and east Midland towns, have nothing to do with entrances and exits, but are derived instead from a Saxon word meaning street or walkway. Westgate has some fine Georgian and Victorian houses, with Westgate Place running off it, a pretty little alley going down to the River Lud. Alfred Tennyson lodged there while attending Louth Grammar School and there, at the age of 18, and aided by his brother, he produced his first book of verse. It was published by a local bookshop, which is still in Mercer Row, and half his fee was paid in books, with a cigar thrown in as a bonus.

LUDLOW *Shropshire*

In the same year as the Conquest, William I granted a number of manors along the Welsh borders to Walter de Lacy, one of the knights who had followed him from Normandy. With the grant came a sizeable share in the responsibility of holding the still unconquered Welsh at bay. Perhaps Walter was too busy soldiering to create an established base, for it was not until 1085 that his son, Roger, took advantage of the superb clifftop site above the River Teme and built his castle upon it. Much of Roger de Lacy's great keep and bailey still stands, but so vital a role did the fortress play in English and Welsh affairs during the ensuing six centuries that it was constantly adapted and altered to suit changing needs and fancies.

The period of the fortress's greatest brilliance was between 1525 and 1642, when it became the home of the Council in the Marches of Wales, from which the entire Principality and several English border shires were ruled. The President of the Council was, in effect, a Viceroy, and lived in a state to accord with his rank – hence the vast amount of Elizabethan building that can be seen among the ruins.

The great days passed with the Civil War, when a Royalist garrison besieged in the castle realised that

SATIRE IN WOOD *In 1447 the Palmers' Guild, a body of laymen working for the support of the Church, bought '100 planks' to make new stalls for the priests and deacons of St Laurence's, Ludlow. The 32 stalls are still there, equipped with one of the finest sets of misericords in England. This one is carved with a scene satirising the elaborate headdresses worn by wealthy women of the period.*

the venerable building was no match for Parliamentarian artillery and surrendered without a shot being fired. Thereafter it was abandoned.

Looked at in one way, what can be seen in the town very precisely mirrors the fortunes of the castle down the centuries – medieval prosperity, Elizabethan and Stuart grandeur, modern tourist attraction. Medieval Ludlow made its living in the cloth trade – hence Mill Street and Silk Mill Lane – and as a market, but in the days when the castle was an administrative centre, the town catered enthusiastically for visiting nobility and gentry. This accounts for the large number of 16th and 17th-century inns, some of which have been converted to other uses, though others are still offering the hospitality they were built for 300 and more years ago. The many Georgian houses, however, hark back to the time when the castle was already abandoned and crumbling and its outer defences turned into a walk for the fashionable gentry of the surrounding countryside, who maintained town establishments for the season. Now, the old fortress's most important role is as a theatre and centre for the Ludlow Festival, an annual feast of music and drama.

Perhaps the best way of gaining an insight into Ludlow's many good things is to begin at the Butter Cross, a worn piece of 18th-century classicism that marks the old market centre. The market looks down Broad Street, a fair contender for the title of the noblest small-town thoroughfare in England. It makes a steep plunge down to the line of the town wall and in its mixture of periods and styles sums up all of Ludlow's history. See especially the wonderful collection of black-and-white timber-framed houses and shops at the top. Fronted by a colonnade borne on delicate pillars, it culminates in the inn that has been called The Angel since at least the 1550s; Lord Nelson was made a freeman of the town there in 1803. A blending of 16th-century black and white, red-brick Georgian and Victorian continues down the hill until it dives into the tunnel of 13th-century Broad Gate, the sole survivor of Ludlow's town gates.

Beyond, Lower Broad Street runs on to triple-arched Ludford Bridge which bears modern traffic as easily as it bore medieval pack-horses. Below it, the River Teme swirls dark green and white, and local children in kayaks negotiate the rapids with enviable ease. The only other bridge is Dinham Bridge of 1823, which lies just beyond the site of Dinham Gate; near by is St Thomas's Chapel which dates from the 1180s.

Parallel with Broad Street is Mill Street which, if you have not seen Broad Street first, is likely to impress as the grandest urban scene in this part of the country. It too is lined with some pretty Georgian houses, among which survives the magnificent 15th-century Guildhall, lightly masked by a new frontage added in 1768. Farther down is Ludlow College, which is housed partly in modern buildings and partly in the 14th-century hall of the Palmers' Guild.

Back at the Butter Cross and facing down Broad Street, the area to the right is pure medieval, in outline at least, even if there has been some considerable patching and in-filling since. Across Harp

CRUSADER'S CHAPEL *The round chapel of Ludlow Castle was probably the work of a crusader who had seen the round churches of the Templars in the Holy Land.*

Lane, for example, upper gables lean forward almost to touch one another, while the little non-touristy shops below must occupy exactly the same spaces as their medieval forbears. Then there is the tiny Quality Square where, so it is said, there was a theatre where Sarah Siddons played. Beyond is King Street and the Bull Ring, formerly the Beastmarket, a place of famous pubs, such as Ye Olde Bull Ring and Keysell's Counting House Tavern. Most famed is The Feathers, a black-and-white structure of 1603, every inch of whose timbers are intricately and amazingly carved.

Over all, and commanding the entire town, stands the tower of St Laurence's Church. Without doubt, St Laurence's is one of the greatest of English parish churches. Grouped about it are the Reader's House, the Rectory and Hosyer's Almshouses, all of great age, while the interior is a medieval hymn of glory. From the west end, there is a deep, theatrical view towards the rood screen and carved reredos, beneath a red, green and gold ceiling supported by angels, all illuminated by the light from the high lantern tower.

All about are splendid coloured monuments, ruffed, armoured and scarlet cloaked and gowned, to Lords Presidents of the Marches and their relatives, looking more regal than any monarchs. At the other end of the scale are the misericords, carved wooden supports in the choir stalls for exhausted choristers to rest upon during long services. Some misericord carvings exhibit heraldic devices, while others seem to be simply doodlings from the 15th-century carver's fancy – a mermaid with a mirror, an ale-wife being dragged off to Hell by a demon, small boys making fun of an ugly woman in a fancy headdress. It is easy to smile with the craftsman of long ago and, indeed, the entire church evokes a warm sympathy with the past. It is not just its tower that speaks of permanence.

MALDON *Essex*

Those who lament the passing of the days of sail may take heart from a stroll down to the quayside, called The Hythe, at Maldon. True, the vessels tied up there – *Trilby*, *Alice Maud*, *Thalatta*, *Adrianus Johanna* and their companions – are not tea-clippers or men-o'-war, but they are working sailing craft, with a real task to perform, even in the last decades of the 20th century. They are sailing barges, surprisingly large, with vast brown sails hanging from massive yards, and blocks, cables, black-tarred rudders and anchors that would not look out of place on the *Victory*. Their timbers are hugely strong, yet handsomely curved, embracing deep holds and snug cabins. Fresh tar, new paint and polished brass gleam everywhere, and *Emily Barratt* has a little praying angel for a figure-head, making the occasional, neglected, rotting barge heart-rendingly pathetic by comparison. Along the quay, the Maldon Maritime Centre tells the visitor all about the past, present and future of sailing barges, and also shows how the East Coast Sail Trust provides adventure holidays for children.

Farther out along the Blackwater estuary is a lonely and faintly hostile place, a country of salt-marshes, creeks and islands. There the great Battle of Maldon between the English and the Danes took place in August, 991. Brihnoth, Governor of Essex, and his followers were massacred by the Danes, but achieved immortality in *The Battle of Maldon*, one of the most vivid of the early English epic poems.

Immediately behind The Hythe, and most pictur-esquely framed by the masts and sails of the barges, is the Church of St Mary the Virgin which dates from about 1150, though with many patches and restora-tions. The four-square stone tower has a jaunty little white wooden spire on top that is, and has been for many years, a daytime market for mariners. At night, it used to be lit by a lantern.

ANCIENT LIBRARY *One of the oldest public libraries in Britain was founded in Maldon at the end of the 17th century by a local benefactor, Dr Thomas Plume. He built the fine brick building which houses his collection of manuscripts, books and pamphlets on the site of the nave of St Peter's Church which had collapsed in 1665 – hence the library's ecclesiastical appearance.*

Maldon's principal thoroughfare is the High Street, which makes a long, curving climb from the river, gaining in the quality of its attractions as it gains altitude. No. 71 is an attractive little 16th-century house used as the local museum; it contains memorabilia of Edward Bright, who lived a little farther along the road in the early 18th century, and achieved a national record for his time by reaching the astonishing weight of 42 stone. Near by is the 15th-century tower of St Peter's Church, though the 17th-century red-brick building attached to it is not a church at all, but the public library.

About here, the architecture of the High Street is considerably mixed – some post-war brick, some Georgian and Victorian, though much invaded by modern shop fronts. There are also a number of pubs of quite amazing antiquity; the White Swan of 1540, the slightly more elderly King's Head, which has a remarkably grim portrait of Henry VIII for a sign and, round the corner, the pretty Blue Boar, part of which dates from the 14th century, as do some of the houses round about, despite later frontages. This is the top of the High Street, where Maldon reaches its attractive climax in little back streets of white Essex weather-boarding, cosy, chintzy restaurants and opulent licensed grocers.

There too, at the top of the High Street, is the parish church of All Saints, constructed of massive and timeless stone and flint enabling the 13th-century tower and some early 20th-century representations of local worthies – Brihnoth and Dr Plume among them – to mingle unconcernedly together. The 14th-century carving in the interior is some of the finest in Essex, and there is a chapel and monuments to the D'Arcy family, medieval lords of the manor. The Washington Window is something of a surprise. It was presented, in 1928, by the citizens of Malden, Massachusetts – founded by a Maldon man – in memory of Lawrence Washington, the first president's great-great-grand-father who was buried in the churchyard in 1652, though no one is quite sure where. There are also monuments in the church to Thomas Cammock, who died in 1602 having had 22 children by two wives, and to poor, overweight Edward Bright. No one should leave the vicinity of the church without a glance at the splendid white and black-timbered building behind the churchyard; this has been the Vicarage of All Saints since the middle of the 15th century.

A little way down the High Street from All Saints', the pavement is straddled by a fine wooden and wrought-iron porch which is the entrance to the Moot Hall, or town hall. The porch is Regency, but the Moot Hall itself was built about 1400 as the tower of a mansion which apparently never proceeded any further. It now contains the old magistrates' court, and there are magnificent views from the top, reaching far beyond the town itself to the misty distances of the Essex coast.

WORKING SAILS *The odd smoke-stack looks out of place among the masts and spars of the old sailing barges which crowd The Hythe at Maldon.*

MALMESBURY *Wiltshire*

This fine old Wiltshire town, built on a ridge between two rivers, claims a unique and delightfully eccentric place in the history of flight. During the 11th century it witnessed man's first authenticated attempt to fly.

The intrepid pioneer was Elmer, a monk who made himself a pair of wings, dived off the abbey's west tower and flew more than 200 yds before gravity claimed its victim. The exploit was recorded by a medieval chronicler: 'Agitated by the violence of the wind and the swirling of the air, as well as awareness of his rashness, he fell and broke both legs and was lame ever after.' The first 'aeronaut' is recalled by a stained-glass window in the abbey.

The town's first charter is said to have been granted by Alfred the Great in AD 880, but that is open to doubt. The date accepted by historians is AD 924, the year when Malmesbury men helped Alfred's son, Edward the Elder, defeat the marauding Danes. Alfred's grandson, Athelstan, confirmed the honour 12 years later. He also granted common rights to the men who fought with him and to their descendants for ever. The ancient traditions are kept alive by the Old Corporation of Malmesbury which meets four times a year in the former Court House in St John's Street.

Malmesbury Abbey traces its roots back more than 1,300 years to a community founded by Maildulph, a Celtic monk, at the start of the 7th century. It became one of England's greatest monastic houses, but was closed by order of Henry VIII in 1539 and sold for £1,517 to William Stumpe, a wealthy clothier who installed weavers and their looms in the nave.

Most of the buildings have gone, but their focal point, the Abbey Church of St Peter and St Paul, has survived as a memorable example of 12th-century architecture. Its magnificent south porch ranks among the finest examples of Norman craftsmanship in England and illustrates many scenes from the Bible. Inside, an effigy carved during the medieval period marks the grave of King Athelstan who died in AD 940.

Near by, a spire is all that remains of St Paul's, the parish church that was abandoned in favour of the abbey church in 1541. It overlooks the battlemented, 18th-century Tolsey Gate – an archway flanked by two cells built as the town's lock-up for petty offenders. Beyond the gate stands one of the finest market crosses in the country. Built at the end of the 15th century, it rises from an octagonal base to an elaborate 'spire' carved with statuettes of saints and a crucifixion scene. According to John Leland, the 16th-century traveller and chronicler, it was built 'for poore market folkes to stande dry when rayne commith'.

MALVERN *Hereford & Worcester*

The Malvern Hills have all the majesty of mountains, despite their highest point being only 1,394 ft above sea level. The range provides a superb setting for Georgian and Victorian buildings typical of the elegant spa towns of 19th-century England.

In fact there are six Malverns – Great and Little, North and West, Malvern Wells and Malvern Link – spread around the hills. Malvern Link is well known to motoring enthusiasts all over the world as the home of the Morgan sports car company started by H. F. S. Morgan in 1910 and still run as a family business.

Great Malvern grew up around a Benedictine priory founded in 1085 and dissolved by order of Henry VIII in 1538. Its 15th-century church was later bought by the villagers for £20 and now stands high among the finest parish churches in Britain. One of the magnificent stained-glass windows was given by Richard III when he was Duke of Gloucester and Lord of Malvern Chase. Another was the gift of Henry VII, who founded the Tudor dynasty after defeating Richard at the Battle of Bosworth Field in 1485.

Springs gushing from the hillside had been credited with healing powers for at least 500 years before they were analysed and publicised by Dr John Wall, one of the founders of the Worcester Royal Infirmary, in 1757.

St Ann's Well and Holy Well – first recorded in 1558 – have buildings which recall the area's heyday as a health resort patronised by such notables as Queen Adelaide, the future Queen Victoria, Charles Dickens, Lord Tennyson and Charles Darwin. In addition, Malvern Water has been bottled and sold since the 18th century. It is now marketed all over the world.

The composer Sir Edward Elgar, born near Worcester in 1857, had homes in Great Malvern, Malvern Link and Malvern Wells. Long walks on the hills inspired him to write such famous works as *The Dream of Gerontius* and the *Enigma Variations*. Sir Edward and Lady Elgar are buried at St Wulstan's Roman Catholic church in Little Malvern.

Wynd's Point, a house near Little Malvern's 12th-century priory, was the last home of Jenny Lind, the 19th-century soprano known as The Swedish Nightingale who died there in 1887.

BACKWATER *For centuries the main road from the south was carried over the River Avon into Malmesbury by the old stone bridge known variously as St John's Bridge or the Town Bridge. Today there is a bypass, so the traffic over the bridge is reduced to those with business in the town or those who wish to explore its ancient buildings and byways.*

MARKET HARBOROUGH
Leicestershire

Markets are known to have been held in Market Harborough since 1204, shortly after the 'new town' was created during Henry II's reign. Cattle, sheep, pigs and poultry changed hands in The Square until 1903, when new premises were opened across the River Welland in Springfield Street. The weekly produce market was also held in The Square before moving to Northampton Road 35 years later.

The 14th-century parish church, one of the few dedicated to St Dyonisius, gracefully dominates the town with a superb broach spire 161 ft high. Many of the 5,000 Royalist troops captured during the great Civil War battle at nearby Naseby in 1645 were held prisoner in the church. Charles I made Market Harborough his headquarters before the battle, and it was there that Oliver Cromwell wrote to Parliament with news of his decisive victory.

The 17th century's early years were also notable for the building of the picturesque, timber-framed Old Grammar School by Robert Smythe. The son of penniless parents, Smythe became Comptroller of the City of London before founding the school in 1614.

The town centre was designated a conservation area in 1969 and has a wealth of Georgian architecture. The broad High Street is particularly attractive and recalls

SCHOOL ON STILTS *When Market Harborough's Grammar School was built in 1614, the lord of the manor ruled that it had to 'stand uppon posts . . . to keep the markett people dry in tyme of foule weather'.*

the time when Market Harborough echoed to the clatter of stagecoaches. Some called at the 18th-century Angel Hotel where as many as 90 horses could be stabled. Others patronised the Three Swans whose wrought-iron sign is one of the street's most eye-catching features.

The imposing Town Hall was built in 1788 by the Earl of Harborough whose coat of arms, carved in stone, decorates the western pediment. Its arcaded ground floor was originally used as a meat market. Catherwood House, with its Gothic façade, dates from 1876 and was the home of Sir William Henry Bragg, winner of the Nobel Prize for physics in 1915.

Market Harborough's 19th-century prosperity owed much to the Symington family whose corset factory – home of the 'liberty bodice' – now houses the local council offices and museum.

MARLBOROUGH *Wiltshire*

With its strawberry-red brick and tile, its gilded signs gleaming in the sun and its wide and gracious High Street, Marlborough looks like the setting for a dukedom, which, of course, it is. However, neither the present Duke of Marlborough, nor his ancestor, the great 1st Duke seem to have had anything much to do with the place. The Churchills came from Devon.

The town grew up, like many others, in the lee of a great Norman castle which stood on The Mound, an artificial hill now in the grounds of Marlborough

DRY BOOKS *Second-hand books are safe from the weather in the display under the arcade outside The White Horse Bookshop in Marlborough's High Street. Anyone wanting a book when the shop is closed just puts the money through the door. A little farther along the street, another shopfront is covered with carvings dating from the early years of this century. The one above commemorates King John, who gave the borough its first charter in 1204.*

College. For once, the Normans did not have to build a mound for their fortifications; it had been constructed long, long before and its purpose forgotten, like those of other monuments in this area of prehistoric wonders. Local legend says firmly that The Mound is the grave of Merlin, and rather more doubtfully that the name of the town is derived from that of the wizard. For much of its existence, the castle was a royal residence; William the Conqueror established a mint there and King John was married in the chapel.

After the Wars of the Roses, parts of the castle fell into disrepair and, later, Edward VI gave it to his mother's family, the Seymours, together with the surrounding Savernake estates. The castle must have been back in repair by the Civil War, since the Seymours held it for the Royalist cause, though the town was solidly for Parliament. This unfortunate division led to some bitter fighting; the Royalists, bellowing 'A town for King Charles!', stormed Marlborough in December 1642 while the Parliamentarians made their last stand in the Church of St Mary, as the scars of pistol and cannon balls still bear witness.

Lying among the Wiltshire Downs, Marlborough has been a centre of human settlement for at least 10,000 years. The Mound, in the grounds of Marlborough College, is just one of many earthworks that were scattered over the turf-clad downs by forgotten races of men who raised other monuments such as Stonehenge, Avebury and Silbury Hill.

By the Restoration, the castle had vanished from history and existence, and the Seymours built a mansion in what had been the bailey. Later, this became the extremely grand Castle Inn, patronised by royalty, nobility and gentry on their way to Bath. The venture was slain by the railway, but the 18th-century building made an ideal nucleus for Marlborough College, founded for the sons of clergymen in 1843; it is now called, somewhat prosaically, C House.

In 1653, the town at the castle's doorstep suffered a disastrous fire in which 250 houses were destroyed, and the Church of St Mary gutted. A petition to Cromwell, Lord Protector of the realm, produced a national appeal which provided for rebuilding and a puritanical interior for St Mary's, a little at odds with the shell, which dates from the 15th century and beyond.

Nevertheless, the general aspect of the present High Street is purely Georgian, though there are some much older buildings in the lanes running down to the River Kennet. It is of immense width, maybe the widest high street in England, and quite capable of coping with the stalls of market day, parked cars and an even flow of traffic all at once. It stretches from the 15th-century Church of St Peter and St Paul, where the future Cardinal Wolsey was ordained – it is now the Tourist Information Centre – to the late Victorian Town Hall, and behind it, St Mary's Church. The reason for the extraordinary width was that Marlborough straddled the main road to the west (and continued to do so until the building of the M4), and

made its living by catering for travellers. A few of the old coaching inns are still in business, most notably the immense Castle and Ball Hotel, whose sign resembles a huge gold ball-cock; the name is probably a corruption of castle and bull, both of which symbols appear in the town's coat of arms. It is a very attractive street with many of the old arcades bridging the pavement still in position. Samuel Pepys mentioned these when he stayed at the Hart Inn, now Nos. 111–113: 'Penthouses with pillars which makes a good walk.' He probably needed the walk, since he reported too that the Hart dined him so well that all five London coaches had departed before he awoke.

Most of the modern shops and supermarkets have done their best to conform with the general pattern of the High Street, and indeed, many of them occupy old premises. Visitors will also notice a much higher than average number of pretty, bow-fronted tea shops, agleam with copper kettles and warming pans, and presenting a rich array of confectionery to the passer-by.

MELTON MOWBRAY *Leicestershire*

Paintings in the Melton Carnegie Museum are colourful reminders that this ancient Leicestershire town has been England's fox-hunting 'capital' for more than 200 years. A 19th-century guide described it as 'one of the brightest and busiest resorts in England' during the winter months when the fashionable Quorn, Cottesmore and Belvoir hunts attracted wealthy, high-spirited sportsmen from all over the country.

Many of Melton Mowbray's finest buildings were originally clubs and 'hunting lodges' where champagne flowed like water as royalty mingled with prominent politicians, captains of industry, wealthy young bucks and high-ranking army officers. Prominent visitors have included the Duke of Wellington, the Prince Regent, Beau Brummel, Winston Churchill and Edward VII when Prince of Wales.

Egerton Lodge, built in 1829 and now the local council offices, was the town's most fashionable address in the 19th century. For many years it was the hunting-season home of the second Earl of Wilton, the 'King of Melton'. Born in 1779, he followed the hounds until a few days before his death in 1882. Another prominent resident and huntsman was the Earl of Cardigan, leader of the Charge of the Light Brigade at Balaclava in 1854. His home, Cardigan House, still stands in Burton Street.

Hard days in the saddle were followed by heavy drinking and wild escapades. In 1837 the Marquis of Waterford and his friends literally 'painted the town red' and gave a new expression to the English language.

The town is also famous for Stilton Cheese and pork pies, noted for their hand-raised crust. Ye Olde Pork

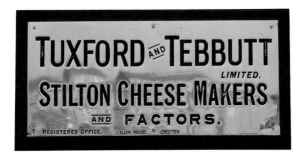

CHEESE TOWN *Stilton takes its name from a village where it was once sold. But this sign in the town is a reminder that Melton Mowbray is where it is made.*

Pie Shoppe in Nottingham Street has been in business since 1850. There is a link between the cheese and the pies – pigs are fed on the whey left over from cheese-making.

'Medeltune' is mentioned in the Domesday Book of 1086 and its magnificent parish church of St Mary was built about 200 years later. It is one of only four parish churches in England whose transepts are flanked by aisles and has the dignity of a small, perfectly proportioned cathedral. The lovely old building shelters an effigy known as the Alabaster Lady, her head resting on a pillow supported by two angels, and the chain-mailed figure of a crusader.

St Mary's eight-pinnacled tower is 100 ft high and overlooks Anne of Cleves House in Burton Street. The house was built in 1384 and given to Anne after she had been divorced by Henry VIII. On the opposite side of the street stands Maison Dieu, also known as Bede House, built by Robert Hudson in 1640 for 'six poor bachelors or widowers'. It was later extended to accommodate six old ladies.

MIDHURST *West Sussex*

Many south-country people firmly believe that Midhurst is the very image of a country town. One of them, E. V. Lucas, writing in 1903, even made it the starting point of his classic *Highways and Byways in Sussex*, though there is little geographic logic in doing so.

However, he enjoyed putting best things first, and felt about Midhurst that 'no other spot has so much to offer; a quiet country town, gabled and venerable, unmodernised and unambitious, with a river, a Tudor ruin, a park of deer, heather commons, immense woods and the Downs only three miles distant ...'

And though nowadays Midhurst has its share of traffic – rather more than its share when a polo match is being played at Cowdray Park – in essence, the older part of the town at least remains much as Lucas described it. Perhaps there were more grocers and bakers in his day, and fewer antique shops; and, of course, the need for the war memorial had not yet arrived; but these apart, the view up South Street to Market Square and Church Hill beyond, must have been almost exactly the same.

This is quite a good way to come to Midhurst, from the south, when the town seems to grow abruptly out

IRON TOWN *The roofs and chimneys of old Midhurst rise towards Church Hill above the rust-red waters of South Pond. The colour of the water comes from the iron which underlies the soil in this part of Sussex and was the foundation of the county's prosperity in medieval times.*

of the fields bordering the Chichester road. The curtain raiser is South Pond, a pretty lake attended by a chorus of quacking waterfowl. Elizabeth I used to take the air by the side of the stream that feeds it, and the path she took was turned into a nature trail in 1977 to mark the Jubilee of Elizabeth II. On the other side of the pond is a street called The Wharf, a reminder of the canal that brought prosperity to the town in the early 19th century, but was killed by the railway; there is little to be seen of it now. In the background is tree-capped St Ann's Hill, which was where Midhurst really began. Shortly after the Norman Conquest, the de

Bohuns built a castle on the hill – its foundations can still be traced. The family moved to the Cowdray site on the banks of the River Rother in the 13th century, but long before the castle was deserted the compact pattern of the town at its gates was well established, and no one has seen any reason to change it since.

The isolated timber-and-brick building at the top of South Street is Market Hall. Dating from the 1540s, it was a meeting place for the traders and craftsmen who built their houses and shops in and around Market Square. In 1674, one of them, a bedspread maker, bequeathed money to found a Grammar School in the loft of the hall. The school still exists, in handsome early 19th-century buildings in North Street. Among its distinguished old boys was H. G. Wells.

Close by Market Hall is the Spread Eagle, an enormous coaching inn said to date from 1430. Most of the buildings in and about Church Hill and Market Square are of great but indeterminate age, since, as is the pleasant way with small and ancient towns, they have all been added to or modified many times down the centuries. Even so, here and there, it is possible to pick out details – timbers, the line of a roof or the shape of a window – that tell of medieval or Tudor origins. There is no doubt, however, about the antecedents of Elizabeth House, now a restaurant, whose white plaster and black timber framing are almost aggressively Tudor. So much so, in fact, that it is no great surprise to learn that it was much restored in the 19th century.

The curiously shaped, shingled spire of the Church of St Mary Magdalene and St Denys dominates the old part of the town. Perhaps the best-known story about the church is its 8 p.m. curfew, said to have been rung for centuries, ever since a traveller, lost in the neighbouring forest, was guided to Midhurst and safety by the ringing of the bells. In case any future wanderer should find himself in the same predicament, he willed a piece of land the rent from which would provide for an evening ringing of the bell in perpetuity; and it is rung still, whenever a ringer is available. Similar stories are told in a number of British towns and villages, but the Midhurst tale at least is backed by some land, still called Curfew Garden, near the lovely 17th-century County Library in Knockhundred Row.

This oddly named street also contains the Knockhundred Market, an arcade of half a dozen very pretty shops, above which hangs a huge painting depicting what is probably Cowdray House in its heyday. It bears the intriguing inscription, 'As in the Armada's day, so in our own. Thanks for Deliverance'. Such touches of the unexpected occur everywhere in Midhurst, from the fine old buildings that breast through the supermarkets in North Street, to the way that almost every road, sooner or later, seems to present a view of the pigeon-haunted towers and skeletal mullions of Cowdray House.

Without doubt, Cowdray is one of the noblest of Tudor ruins, just as in the days of its prime it was one of the greatest houses of the realm. It was gutted by fire in 1793. The present owner, Lord Cowdray, has converted much of the park to sports fields and opened the ruined house to the public. Smoke stains and evidences of former grandeur remain very much apparent.

MUCH WENLOCK *Shropshire*

The heart of Much Wenlock lies just off the main road between Shrewsbury and Bridgnorth as it swings hard right after swooping down from Wenlock Edge. The town's narrow streets and ancient buildings developed around a now-ruined priory founded by St Milburga, daughter of King Merewald of Mercia, about AD 680. It was sacked by Danish raiders 200 years later, but was revived in the 11th century by Earl Leofric, Lady Godiva's husband, and became an abbey shortly after the Norman Conquest.

Like the other monastic foundations in England and Wales, Much Wenlock's abbey or priory was closed by order of Henry VIII in the 1530s, became derelict and was used for building material by many generations of local stonemasons. Most of the building vanished long ago, but walls rising to more than 70 ft in places provide a strong impression of its medieval size and splendour. The former infirmary and Prior's Lodge, built about 1500, have survived intact and now form a private house that is one of the finest examples of domestic architecture from that period in England.

The town centre is a delight. Holy Trinity Church, built in the 13th century, overlooks the black-and-white Guildhall whose most recent additions are more than 400 years old. The interior is equally enchanting with oak panels, a fine old tie-beam roof and Elizabeth I's coat of arms as features of the old court room. Outside stand the mobile stocks, last used in 1852. One of the Guildhall's oak posts also retains the iron hoops which secured a prisoner's wrists during public floggings.

High Street's architectural heritage includes Raynalds' Mansion – built in 1682 for John and Mary Raynald – and Ashfield Hall, where Charles I is believed to have spent a night in 1642, just after the start of the Civil War.

NANTWICH *Cheshire*

Timber-framed buildings give the streets of Nantwich an atmosphere of timeless charm and tranquillity which belies the town's turbulent history. It was reduced to a single house when the Earl of Mercia fought a bloody, last-ditch battle with the Normans in the 11th century. In the Middle Ages it was attacked and devastated by the Welsh who called the town Hellath Wen or White Salt Pit. A great fire raged for nearly three weeks in 1583, but St Mary's Church, Sweet Briar Hall and Churche's Mansion survived.

Rebuilding the town cost £30,000 – many millions of pounds in today's money – and contributions included £2,000 from Elizabeth I who ordered a collection to be made throughout England. Queen's Aid House in The Square has an inscription thanking Elizabeth I for her help in rebuilding Nantwich:

> '*God grant our Ryal Queen*
> *In England longe to Raign*
> *For she hath put her helping*
> *Hand to bild this towne again.*'

Nantwich was one of the greatest salt-producing towns in England from Roman times until the middle of the 19th century. Eight 'salt houses' where brine was evaporated were recorded in the Domesday Book of 1085 and there were 300 in use when the chronicler John Leland visited Nantwich during Henry VIII's reign. Most of the salt was used to preserve food, but 18th-century Nantwich was also a modest health resort whose brine baths were said to cure epileptic fits, indigestion and rheumatism. The town's swimming pool is still fed by a saline spring that has been used since Roman times.

The 14th-century parish church of St Mary has an octagonal tower and is notable for some of the finest carved choir stalls in England. The misericords depict such things as a woman beating her husband with a ladle, the Devil pulling a nun's mouth open, St George and the dragon, a pelican feeding her young, and a mermaid combing her hair.

Sweet Briar Hall in Hospital Street dates from 1450, while Churche's Mansion at the junction with London Road was built in 1577 for Richard and Margery Churche. Their carved portraits are a feature of the porch. The mansion is a superb example of Cheshire decorative half-timbering with large gables, mullioned windows and leaded lights. It is now a restaurant and the upper floor, furnished in 16th-century style, is open to the public in the summer.

Another fine building, the three-storey Crown Hotel in High Street, dates from 1585. Its impressive black-and-white frontage, with close-set timbers leaning at alarming angles, is topped by a window running the entire length of the second floor.

SAVED FROM FIRE *Sweet Briar Hall, in Hospital Street, was one of the few houses to escape the great fire of Nantwich, which raged through the town for 20 days in 1583.*

NEWMARKET *Suffolk*

The sport of kings may not be to everyone's taste, but no one could fail to be moved by the sight of early morning training on Newmarket Heath – the long lines of horses, tall and grave against the pearly mist, each with a mackintoshed apprentice perched high on top, the miles of undulating, velvety turf, broken only here and there by Scots pines permanently bent over by winter gales, and by trainers anxiously studying stop watches. Visitors who see such a sight should make the best of it, for unless a race meeting or a sale is being held, they are unlikely to see another horse all day. There are plenty of things in and around Newmarket that are constant reminders that this is the headquarters of horse racing; transporters, stable blocks, saddlers and breeches makers, streets named after heroes of the turf, miles of the neat, white railings known as Newmarket fencing, but for some reason, seldom any sign of the horses themselves.

The white railings and the marked training gallops begin at least 2 miles out on the Cambridge road, a wide, straight, pleasant route, flanked by stately banks of tall beeches. The National Stud is thereabouts, blocks of neat cream and red-tile stabling, to which admission may be obtained by appointment in August and September week-ends. The racecourses are near by and on the edge of the town is Tattersalls, the most elegant emporium in the world, where racehorses are bought and sold.

Newmarket's High Street is simply a pause in the Cambridge–Bury road, wide and elegant. The most impressive buildings in the street are the part-Georgian Rutland Arms, and racing's holy-of-holies, the Jockey Club, in Georgian style though much of what can be seen from the road dates from 1933. There are some old, pretty streets of flint and coloured plaster behind the Rutland Arms; one of them is Palace Street which has the black-shuttered Nell Gwynne House, where Nell resided when her royal lover was at the races.

Even people whose interest in the turf is restricted to a very occasional flutter on the Derby or the Grand National should make a special effort to visit the National Horseracing Museum. It is contained in some handsome rooms in the Jockey Club. There, in a comprehensive collection of paintings, drawings, relics and documents, is presented a picture of an extraordinarily lively part of the British social scene over three centuries.

NEWPORT *Isle of Wight*

The Isle of Wight's attractive old 'capital' stands on the tidal River Medina and is overlooked from the west by the stern battlements and towers of Carisbrooke Castle. Town and castle both have sad memories of Charles I. King Charles went to the castle at the end of 1647, hoping to rally support from the governor for the Royalist cause, but found himself treated as a prisoner rather than an honoured guest.

During his year on the island he was placed on parole and lived in the Old Grammar School, founded in 1614. Its style is typical Jacobean, with steep gables, tall chimneys and mullioned windows set in walls of undressed stone. The parish church of St Thomas dominates the heart of the town. Built in 1854–7 on the site of an earlier church, its foundation stone was laid by Prince Albert. Princess Elizabeth, second daughter of Charles I, was buried in the old church. A brass plate marks her grave.

The town's history is punctuated with disasters. The Black Death killed many inhabitants in 1349, and Newport was completely destroyed by French raiders in 1377, during the Hundred Years War. The plague struck again in 1583 when, according to legend, only one house was free from death. Its site is now occupied by God's Providence House, built in 1701 and notable for a beautiful, shell-like canopy over the front door. It stands in St Thomas's Square.

The High Street has an imposing Guildhall built by John Nash in 1816. Its slender Ionic columns contrast with the clock-tower built in 1887 to mark Queen Victoria's Golden Jubilee. The Castle, said to be the Isle of Wight's oldest public house, dates from 1684 and was a popular cock-fighting venue.

MEMORABLE STYLE *The ornate memorial in St James Square, Newport was erected in memory of Queen Victoria in 1901, the year in which she died.*

NORTH BERWICK *Lothian*

Anywhere on the Firth of Forth, and quite a long way down towards the English Border also, the 613 ft pyramid of North Berwick Law stands always at the corner of the eye. Like the Bass Rock, with its screaming population of gannets offshore, the rock of Edinburgh Castle and a number of other heights in this part of eastern Scotland, it is a plug of solidified lava that was once the core of a volcano. This accounts

ODD MAN OUT *The elaborate fountain at the Cambridge end of Newmarket's High Street commemorates Sir Daniel Cooper, a deputy lieutenant for Cambridgeshire, who died in 1910. As far as is known, Sir Daniel had little or no connection with horse racing – the principal activity in and around Newmarket.*

PILGRIMS' WAY *The sturdy stone breakwater which encloses the harbour at North Berwick dates from 1887. But long before that, North Berwick had been a ferry port for pilgrims crossing the Firth of Forth on their way to the shrine of St Andrew at St Andrews in Fife.*

for its symmetry. At the summit are a look-out post constructed during the Napoleonic Wars, another one dating from the Second World War – logical-enough structures, considering the enormous views from the top. But there is no such accounting for an arch made from the jawbones of a whale.

The charming and ancient burgh of North Berwick lies between the woods that were planted on the side of the Law in 1707 to celebrate the Union of Parliaments, and the harbour, where there are generally a few fishing boats tied up. Yachts, however, are the more characteristic craft, complementing the pleasantly opulent, turn-of-the century air the town now possesses. In the 1880s, the medieval fishing port and market town began to change its identity as holiday-makers took note of the salubrity of its air. They were followed not long afterwards by Edinburgh commuters. The two principal streets, Quality Street and High Street, are lined with decorous shops and hotels, and every yard along the seafront, it seems, has been shaped and shaven into a golf course. In the rest of Scotland, golfing is merely a passion, but on the south-east coast it is a religion.

Nevertheless, supplementing the Edwardian villas, there are reminders of a more ancient Berwick. In Old Abbey Road, there are the remains of a 12th-century Cistercian nunnery, while the darkly handsome parish church was probably built in about the 1650s, as was the Tower House in the High Street. The Lodge, a group of modern flats in Quality Street, was carved out of the 18th-century Laird's House by the National Trust for Scotland.

By the harbour wall, there is another survivor, the tattered remnants of the 12th-century Kirk of St Andrew that is also the last memento of a scandal that set all Europe a-buzz. In 1590, it is said, 200 witches met there under the personal presidency of the Devil to bring about the death of James VI, who was returning from Oslo with his new bride, Anne of Denmark. The method chosen was to sink his ship in a storm that would be raised by tying portions of a hanged man to a cat that would then be cast into the sea – or at least, so went the evidence that was later wrung by torture from some of the unfortunate women involved. In any event, their efforts were unsuccessful, for the king survived and took an active part in the subsequent trial, as a result of which several of the so-called witches concerned were strangled and burned on Castle Hill in Edinburgh.

OAKHAM *Leicestershire*

For nearly 700 years this pleasant old market town was the proud 'capital' of Rutland, England's smallest county. It kept the honour until 1974 when Rutland was merged with Leicestershire during local government reorganisation.

The town centre with buildings of mellow stone has much to reward the explorer on foot. All Saints' 14th-century spire, a great landmark in the fertile Vale of Catmose, rises gracefully above the 12th-century banqueting hall of Oakham Castle. The hall, built by Walkelin de Ferrers, is the most complete survivor of its type and period in England. Inside, more than 200 replica horseshoes illustrate the ancient custom of charging every peer of the realm who visits Oakham either a shoe from his horse or the money to have one made. The origins of the 'tax' are not known, but it is believed to have been levied by the de Ferrers to emphasise their lord-of-the-manor status.

Close by the castle, in the Market Place, is the old Butter Cross whose ancient stone-clad roof, supported by eight pillars of weathered oak, surrounds a central column of stone. The same roof shelters the stocks.

In the High Street, which runs off the Market Place, is Flore's House, an early 14th-century stone house, named for one of Oakham's most famous sons, Roger Flore, Speaker in four Parliaments between 1416 and 1422. More famous still is the dwarf Jeffrey Hudson (1619–82), the son of an Oakham butcher who was 'served' to Charles I and Queen Henrietta in a cold pie while they were hunting near the town in 1628. Queen Henrietta took Jeffrey as a page and he became one of her most trusted servants. By a strange coincidence, towards the end of his life he fell foul of the machinations of Oakham's most infamous son, Titus Oates (1649–1705), fabricator of the 'Popish Plot' of 1678. Oates alleged that Roman Catholics were plotting to murder Charles II. Many Catholics were executed while others were imprisoned, including Hudson. He was later released and received a small pension from Charles II's secret-service fund.

Oakham School, one of the oldest in England, was founded in 1584 by Archdeacon Robert Johnson of Leicester and is now claimed to be the largest co-educational public school in the country. Its original premises near the church have become a theatre.

The Rutland County Museum, in Catmose Street, occupies what was originally a riding school built in the 1790s for the Rutland Fencibles, one of many militia units raised to defend Britain during the Napoleonic Wars. The museum's exhibits range from fossils to traditional farm wagons, the oldest of which dates from the same period as the building.

Rutland Water almost laps the south-eastern outskirts of Oakham and is England's biggest man-made lake with a 24 mile perimeter. Its earth-fill dam rises from a base half a mile wide and holds back 27,300 million gallons of water.

OBAN *Strathclyde*

In the course of the immortal Highland Jaunt in 1773, Dr Johnson and Mr Boswell came to Oban, then no more than a collection of cottages by the shore. Nonetheless, these pioneers of the Highland tourist industry were able to find 'a tolerable inn', somewhere about where Argyll Square is now. Were they on the same spot today, they would have a hundred or so to choose from, as well as a fair number that are considerably better than tolerable.

Shielded by the long island of Kerrera, Oban Bay is the largest and finest harbour in the north-west. By the piers, there is a constant coming and going of fishing

COVERED STOCKS *The stone slab roof, supported on stout oak timbers, which covers the Butter Cross in Oakham Market also shelters the town stocks. This does not mean that the townsfolk were over-concerned for the welfare of offenders – just that they wanted to preserve the stocks.*

boats, of ferries big and small, and of puffers, the much-loved little coasters that turn up, sooner or later, in every harbour and inlet in the Highlands and Islands. There is, too, a sense of outwardness and adventure, for this is the gateway to the west, to Mull and Tiree and Iona and Staffa, and farther out still to places with magical, musical names like Mingulay and Barra and Benbecula and Rodal. It is a feeling that puts a bounce in the step, and if Oban is not the end of the 'Road to the Isles', as described in the song (actually, Morar, near Mallaig is) there is a distinct sense that it should be. Climb up Pulpit Hill behind the harbour as the evening fades and look out to Mull and the smaller islands as the lighthouses give forth their first jewel-like sparkling, and it is possible to share the old Celtic belief that Paradise lies somewhere to the west.

Oban looks after its visitors very well. There are masses of hotels, of which the grandest and most Edwardian-gracious are along the curve of the Corran Esplanade near the pink granite Cathedral of St Columba, and there are ceilidhs, summer shows and shinty matches galore – shinty being a brand of hockey that was substituted for clan warfare. Then there are the Highland Games held in mid-August, that are second in importance only to the games at Braemar, attracting pipers and athletes from all over the country, and enthusiasts from all over the world.

The visitor would be forgiven for thinking that the Colosseum-like structure balanced on top of the town like an ill-fitting hat might have something to do with the games; but it has not. This is McCaig's Tower, or McCaig's Folly, a vast granite structure that the banker and art critic, John McCaig, had built between 1890 and 1900 to give work to local masons. It was never finished and now contains an attractive garden and shrubbery and, take it all for all, it would be a pity if it were ever demolished. Besides, for eccentricity, it goes very well with the shell of the never-completed hydropathic, and the blue-and-white wooden railway station that looks as though it had been constructed out of marzipan.

At the end of the esplanade, and standing imposingly on a crag overlooking the bay, is the creeper-clad ruin of Dunollie Castle. Dating from perhaps the 12th century, it was the stronghold of the MacDougall Lords of Lorn, and was practically impregnable, since it was successfully held against General Leslie's Covenanters in 1647, and also withstood an attack by government forces in the Rising of 1715. Presumably the castle was eventually abandoned only for reasons of comfort, since the MacDougall chieftain still lives in a mansion near by.

SNUG TOWN *Oban huddles down snugly beneath its snow-clad roofs, making a cosy contrast with the bleak outlook across an icy sea to Kerrera and the mountains of Mull.*

PEEBLES *Borders*

GOOD ORDER *The neatly ordered streets of Peebles speak of prosperity as they spread out across the valley of the River Tweed. Beyond, the gentle green hills of the borderland repeat the theme of an ordered way of life.*

ENDURING STONE *One of the best-preserved medieval castles in Scotland stands about a mile outside Peebles on a beautiful site above the River Tweed. Neidpath Castle, which dates in part from the 14th century, owes its survival to massive stone walls, up to 11 ft thick in places.*

The town's motto means, roughly, 'Flourish against the stream', a neat exhortation meant to appeal equally to the salmon in the tranquil Tweed, and to the stern and striving spirits of the people of the Borders. The salmon seem to do very well, and as for the people, Peebles is one of those Scottish towns whose expertise is the nurturing of Great Men. It produced the Chambers brothers, famed for their dictionaries, encyclopaedias and generosity, numerous professors and writers, and provided Sir Walter Scott and Robert Louis Stevenson with material for their novels. Mungo Park, the African explorer, had a large medical practice in Peebles for several years before setting out on his last, and fatal, expedition in 1805. Even William Douglas, 4th Duke of Queensberry, born there in 1724, achieved greatness of a kind as 'Old Q', sportsman, rake, dandy and object of a sonnet by William Wordsworth. The poet, inspired by the felling of ancient trees on the Queensberry estate at Neidpath Castle, a mile or so outside the town, addressed the duke thus:

> *Degenerate Douglas! Oh, the unworthy Lord...*

'Mellow' is an adjective that is much overworked when describing old towns, but Peebles deserves it more than most, especially in spring and autumn when the light mingles the river, the ancient bridge, the crown-topped tower of the Old Parish Church, and the wooded hills behind into a warm harmony exactly reminiscent of an 18th-century print. Actually, in spite of its name the Old Parish Church is not especially old, rather less than 100 years in fact, and a mere child when compared with the ruined Cross Kirk. There, in 1261, 'in the presence of various honest men, ministers and burghers', a cross was discovered beside a slab bearing the words 'The Place of St Nicholas the Bishop', and near it a funeral urn containing ashes. It was assumed that the cross had been buried in about 296, the period of the Roman persecution of the Christians in Britain. The ashes were presumably those of the bishop himself who, incidentally, had nothing to do with the Nicholas of Santa Claus fame, and must instead have been a local divine of the Celtic Church, about whom nothing whatsoever is known. Nevertheless, a number of miraculous cures were reported at the site of the discovery, and Alexander III built the Church of the Holy Cross over it. For many years it was a famous place of pilgrimage, but oddly enough there is no further mention anywhere of either the cross or the ashes, which seem to have vanished as mysteriously as they arrived. At any rate, they had long gone by the Reformation, when the Cross Kirk became the parish church. It was abandoned in the late 18th century and

SNOW CHANGE *A light covering of snow, a touch of hoar frost and the bright winter sun transform Peebles into a perfect model for a Christmas card. The Victorian sundial (below) is one of the many details that enliven the great variety of buildings in the High Street.*

fell gradually into ruin, though in fairly recent years it has been to some extent restored, and open-air services are occasionally held there. Close by is the tower and a fragment of wall of an even more venerable parish church that was dedicated to St Andrew by the Bishop of Glasgow in 1195.

The High Street is attractively formal, of all sorts of periods, with uneven roofs underlining the high, dark forests behind. At one end there is the old Mercat Cross, which figures in the midsummer Beltane Festival, when all the children parade in historical costume. Near by is the 16th-century, turreted Chambers Institution. It used to be known as the Queensberry Lodging and it was there that Old Q, that 'polish'd, sin-worn fragment of the Court', as someone called him, was born. The building was converted into a library, museum and art gallery by the Chambers brothers, who presented it to the town in 1859. Almost next door is the Town House, which was built in 1753 as the civic centre; during the Napoleonic Wars, the upper room was taken over as a theatre by paroled French officer-prisoners, where they entertained the town with the plays of Molière and Corneille.

Off High Street is the cobbled Parliament Square, surrounded by handsome, 18th-century houses. It got its name from the emergency session of the Scottish Parliament that was held there in 1346, after David II was captured by the English at the Battle of Neville's Cross. Running off the square is the not so gracefully named Stinkin' Stair, though it is called so for no worse a reason than there used to be a brewery at its foot from which the smell of malt once emanated.

One of Peebles' pleasant features is its higher than average number of old inns, several of them with interesting stories and associations. The Tontine, which was a favourite haunt of the French prisoners of war and has a most elegant dining-room with a music gallery, was financed by the old Tontine form of life insurance in which a group of people invested in a joint enterprise or loan and the last living investor of a group inherited the lot. In the days when the County Hotel was the Harrow Inn, it was the starting-place for the Peebles–Edinburgh stagecoach, while the Cross Keys plays a role in one of Sir Walter Scott's novels. It is the Cleikum Inn of *St Ronan's Well*, while Meg Ritchie, the landlady in Scott's day, gained immortality as Meg Dodds.

PEMBROKE *Dyfed*

The castle round which Pembroke grew rises majestically from a narrow-necked tidal creek, while the oldest part of the town is squeezed on to a long, low ridge flanked by the Pembroke river. Natural defences were enhanced in the 13th century when William de Valence, Henry III's half-brother, built a town wall just over a mile long, most of which has survived. Its prominent features include the Barnard Tower, near the junction of Mill Pond Walk and Blackhorse Walk.

Much of the town was rebuilt during the Georgian and Victorian periods, but St Mary's Church dates from the 13th century and there are medieval cottages on Westgate Hill. St Michael's Church is another link with the Middle Ages, when Pembroke gave its name to Pembrokeshire and became the symbol of English rule in the far west of Wales.

Monkton, just beyond the town walls, has memories of a Benedictine priory founded by the Norman invaders in 1098. Its ruined walls stand near the restored Church of St Nicholas. Near by, the 15th-century Old Hall served as the priory's guest house until the monks who gave the place its name were driven out by order of Henry VIII in the 1530s.

The mill-pond, formed by holding the Pembroke river back with a sluice-gated causeway, is one of the town's most delightful assets. Stately swans patrol its tranquil waters while mallard, coot, moorhen, teal, wigeon and little grebe can be seen from Mill Pond Walk. Colonies of grey heron also nest near the pond.

The original castle, a 'slender fortress of stakes and turf', was replaced by a stone castle in the 12th century after Gilbert de Clare became the first Earl of Pembroke. His son, Richard, a mighty warrior known as 'Strongbow', used it as his base for the conquest of Ireland in 1148. Strongbow's son-in-law, William Marshal, built the impressive keep whose lower walls are 20 ft thick. The outer defences were completed by William de Valence midway through the 13th century. They include a splendid gatehouse whose drum-towers dominate westward views along Main Street.

John Poyer, Mayor of Pembroke, made the castle

ROYAL BIRTHPLACE *The mighty castle whose walls and towers have watched over Pembroke for more than 800 years is the place where Henry Tudor, founder of the Tudor dynasty, was born on January 28, 1457.*

one of Parliament's most important strongholds during the Civil War, holding it from 1642 until 1647, the year when King Charles surrendered. For some astonishing reason he then came out in support of the doomed Royalist cause. Cromwell himself marched on Pembroke and directed a 48 day siege which ended in Poyer's surrender. He and his second-in-command were allowed to draw lots to decide who would pay the traitor's penalty. The mayor lost, was taken to London and executed in Covent Garden in 1649.

Pembroke's neighbour, Pembroke Dock, was founded as a naval base and shipyard early in the 19th century. Grey buildings flank broad, straight streets set out in a neat gridiron pattern reminiscent of Milford Haven, which is slightly older. More than 250 ships went down the slipways before the Royal Navy Dockyard was closed in 1926. They included HMS *Warrior*, Britain's first iron-clad warship.

PITLOCHRY *Tayside*

To set out on The Road to the Isles, 'by Tummel and Loch Rannoch and Lochaber', the route recommended in the song, it is almost essential to begin at Pitlochry, the glittering little granite town on the banks of the River Tummel. It is not quite Highland, and certainly not Lowland, but situated as it is on almost the geographical centre of Scotland, it is able to present a good many of the advantages of both. The scenery in the immediate vicinity is grand and gracious, rather than wild; and, at the same time, the great mountains are close enough to be admired without having to reside among their threatening splendour. But the area is Highland enough for old echoes not quite to have died away. The marching feet of Prince Charlie's men as they marched to, and fled from, Culloden Moor, or the clash of steel from the battlefield of Killiecrankie, just down the road. There, in 1689, Graham of Claverhouse, Viscount Dundee – 'Bonnie' Dundee, or 'Bluidy Clavers', according to political sympathies – died in the moment of victory, fighting for James II.

Pitlochry itself, however, is purely, almost flamboyantly, Victorian, with more reason than most such places, since Victoria herself was very fond of the area. Everywhere there are the towers and turrets of Scots baronial, gables with scalloped edges or hung with fretwork, and slate roofs capped with cast-iron bits and pieces. And though it makes world-famous whisky and knitwear, the town's chief dedication is to the well-being of the holidaymaker.

It all began in the middle decade of the 19th century, when some shrewd people began to promote the healthful qualities of the waters of the Moulin burn that joins the Tummel at Pitlochry's present site. This, combined with the pure air sweeping down from the mountains, made the place irresistible to that

ROYAL FAVOURITE *Queen Victoria loved the Highlands – at least those parts that were romantic and beautiful without being too rugged. Pitlochry stands in just such a setting on the banks of the River Tummel below the heather-clad slopes of Ben Vrackie. Her favourite view was from a spot overlooking Loch Tummel, just west of the town.*

hypochondriacal age. In no time, hotels by the dozen were shooting up along the hillside, among them a hydropathic, that combination of hotel and pump-room, with a slight touch of convalescent home, so dear to the Scottish heart. It still stands and it is still possible to take the waters there.

Even today it seems that half the buildings in Pitlochry are hotels, and half the other half are guest houses. Then, having accommodated its visitors, the town ensures they will stay and return again next year, by providing a programme of activities and entertainments that is not bettered in any resort of its size in the kingdom. There are walks and light mountaineering on Ben Vrackie and Schiehallion, golf, sailing and all kinds of sports, battlefields and a stately home – Blair Castle – to visit, splendid Highland Games to see in September, and biggest draw of all, perhaps, the Festival Theatre. Ever since its founding in a tent in

1951, the theatre has grown steadily in reputation, and now attracts audiences and players from all over the world.

PORTREE   *Isle of Skye*

Port-an-Righ (the port of the king), was called Kiltaraglen, meaning 'the Chapel at the glen's foot', until 1540, when James V anchored 12 warships in the bay as a genial hint to the Hebridean chieftains that it was time to cease their endless bickering and submit to himself as the central authority. All those who could be rounded up swore allegiance to him in what is now Somerled Square, where he also passed judgment upon several ancient disputes. These matters accomplished, he sailed away, and Skye's little capital has borne his title ever since.

Small it may be, but its siting under the guardian

ISLAND CAPITAL *Spread out neatly round the shore of its bay, Portree is smart enough – if not overly large – to be the capital of Skye. The pier jutting out into the bay is the terminal for a ferry to the mainland.*

presence of mighty Vriskaig Point, and with the dark Cuillins spilling mist down their flanks in the background, it is quite unforgettable. Portree's buildings are mostly two-storey, white-painted and slate-roofed houses and shops along the harbour wall, and climbing up the slope behind, with here and there a block or two of post-war concrete and glass. There are a large number of banks and of churches of various denominations, signifying a well-balanced community and, as in other Highland towns, many guest houses and hotels. One of these, the Royal Hotel, stands on the site of MacNab's Inn, where in June 1746, there took place one of the most treasured of history's romantic moments – the parting of Prince Charles Edward from Flora MacDonald, after she had conveyed him 'over the sea to Skye' from Benbecula a few days earlier.

Some 27 years later, that ubiquitous pair of Highland travellers, Dr Johnson and James Boswell, also stayed at the inn. During their stay they were introduced to Flora who, long before, had married her kinsman, MacDonald of Kingsburgh. Despite their ten children, she still retained a good deal of her youthful grace. Johnson was much impressed by her gentle manners and elegant presence.

Memories are strong at Portree, but they are by no means its only attraction. There is a famous modern High School that serves a large part of the Hebrides, and the steep streets are full of busy, pleasant shops. Some of the streets, incidentally, have surprisingly English names – Wentworth Street, Bosworth Street, and so on; most of them commemorate the English wives of 18th-century MacDonald chieftains. Then, too, all roads to and from Skye's tentacle-like peninsulas meet at Portree, making it the best of all centres for touring the island, and the natural place to hold such splendid annual festivals as the Highland Games and the Agricultural Show, and the occasional National Mod – the Gaelic Eisteddfod which attracts people with Highland names from all over the world.

RHAYADER *Powys*

Racing down from its source on Plynlimon, 20 miles away, the River Wye passes through this tiny town in the green heart of Wales. Its character has remained essentially unchanged since the middle of the 19th century when a Victorian guidebook praised 'a situation of much beauty amid barren hills' and extolled Rhayader's virtues as a tourist centre.

The town grew up in the shelter of a 12th-century castle built by Rhys ap Gruffydd, Prince of South

THE YOUNG WYE *At Rhayader the River Wye, still fresh from its mountain source, rushes and foams through the town. The rapids below the bridge, which dates from 1780, gave the town it Welsh name* Rhaedr Gwy, *meaning 'cataract of the Wye'.*

Wales, which was burned by Llewelyn the Great in 1231 and finally demolished during the Civil War. No traces remain, but the Old Swan in South Street and the Cwmdeuddwr Arms in West Street, Rhayader's oldest building, are eye-catching links with the 17th century. The town's 18th-century oak-bark tannery, the last of its kind in Wales, now forms part of the Welsh Folk Museum at St Fagans.

Before the coming of the railways, Rhayader was a resting place for the hardy drovers who trekked over the mountains with livestock for the markets of England. Sheep reared on the surrounding hills also made it a centre for the Welsh wool trade. Both have gone, but the town now attracts pony-trekkers, walkers and anglers who fish for trout in the Elan Valley reservoirs west of the town.

Four of the man-made lakes were completed in 1904, while Claerwen, the fifth and largest, was inaugurated in 1952. Their combined surface area is about 1,500 acres, and the reservoirs send some 75 million gallons of water to Birmingham every day. Walkers, pony-trekkers and four-wheel-drive vehicles can follow an old drover's road which runs from the Claerwen reservoir to Ffair Rhos on the B4343 between Devil's Bridge and Tregaron.

RICHMOND *North Yorkshire*

Probably it will never be settled for certain whether The Lass of Richmond Hill of the song lived in Richmond, Yorkshire or in Richmond, Surrey or, indeed, in both. Yorkshire being Yorkshire, its people are certain that she belonged to their Richmond; that she was a Miss Frances l'Anson who lived there in Hill House, where she was wooed by the author of the lyric, Leonard McNally, in 1785. All very well, says Surrey, but the composer of the tune had the work performed on several occasions in its Richmond Theatre, and points to its famous pub, The Lass, on Richmond Hill; then there is the fact that McNally, having won his bride, went to live in Surrey. On the other hand, the song may have nothing to do with McNally at all, but is instead a satirical reference either to Charles II's mistress, the Duchess of Richmond (Yorks), or to Mrs Fitzherbert, the morganatic wife of the Prince Regent, who lived in Richmond (Surrey); hence the line, 'I'd crowns resign to call her mine ...'

Be all that as it may, there is no doubt that the Yorkshire town is the earliest of all the world's 70 Richmonds and the one from which the others, including Surrey's, take their names. It, or rather the castle that gave it birth, was begun in 1071 by Alan Rufus, the friend of William of Normandy, in the days when the boundary of conquered England ran only a little to the north. Even in this area of dramatic – and strategically powerful – sites, Rufus could hardly have chosen better than his sheer promontory at the head of Swaledale, with the Swale hurrying below. The castle was about two centuries in the building, and the

ANCIENT MARKET *On Saturday – market day – Richmond comes into its own. Then, the vast cobbled Market Place (rounded here by the camera's wide-angle lens) is set out with stalls, just as it has been for more than 800 years. The obelisk was erected to replace the old market cross in the 18th century – at the same time as most of the houses round the square were built.*

100 ft tower that stares out over the steep narrow streets and the cobbled Market Place to the wide Dales beyond was one of the last additions. Scolland Hall, the great hall named after the castle's first butler, is at least 100 years older, and may in fact be the oldest domestic building in England, while the remainder of the crumbling walls and towers were built at various times between the two. Perhaps it was the castle's unassailable appearance, or perhaps it was sheer luck, but throughout its long existence it does not appear to have been attacked by anyone, and its very occasional emergence from the wings of history was generally as a royal prison. Two medieval Scottish kings, William the Lion and David II, were held there, and so was Charles I on his melancholy journey south after the Scots handed him over to the Parliamentarian army in 1647.

But what the place lacks in military history is compensated for by legend. King Arthur and his knights are said to lie in an enchanted sleep in a cavern beneath the castle, where they were discovered one day long ago by a potter named Thompson. A sword and a hunting horn lay by the king's side, and as the potter picked up the sword, the knights stirred and began to wake. Thompson cast the weapon aside and fled in terror with a great voice booming down the cave after him:

'Potter Thompson, Potter Thompson,
If thou hadst drawn the sword or blown the horn,
Thou hadst been the luckiest man e'er born!'

– though the story does not say why. Whatever may lie in the caves, any visitor should make a point of exploring the castle. The view from the top of the tower, reached by steep staircases in the thickness of the walls, is quite astonishing, taking in all of the town and beautiful Swaledale, while Castle Walk provides a pleasant aspect of the 18th-century Town Bridge, the turbulent river, and a scene that has made an easy adaptation to the passing years. The football ground was very likely the castle's jousting field, and within the view there is an extraordinary, octagonal Gothic structure. This is the Culloden Tower, built by the Yorke family in 1746 to celebrate the safe return of one of its sons from fighting the Young Pretender's clansmen. Not everyone loved Prince Charlie.

Though the town, with its fragments of ancient defensive walls, is medieval in layout, its general aspect is Georgian. Apart from some regrettable modern intrusions, that is. The centre is, and has been since the 12th century, the Market Place where a tall obelisk of 1771 replaces a long succession of Market Crosses. There are several fine Georgian buildings there, including the Town Hall and the King's Arms Hotel, and there is, too, the chapel of the Holy Trinity, founded in 1135, but with a chequered career since. It has been a school, gaol, courtroom and warehouse, and now houses the museum of that famous Yorkshire regiment, the Green Howards. There are some attractive streets round about, especially the steeply plunging Cornforth Hill, Newbiggin and Finkle (bent) Street, and a little north of the market, there is a little

jewel of a Georgian theatre. It was founded in 1788, and many famous players performed there, including Kean, Kemble, Macready and Mrs Siddons, but declining audiences forced its closure in about 1848, after which it went through a long and dolorous period as an auction room, a corn chandler's, a furniture repository and, during the Second World War, a salvage depot. Then, in 1963, after much research and a great deal of hard work, it was perfectly restored to its former splendour, and is once again a full-time working theatre.

Opposite the theatre is the stone Greyfriars tower, all that remains of a monastic church founded in 1288 and quashed at the Reformation; whatever else there is of the building lies beneath the little green park that surrounds it. The parish church, in Frenchgate, dates from much the same period as Greyfriars, but was almost entirely reconstructed in 1864. However, it still has some fine medieval choir stalls.

In some ways, the old Railway Station near by is as worthy of praise as the theatre. Axed, like so many others, in 1963, it is a splendid stone Victorian-Gothic building, some of whose parts would not have looked out of place attached to the abbey. Wisely, the District Council has given it a face-lift, and it is now an unusual and thriving garden centre.

PROUD KEEP *Centuries of advance in building and engineering techniques have failed to produce a rival to the great keep of Richmond Castle as the dominant feature of the town. After 700 years it still looks down on every edifice that succeeding generations have raised.*

CASTLE VIEW *(opposite) The roofs of Richmond spread out towards the surrounding hills in this archer's-eye view of the town, framed by an arrow-slit in the castle walls.*

MOUNTBATTEN'S HOME
Broadlands, on the outskirts of Romsey, is a magnificent Palladian mansion standing in a park designed by Capability Brown. Inside are fine paintings and furniture, and memorabilia of Lord Mountbatten and Lord Palmerston, the great Victorian Prime Minister, who was a previous owner.

ROMSEY *Hampshire*

Just outside the town on the Winchester, or London, side, there are a pair of gates whose restrained elegance announces the proximity of a country house of note. The park beyond is in the same mood; smooth acres of turf embroidered with curving gravel paths and nobly thewed chestnuts planted 200 years ago with the careless precision that lesser establishments devote to tulip bulbs. The River Test moves sinuously through, swift and quiet as fast-poured syrup, and over all there is suspended that mellow silence that is the special prerogative of Capability Brown-designed parks.

Until his tragic and wasteful death in 1979 Broadlands was the home of Earl Mountbatten of Burma who, the year before he died, opened the house to the public. His grandson, Lord Romsey, has continued to do so.

Romsey's Market Place, presided over by a greeny-

black bronze statue of Lord Palmerston and the big, square tower of the Abbey Church, is only yards from Broadlands' gates. Like the rest of the town, it is mostly red brick, old and new; the old brick a pretty strawberry colour often mingled with timber. Some of Romsey's new building is very attractive too; the housing estates by the river for example, and Edwina Mountbatten House – flats for old people – with a little fountain splashing in a central courtyard. Most of the façades in the Market Square are Georgian brick, though some of them are simply masks stuck on the fronts of much older buildings. An exception is the Old Swan Inn, now the Conservative Club, which is white and black timbered.

Below the Market Place is the Corn Market with a sprightly painted Corn Exchange decorated with gilded sheaves, a sickle and a pitchfork. It stands close by the Tudor Rose pub, whose upper storeys contain a great deal of medieval timber and a handsome 16th-century fireplace. Near the pub, and just before the

Corn Market becomes a street called The Hundred, one is standing above the Fishlake stream, which has made a brief plunge underground.

The Hundred is a pleasant thoroughfare of varying periods, as is its extension, Palmerston Street, where stands the Manor House, one of the few obviously Tudor buildings in the town. Built about 1540, it was the home of the St Barbe family until they inherited Broadlands in the early 17th century. Venerable though it is, it was born but yesterday when compared with King John's House, which lies off Church Street to the north of the Market Place. It is a hall house, built about 1230, so it is doubtful if it could have had much to do with King John since he died 14 years earlier. Still, it is a tremendous age for a domestic building. It is now a museum.

Just over the way is the solid, square-cut block of the Abbey Church of St Mary the Virgin and St Aethelflaeda, which was built in about 1120 as the church of a Benedictine convent. When the convent was dissolved by Henry VIII, he sold its church to the townspeople for £100; they made an excellent bargain. The fortress-like exterior is quite belied by the interior – tier upon tier of pillared, rounded Norman arches topped by clerestories pouring shafts of light upon the brown-grey stone and a myriad treasures. There is a Saxon crucifix, dating from about AD 1000, for example, and a painted wooden reredos of 1525 depicting Christ rising from the tomb to the astonishment of a group of Roman soldiers in medieval armour. Among the splendid monuments is the enchanting tomb of Alice Taylor, a little girl curled up in sleep, and the coloured busts of Henry and Grissel St Barbe, who lived at Broadlands and died on the same day in 1658. Close beside this monument, a later owner of Broadlands lies beneath a plain slab that bears the simple inscription: 'Admiral of the Fleet Earl Mountbatten of Burma 1900–1979. In Honour Bound.'

ROSS-ON-WYE

Hereford & Worcester

The *Moral Essays* of Alexander Pope, the early 18th-century poet and satirist, is a work not widely quoted nowadays. Except, that is, in this charming town, balanced on a curve of the Wye, where long ago there lived a good and generous man named John Kyrle. Pope dubbed him the Man of Ross, and in one of the essays, *Of the Use of Riches*, extols him at some length:

> *Behold the market-place with poor o'erspread!*
> *The Man of Ross divides the weekly bread:*
> *He feeds yon almshouse, neat but want of state,*
> *Where age and want sit smiling at the gate;*
> *Him portion'd maids, apprenticed orphans blest*

– and did many other things that are still, with Pope's aid, warmly remembered in the town. Born in Dymock in 1637, Kyrle spent most of his 87 years in Ross, to which he donated, in one way or another, a very large proportion of his considerable income. As well as gifts to individuals, he gave to the town he loved a water supply, a raised causeway to serve Wilton Bridge, and the church's slender spire and pinnacles that soar above the trees and are mirrored shakily in the ripples of the Wye at the bottom of the steep hill. But most delightful, and perhaps now best appreciated of his gifts, is The Prospect, a walled public garden by the church, which has tall, dignified gates bearing his cypher and the date 1700.

John Kyrle lived in the High Street, in a house that is now a pair of shops, one of which bears his bust above it. The house is on the edge of Market Square, with the Market House, built of the local red sandstone in 1674, just opposite. Sandstone is an attractive material, but not durable, so that the pillars that support the Market House's open ground floor have a wrinkled look, like the skin of old elephants.

Also in the High Street is a handsome black-and-white building with overhanging storeys, which used to be The Saracen's Head. This is one of several inns, existing or pensioned off, that recall the town's importance on the western coaching routes; another is the Royal Hotel, where a plaque reminds the visitor

TOWN AND COUNTRY *Few towns are set more firmly in the country than Ross, perched on its hill above the River Wye. The cattle which graze the water meadows are as much a part of the Ross scene as the spire of St Mary's Church soaring above the dense array of rooftops.*

that this was where Charles Dickens first met his biographer, John Forster. Though interspersed with the usual modern shop fronts, and a number of 17th-century buildings, the general appearance of the town's steep streets is Georgian.

Everywhere, however, the eye is drawn to the crowning height of the Church of St Mary, part of which dates from about 1200, and most of the rest between 100 and 150 years later. It is a large and gracious building, containing an extraordinary variety of monuments, mostly to the Rudhall family. The Man of Ross is also there, but as might be expected of him, his monument is a modest one. Outside, in the churchyard, there is a cross bearing the sobering inscription, 'Plague Ano Dom 1637 Burials 315 Libera nos Domine', and there is also a memorial to 22 Chelsea Pensioners who died between 1939–45, when Chelsea Hospital was evacuated to nearby Rudhall Manor.

By Banky Meadows leading down to the river, there is something of a curiosity – great red fortress walls with arrow slits and a massive medieval tower, all of which, for some reason, were built in the 1830s. But the ruins that peep over the trees by the river are genuine enough. They are all that remain of Wilton Castle, built in the 13th century to guard the ford.

FORTRESS RESORT *Below the stone roofs of the old town, Rothesay pier juts out into the bay. This pier was a prime destination for Glasgow paddle steamers in Victorian and Edwardian days, and helped to turn the royal fortress town of Rothesay into one of the most popular resorts on the Clyde.*

ROTHESAY *Isle of Bute*

Though a little wistful, now that so many of its old customers have opted for the Costa del Sol, Rothesay yet maintains its firm hold upon Glasgow's heart. Probably it is the best loved, and certainly the most Highland, of all the Clyde resorts.

As a resort, it is very much the product of the paddle steamers, the *Duchess of Hamilton*, the *Glen Sannox*, the *Queen Mary II* and other such legendary craft that tore into the bay pouring smoke from their rakish funnels, before their skippers spun them alongside the pier with a precision that no destroyer captain would dare to emulate. They brought generation after generation of Glaswegians 'doon the watter' for their annual holiday.

Nostalgia, however, is not the town's chief preoccupation. True, the Winter Garden that was played by generations of top music hall artistes is shuttered and shabby now, but the municipal gardens that surround it are as immaculate as ever, and the tall, 19th-century houses behind the broad esplanade as brightly painted. Maybe Rothesay is in a period of transition, and is looking towards a different kind of holiday-maker; a clue is the yachts and dinghies that crowd the clear waters of its harbour. But above it hangs the

Skipper Woods, as pretty and romantic as when courting couples wandered them in the days before the First World War. Rothesay did not spring full-blown to life as a holiday resort. Centuries before the steamers came, it was a fishing port and market town that grew up about the castle whose substantial and also romantic remains occupy a moated knoll in the centre. Even by the standards of Scottish fortresses in general, Rothesay Castle has a picturesque story. It was always a royal castle, and makes an abrupt entrance into history in 1230, when it was held by the High Steward of Scotland against the Vikings.

Later, the castle was sacked by Cromwell and burned by Campbell of Argyll in 1685. It was never occupied again, though recent Marquesses of Bute have partly restored it as a tourist attraction. Much of its story is told in the fine local museum beside the castle. Begin your tour of Bute at the museum, is the suggestion.

It is not a bad point, either, from which to start exploring Rothesay. All the old streets are gathered about the museum and the castle, a pleasant mixture of seasidery and Scottish sedateness that runs down to the esplanade and Battery Place, so called because cannon were mounted there to guard against the invading armies of Napoleon. Fortunately, they did not arrive, and the gun barrels are now set vertically into the quays as bollards.

Off the High Street there is the Mansion House, a grand 17th-century town house that was occupied by the Marquess of Bute after Argyll fired the castle. Following the High Street farther inland, there is the High Kirk of St Mary and St Bruoc, with its marvellous array of ancient tombs. Though Napoleon never got to Rothesay, his niece, Stephanie Hortense Bonaparte, did, and was buried in the church in 1885.

ROYAL TUNBRIDGE WELLS

Kent

Few towns may be said to have been born out of a hangover, yet this, more or less, was the beginning of Royal Tunbridge Wells. In 1606, Lord North, on the advice of his doctor, absented himself from the hurly-burly of court life and submitted to the notion of a lonely, but healthful, stay on the Eridge estate of his friend, Lord Bergavenny, in Kent. On a solitary ride, he paused to refresh himself at a spring whose appearance, bubbling through rust-coloured mud, reminded him of the chalybeate, or iron-laden, waters of Spa in the Ardennes which he had imbibed, to beneficial effect, during an earlier crisis in his life. A new man, he hastened to tell the fashionable world of his discovery.

At first, little provision was made to accommodate the thousands of people who came to sample the waters' rather vaguely defined curative properties, and even when Queen Henrietta Maria paid a visit in 1630 to help her to recuperate from the birth of the future Charles II, she and her retinue had to camp on what is now the Common. The stamp of Royal

approval, however, was just what the place needed. Hostels and a coffee house were built, the Upper and Lower Walks to the spring were levelled and shaded with lime trees.

So frivolous an enterprise could not be expected to thrive under the Commonwealth, but with the Restoration, the place grew ever more prosperous. Charles II and his court were frequent visitors, especially in time of plague, and to accommodate them and all the fashionable world that followed in their wake, building proceeded apace, along the Walks and up the hill that was already called Mount Sion. Towards the end of the 17th century, the delightful little Church of King Charles the Martyr, with its exquisitely moulded ceiling, was built in memory of, and in gratitude to, the husband of Tunbridge Wells's first royal patron, and it was at about this time, too, that the Walks were paved. The material used was a hard, flat, red tile known locally as pantile, and the area has been known as The Pantiles ever since.

Though this part of the town was well established by the end of the 17th century, The Pantiles really belong to the ensuing 100 years or so. The Assembly Rooms and the theatre where Kean and Garrick played are patched and faded now, and long converted to other uses, but the Lower and Upper Walks between the trees and the solidly elegant, wooden pillared colonnade are as glorious as ever. So, too, are the pretty places in which to eat and drink, and the high-class shops. All owe a good deal to two particular ghosts, those of Bell Causey and Beau Nash. Bell was a former London orange-seller and a lady of formidable personality who, from 1725 until her death ten years later, ruled the entertainments, the assembly and gaming rooms, and the love-affairs, of Tunbridge Wells with a rod of iron. Beau Nash, who was Master of Ceremonies at the Wells for a quarter of a century after Bell's death, was the man who created the Tunbridge Wells Season, from May to October, to balance that of Bath, which ran from October to May.

About the turn of the 19th century, Tunbridge Wells began to drift away from its place at the forefront of fashion. But the effect upon the town itself was more beneficial than otherwise. With the departure of the aristocracy and its raffish ways, Tunbridge Wells in its setting among the bosomy fields and wide, dark-wooded horizons of the Weald, had great appeal for the respectable, and rich, middle classes. They built magnificently upon the hills about the Common, with its strange, rocky outcrops, and it is this period that has bequeathed to us the tall-windowed, stone-balus-traded houses and hotels on Mounts Pleasant and Ephraim, and the enchanting Regency buildings, with their delicate, wrought-iron verandas, along the London Road. William Thackeray, the novelist, lived in a white clapboard house, now a little shabby, in the London Road. And Queen Victoria, with her mother, the Duchess of Kent, spent many girlhood summers at 'dear Tunbridge Wells', in a house that is now the Calverley Hotel.

Near the hotel, and at the top of Mount Pleasant, a busy shopping street made bright with hanging

ARTISTRY IN WOOD *For more than 200 years the art of making pictures in wood was practised in Tunbridge Wells. Pictures, such as this view of The Pantiles, were built up like mosaics, using different coloured woods. Oak, holly, pear and yew were among 150 types used, all of which were found locally. The pictures, which usually decorated box lids and are known as Tunbridge ware, ceased to be made in the 1920s.*

THE PANTILES *Tunbridge Wells (opposite) had the most elegant shopping precinct in England long before such things became fashionable elsewhere. The smart shops and eating places behind the colonnade have seen little change over the centuries, except that the paving tiles which gave the place its name have nearly all gone – replaced by stone flags in the 18th century.*

SEA LINK *Since the 16th century the sea has retreated 2 miles from Rye. Now the former seaport's only link with the sea is the River Rother.*

baskets of flowers in summer, there is a tall arch. This marks the boundary of an early 19th-century experiment in urban development that was to utterly change the character of Tunbridge Wells. Known at first as the Calverley Development, it was intended to be a new town that would turn its back on the old spa and offer instead solid middle-class values for solid middle-class money. The architect chosen by John Ward, the landowner, was Decimus Burton who, young though he was, had already gained a reputation as the designer of some of the terraces in London's Regent's Park.

He began work on the Calverley estate in 1828, and over the next 20 years built a school and churches, but most notably, his groupings of stone villas and mansions in the Grecian style. Grandest of these is Calverley Park, a deep half-moon of large houses, bristling with verandas, balustrades and conservatories, each one different, and each one in its own large garden looking on to a private park adorned with stately cedars. But prettiest, perhaps, is Calverley Park Crescent.

Other landlords in the vicinity followed John Ward's example, but no new town developed. The older and newer parts of Tunbridge Wells simply drew together, gaining much from each other's characters, their unity celebrated in the proud prefix of Royal that was awarded to the town in 1909.

RYE *East Sussex*

To observe the manner in which some visitors flatten their noses against the windows of private houses, it must be like living in a glass case in the Victoria and Albert Museum or even in Disneyland. It is therefore much to Ryers' credit that they are so noticeably nice to strangers within their gates. Or perhaps they are simply resigned, accepting that it is a price that has to be paid for residing in such a pretty town.

This is apparent almost at once after passing through the Landgate, the massive medieval entrance beyond which the town sits crammed on its hill with its lovely church at the peak. 'Cute' or 'quaint' are terms that might leap to mind when looking upon the steep, cobbled streets, overhung by houses and pubs of incredible ancientness – one of which is a medieval friary now converted into a pottery – and a myriad antique shops with names like 'A Pocketful of Rye' or 'The Quay Hole'. Add to this tales of smugglers and secret passages, ghosts and great men, French raids and the Armada sailing up the Channel, and it is possible to feel that Rye's scriptwriter has overdone it, and that a peek behind the façades will reveal the scaffolding of a film set.

It isn't so. Every bit of Rye is genuine, and its attractiveness is due to a chain of incidents, historical and geographical, deliberate and accidental, that stretch back to the days when the last Roman legions were summoned home. Until the sea finally retreated from it in the 1600s, it was one of the most important harbours on the south coast, and was (and is) a member of the Cinque Ports. This was a confederation of southern seaports that probably began before the Norman Conquest and in later years had the duty of supplying ships and men for the defence of the realm.

In the 18th century, Rye was the home of the notorious Hawkhurst Gang of smugglers who swaggered armed about the town and no magistrate dared to touch them. Eventually, the exasperated citizens made the arrests themselves, and with grim satisfaction watched the hanging of the ringleaders. However, it was not the 'Gentlemen', as they were called, that were the worst menace, but the French who, between 1250 and 1377, attacked the town four times, on the last occasion virtually burning the place to the ground. Among the few stone buildings to survive were the defences, including the Ypres Tower, the chief fortification. It does not seem to have been very successful in its defensive role, but it later served as a courthouse and gaol and is now the Town Museum. In Tudor times the Gun Garden – a battery – was established next to the tower, but it was never put to the test for the French did not come again.

All kinds of influences, subtle or direct, from home and abroad, have been brought to bear upon Rye, as can be seen from a glance down the steep plunge of Mermaid Street, with its hung tile, Georgian tile and

clapboard, Dutch gables and Tudor black and white. This is one of the most famous small-town streets in England, so pretty that it might be made out of marzipan, and come to think of it, there is something edible about it, like an expensive birthday cake. Henry James, the American novelist, lived in the early 18th-century Lamb House at the top, until his death in 1916.

A little farther down the street is The Mermaid Inn, and facing it an attractive black-and-white house called The House Opposite, while below it there is The House With the Seat because it has a seat in the porch, and next door, The House Without a Seat, because it hasn't. Almost down at the quay, there is the wonderful 15th-century Hartshorn House.

Though the sea has long deserted Rye, the quays on its rivers – which lead to the Channel – are still busy with yachts and fishing boats, presided over by a great white windmill and a fish and chip shop. Here was the Strandgate, the water gate in the old defences, and there are still a number of majestic warehouses left over from the days when Rye was still a name in the coaster trade.

Most of Rye is a delight, and too much to take in during a single visit. But do spare a glance for some of

the smaller streets, such as Trader's Passage, tile-hung and creeper-clad, that was a smugglers' lair, and Turkey Cock Lane that is haunted by a love-lorn monk who expresses his distress by gobbling like a turkey.

In and about Church Square there are a number of medieval and Tudor buildings including the Customs House, the Old Stone House, part of which was the friary of the mendicant order of the Friars of the Sack (from their sackcloth robes), and a house, now a tea-shop, where the Jacobean dramatist John Fletcher was born. There is also a fine, elliptical water tower, built of brick in 1733 to give the town a water supply.

The church, one of the largest in Sussex, was originally built in about 1150, but was reduced almost to a ruin in the raid of 1377, and rebuilt during the following century. It is splendid, a gathering of the skills of all the ages since, from the tower clock of 1560, that is still in perfect working order, to the big, modern stained-glass windows, one of which was presented by E. F. Benson. The magnificent communion table, in carved mahogany, is reputed to be a survivor from a ship of the Spanish Armada, and there are a number of fine tombs.

For those who find a total exploration of the town

MARSH WEALTH *Tourists, overwhelmed by the charm of old Rye, can easily miss its more workaday side. The town lies on the edge of Walland Marsh, one of the finest areas of grazing land in England. The prime sheep raised there are sold in Rye Cattle Market on Wednesdays.*

SUBTLE CLAIM *The sign 'Rebuilt 1420' has a subtle, telling air about it, far more convincing than 'Queen Elizabeth slept here'. And in the case of The Mermaid Inn, Rye, the claim is backed up with inglenooks, secret passages and ghosts. Almost as old as the inn is the 16th-century turret clock on the parish church (left).*

too much – the cobbles can be a sore trial on the feet and ankles – there is a vast scale model of the entire place at the bottom of Mermaid Street. With sound and light it presents the history of the town, including the fire of 1377 and even the unfortunate monk of Turkey Cock Lane.

SAFFRON WALDEN *Essex*

Headscarves, padded waistcoats worn over tweeds, green wellingtons and an estate car with a doggy gate at the rear distinguish the natives of Walden, no matter whether their livelihoods are derived from the countryside, or from the City of London. All mingle happily together in Market Place on Tuesdays and Saturdays, which have been the town's official market days since some time in the 13th century. In the place where a pewterer was burned to death for heresy in the reign of Mary Tudor, stalls are crammed in pleasant disarray. From them, it is possible to buy almost anything from old tools, local honey and eggs to pies and Wehrmacht paratroop boots, and some of the best cheese in eastern England. Or you can queue in the old-fashioned grocery at the corner of the square, where there are cool marble slabs, rows of varnished drawers containing peppers and spices, gleaming brass scales and weights, and scarlet bacon-slicers and coffee-grinders. After waiting for some time in a bouquet composed of a hundred tempting smells, you eventually get served, with great expertise and smiling friendliness.

Like much of Saffron Walden's architecture, that of Market Place is an unobtrusive mingling of periods and styles, and it is not until each building is looked at individually that it begins to seem a little odd. There is the Town Hall, for example, which dates from the 18th century, but has a huge black-and-white Tudor style portico added in the 1870s. An exuberant Regency balcony looks on to a drinking fountain, invariably dry, that starred in the London Exhibition of 1851; its reliefs, of a vaguely Biblical nature, are surmounted by coloured pebbles set in cement. Then there is a bank, whose leaded windows and imposing stone entrance give it the air of a bishop's palace, while the Corn Exchange, now the Public Library, with its tall cupola and gilded clock, has been called 'jolly Italianate'. The huge bunch of golden grapes that hangs outside Boots' chemists is practically all that remains of the 17th-century *Rose and Crown* inn that was burned down, with tragic loss of life, at Christmas, 1969.

New is lightly superimposed upon old throughout the town, and each age left something of itself to those that followed. There are Iron Age ramparts near by and the Saxons built a palisaded village whose boundaries were more or less the lines followed by the High Street, Castle Street and Church Street; they also left a name, *Wealh Denu*, which means 'Valley of the Britons', or perhaps 'Valley of the Serfs'. Shortly after the Norman Conquest, the de Mandeville Earls of Essex built a castle, but no one seems to have regarded it very seriously, since within a century it had fallen into ruin. And so it remains, a glum pile of

clunch and flint whose facing stone was long ago incorporated into the foundations of the church.

Perhaps the townsfolk were too busy making money to spare time for castles, for the Middle Ages were a time of great prosperity in Saffron Walden, or Chipping (market) Walden as it was known in the earlier part of that period. It throve on the wool and cloth trades, and as a market for a wide area; much of the present street plan dates from this time, and so also do a surprising number of buildings. A few specialised crops were grown in the neighbourhood – teasels, for raising the nap on cloth, and caraway and coriander, but most important was the autumn-flowering crocus, *Crocus sativus*, from whose golden stigmas the dye (or flavouring agent, or medicine, or aphrodisiac) saffron was made. The first plant was said to have been smuggled from the Holy Land in the staff of a pilgrim; whether true or not, the light, rich soil about Walden suited it admirably, and the manufacture of saffron soon became a major industry, and remained so for some 400 years. Many writers tell of the surrounding hills and fields empurpled in September – 'looking merrily with most lovely saffron' – and certainly, fairly extensive cultivation was required.

PLASTER ART *Geese and flowers, a giant and a hero adorn the walls of the 15th-century Sun Inn in Saffron Walden. The figures are all moulded in plaster – a form of decoration called pargeting, which has been popular in East Anglia for centuries.*

It needed more than 4,000 crocus flowers to yield one ounce of dye; only the stigmas were used, and after harvest, the discarded petals blew about the streets in purple drifts. But by the end of the 18th century, synthetic and imported dyes had ousted the trade, and now there are no saffron crocuses in Walden. Apart, that is, from the ones that appear on the civic coat of arms – as on the Town Hall portico – and the ones that are carved on high arches in the church.

The Church of St Mary the Virgin reflects the 15th-century climax in the town's fortunes. Of cathedral proportions – the nave is 184 ft long and 50 ft high – it is the largest parish church in Essex. The building is flooded with light from the tall windows, and often it is flooded with music, too; the choir is assiduous in practice. There are a number of fine monuments, including one in the black marble called 'touch', from its curiously soapy texture. It commemorates Lord Audley, who died in 1544; he succeeded Sir Thomas More as Chancellor of England, and presided over the court that sentenced him to death. For this work and for his zeal at the Dissolution of the Monasteries, he was given the lands of Walden Abbey. *Worthies of England*, published about a century later, comments that the stone is not harder than the heart nor blacker than the soul of the man who lies beneath it.

At the beginning of the 17th century, the abbey lands became the property of Thomas Howard, Treasurer to James I, and there he built Audley End, then the largest house in Britain, Hampton Court not excepted. 'Too big for a king, but I suppose it might suit a Lord Treasurer', said James I waspishly. Howard's descendants, unable to afford the running costs of so enormous a place, pulled it all down, save for one wing, which survives as a still large and handsome Jacobean house. They continued to live at Audley End until the Second World War. The house and its grounds, landscaped by Capability Brown, now belong to the Department of the Environment and are open to the public during summer.

But the chief joy of Saffron Walden, surpassing even its great house and magnificent church, is its streets and lanes where the centuries casually brush against each other, and against the present. The crossroads, for example, where Market Hill meets Church Street, is purely late medieval, with overhanging eaves, carved oaken doorposts and window-frames, and red-

TANGLED ROOFS *The lofty tower and spire of Saffron Walden's parish church thrust up above the tangle of medieval roofs in Bridge Street. In comparison, High Street almost has an air of modernity with early 19th-century façades, like that of The Pump House (above).*

tiled roofs all tipped awry. Among them is a 15th-century group of buildings still called The Sun Inn, though it has been an antique shop and booksellers for many years. Its walls are covered with some of the finest examples of pargeting in the country.

This form of decoration, long popular in East Anglia, is created by incising wet plaster, or by moulding it in relief. Almost any theme may be chosen, from abstract patterns to whatever took the plasterer's fancy. The Sun Inn is covered with geese, flowers and scrolls and, on one gable end, a lively representation of two men in combat. One is Tom Hickathrift, the East Anglian folk hero, and the other, his arch enemy, the Wisbech Giant. The giant attacked Tom with an uprooted tree, but Tom overcame him, using an axle as a cudgel and a cartwheel for a shield. Tom is said to have been born in the reign of William the Conqueror, yet the figures on the gable end are dressed in the costume of the 1660s – which was when the relief was cast. Firm tradition relates that Oliver Cromwell stayed at The Sun Inn when he visited Saffron Walden to placate a mutinous Roundhead army encamped on the Common. The soldiers had refused to embark for Ireland until they received 43 weeks back pay due to them.

Ancient pubs are the rule, rather than the exception, in the town. The Cross Keys, The Eight Bells and The Saffron Hotel all date from the 16th century, and many of the shops and houses are as old or older. See the medieval shop fronts in Cross Street, for instance, or the 15th and 16th-century cottages, with their tiny front doors, about the church. Or consider the ancient, timbered maltings, now a youth hostel, in Myddleton Place, or the many old hall houses and weavers' establishments, now converted into shops and flats, and it is possible to sense the soothing

TRADE CENTRE *A 15th-century timber-framed house, now a shop, stands on the corner of Cross Street in Saffron Walden. Cross Street leads to The Rows, a web of narrow lanes where medieval traders once had their stalls and shops. The shops at least are still there – and still trading.*

permanence of Saffron Walden. Even the Georgian houses in the High Street are longer-lived than they seem; when this building style became fashionable, merchants of the town simply added elegant brick fronts with sash windows to their comfortable old timber-framed homes.

There is one curiosity, however, that is out of step with the rhythm of continuity, and that is the maze cut deep into the turf of the Common. It is the largest of its kind in England, but no one knows when it was cut, or what its purpose was, though theories abound. Perhaps monks of the long-vanished abbey used to perambulate the maze on their knees as a penance. Or is it possible that, on Midsummer Eves long ago, the townsfolk of Walden used to throw decorum to the winds and dance wild fertility dances about the twisting paths?

Probably older than the maze are the Battle Ditches, ancient earthworks on land off Abbey Lane, close to the town centre. They are known to be Saxon in origin and are believed to have been part of the town's defences in the Dark Ages.

SANDWICH *Kent*

The suavity of its golf courses is Sandwich's best known attraction. Another, less publicised but rarer, is that there, crammed within its medieval walls, is a small town that tells more of England's story than many a city a dozen times its size. For centuries, it was the country's gateway; the Romans had their chief port at Richborough just down the coast, the Saxons, Danes and numerous saints landed there, and all down the years it has witnessed the comings and goings of men and women whose names read like a cast list of history. Thomas Becket landed there shortly before his murder at Canterbury, Richard the Lion Heart walked barefooted from Sandwich to Canterbury to give thanks for deliverance from his Austrian imprisonment, and the Black Prince, victor of Poitiers, brought the King of France captive to the town in 1357. Equally, it was the great port of embarkation for kings and their armies – those of Henry V and Edward IV, and for many others up to 1944, when the 'Mulberry' prefabricated harbour was constructed at Sandwich and towed across the Channel to the Normandy beaches.

Sandwich is one of the Cinque Ports, the confederation of south-eastern seaports created at about the time of the Norman Conquest, that supplied warships for the defence of the realm in exchange for a relaxation of taxes and Customs dues. In the 13th century, Sandwich was the major port for the export of wool, and its medieval prosperity is apparent in its three, somewhat battered, churches, three hospitals, or almshouses, and the town ramparts, pierced by the mighty Barbican, and Fisher Gates. Though generally advantageous, proximity to the Continent also brought its troubles. On several occasions the town was sacked and burned by the French, despite spirited resistance by the inhabitants. The most devastating raid was in 1457 when, in the course of a day's bitter

street-fighting against 4,000 French troops, the Mayor, John Drury, was killed. Mayors of Sandwich still wear black robes in his memory. But the invaders did not always have it their own way; on St Bartholomew's Day, August 24, 1217, a French fleet was repulsed, and it is said that one of the almshouses, St Bartholomew's Hospital, was built to celebrate the victory.

It was not the French that changed Sandwich from a busy seaport into a backwater, but the forces of nature. Its harbour silted up during the 16th century, and the town would have been hard put to it to survive, had it not been for an influx of Flemish clothworkers, refugees from Spanish persecution, who set up business there in the 1560s. Their influence can still be detected in a number of old buildings. It can be seen, for example, in the stepped gables of the Dutch House and Manwood Court, once the grammar school. Dutch bricks were used for many buildings in the town, most notably in St Peter's Church, which the refugees rebuilt after the tower collapsed in 1661. Despite the industry of the immigrants, the town never regained its early prosperity, and even today it fails to fill its medieval boundaries.

All the same, it is a wonderful place to stroll in, and to savour, in whole or in its parts. The overall picture is best appreciated from a circuit of the raised bank of the town walls, and in particular by getting mildly lost in the maze of the streets. There, watch out for the massive, fortress-like Norman tower of St Clement's Church, and pay a visit to the splendid Guildhall, whose Court Room has scarcely altered since the days of Elizabeth I. There are also some houses of immense age, such as The Pilgrims in Strand Street, merchants' dwellings of the 15th century, and The King's Lodging, which has an early Georgian front masking a much older building that was probably a hostel for pilgrims on their way to Canterbury. Similarly disguised is the old house at the top of Quay Lane that was made the Customs office in the early 1600s, and has a large coat of arms of James I above the main fireplace as a relic of its days of officialdom. An interesting point is that all these houses, and many others, obtained their water supply from the Delf, a stone-lined channel that was constructed in the Middle Ages to bring spring water to the town. Part of the stream can still be seen in Delf Street.

In rather odd contrast to these medieval mementoes, there stands at the end of Upper Strand Street a sumptuous house called The Salutation, designed by Sir Edward Lutyens in 1911. Yet, in another sense, its timing is perfect, for this was precisely the year when the golf links, and their attendant equally grand houses, were being planted along the edge of Sandwich Bay, 2 miles away.

BATTLE CASUALTY *In August 1457, the outlying parishes of Sandwich were devastated in a lightning French raid. The Old Drum, the timbered house in Church Street, was one of many buildings damaged in the battle, but was repaired shortly afterwards. Much of the surrounding parish of St Mary, however, lay in ruins for more than a century.*

THE SURVIVOR *St Peter's, high on its windy hill, is the only one remaining of Shaftesbury's 12 medieval churches that were built to serve pilgrims visiting the shrine of St Edward the Martyr in the nearby abbey. His cult brought riches to the abbey, but both disappeared at the Dissolution.*

SHAFTESBURY *Dorset*

Seven hundred feet up on its windy spur, Shaftesbury gazes deep into the smooth green miles of Wessex – into Wiltshire, Somerset and along the Blackmoor Vale of its own county of Dorset. A wonderful spot for a citadel, it might be surmised, but in fact, the town has had little to do with the military and grew instead about an abbey that King Alfred the Great founded in 880 and presented to its first Abbess, his daughter Aethelgiva. The abbey prospered, especially after 979 when the body of the boy King Edward the Martyr was brought there from his wayside grave at Wareham,

where it had lain for several months following his murder, probably by his stepmother, at Corfe. Miraculous cures were reported at his new tomb, and pilgrims flocked to Shaftesbury, so that by the Middle Ages 12 churches, two hospitals and a market town were crowded alongside the abbey on the hilltop. So rich did the abbey become that it was said at about this time too: 'If the Abbess of Shaftesbury could marry the Abbot of Glastonbury, their heir would own more land than the king.'

Within a year of the Dissolution of the Monasteries, however, the abbey had all but vanished, quarried by the townsfolk for building materials almost as the nuns departed. For centuries, the site was ignored, and it was not until the 1930s that the ruins were fully excavated. While the work was going on, a lead box was discovered, containing the bones of a boy. The box had been hastily buried, apparently at the time of the Dissolution, but whether the bones were Edward's or not will probably remain an enigma. The ruins, green and soothing to stroll through, are open to the public in summer; a medieval cross, formerly in Angel Square in the town, marks the site of the high altar. Near by, a little shrine has been constructed to harbour the mysterious box and its contents.

Close by the abbey is the Church of St Peter, dating in part from 1304, and the only survivor of the pre-Reformation churches in the town. Only occasional services are held there now, and concerts and recitals, but it is a place of great and simple charm with some good, old stained glass and monuments. The crypt is something of a curiosity, since for many years it was used as a cellar by the Sun and Moon Inn – now a private house – next door.

St Peter's stands at the head of the steep, sweet curve of Gold Hill, star of many an advertisement and film whose plot, as often as not, is set far from Shaftesbury. It doesn't matter really; with its cobbles and old stone houses, it is everyone's ideal of a street in an old hill town, wherever they live. Most of the rest of the town is also stone. It has to be, considering the gales that harry its streets, and some of it is very attractive, especially in the St James area at the bottom of the hill, where thatch caps stone and a battery of mullioned windows. Old Pump Court there, a tiny quadrangle with a pump in the middle, is almost as picturesque as Gold Hill. In the High Street there is the town's sole remaining timber-framed building, and The Grosvenor Hotel, an imposing coaching inn of Regency period. It contains a famous sideboard of beautifully carved oak depicting the Scottish border battle of Chevy Chase that took place between the English and the Scots in 1388.

The town museum, behind St Peter's Church, contains an unusually well-presented and comprehensive portrait of the town's history and industries – button and lace-making, mostly. The star exhibit is The Byzant, a totem-like object that used to be carried in an annual ceremony that confirmed ancient rights to drinking water drawn from the neighbouring Manor of Gillingham.

SHERBORNE _Dorset_

As with Tunbridge Wells, Marlborough and a number of the other older, prettier British towns, there is the notion about Sherborne too that it is chiefly occupied by retired colonialists and pedagogues. Certainly it has all the attributes: castles, gracious streets of mellow stone, associations with the great, and the kind of grocer's shop that sells Dorset Blue Vinny cheese. But the few remaining colonial officials tend now to retire to the Costa del Sol, and as for the schoolteachers, in Sherborne at least, there might never be any need for them to retire. With half a score or so of well-known schools, education is a major industry in the town.

Venerable though some of these institutions are – Sherborne, the boys' public school, was founded in 1550 – the town began with the great Saxon abbey founded by King Ine of Wessex and St Aldhelm in 705. After the Norman Conquest, the abbacy of Sherborne became one of the offices of the Bishops of Salisbury who were also Lords of the Manor. It was they who built the Old Castle, which remained a favourite episcopal residence for many years.

As often happened, the abbey church was shared between the monks and the townspeople and, as often happened too, there was not much love lost between them. At the time of the great rebuilding in the 1430s, smouldering enmity flared into open quarrel, and someone shot a fire-arrow into the thatch that was temporarily roofing the choir. The red scars of the conflagration are burned deep into the limestone walls, but the Abbey Church of St Mary survived to become, after the Reformation, Sherborne's parish church which is, without doubt, one of the loveliest in the land. The fan tracery in the ceilings, delicately carved and a miracle of interweaving geometrical precision, is alone worth travelling miles to see. But once there, make a special, additional point of seeing the chapels and the tombs. There is the portrait tomb of Abbot Clement, for example, who died in 1160; 'The Almighty's clemency may Clement feel...' – so runs his epitaph. Then there is the elaborately armoured effigy of Sir John Horsey who, having acquired the abbey church at the Dissolution, sold it to the parish for £66 plus a further £260 for the roof lead and bells – which form, incidentally, the heaviest peal of eight bells in the world.

Cheap (meaning 'market') Street is Sherborne's main thoroughfare, a wonderful mixture of white-and-black timber framing, bowed shop fronts, Georgian

NEXT TO GODLINESS _The early 16th-century Conduit House that stands not far from Sherborne's abbey church, is unique. It formerly featured in the abbey's cloister, where it was the monks' washroom until the abbey was dissolved on March 18, 1539 – according to a note in the parish register. After the Dissolution, the townspeople dismantled the Conduit House and set it up again in Cheap Street as a well head for the town's water supply._

SHREWSBURY *Shropshire*

The ancient heart of Shropshire's county town climbs a steep hill almost islanded by a great loop of the River Severn and guarded by a crag-perched sandstone castle dating from Norman times. But 'Shrozebury' is best known for an abundance of black-and-white Tudor buildings which line a maze of narrow streets bearing such quaint names as Dogpole, Wyle Cop, Mardol, Grope Lane, Shoplatch and Gullet Passage.

The town is believed to have been founded by people who abandoned the nearby Roman city of Viroconium after the legions left Britain at the start of the 5th century AD. River and hill combined to make a fine defensive site whose potential was exploited by Roger de Montgomery, one of William the Conqueror's most powerful supporters. His castle made Shrewsbury one of the keys to the Welsh Marches.

The cliff on which the castle stands looks northwards to where Henry IV and his son, the future Henry V of Agincourt fame, won the Battle of Shrewsbury in 1403. A plaque at the top of High Street marks the spot where the body of their rival, Henry 'Hotspur' Percy, was hacked to pieces. Another plaque tells how Dafydd ap Llewelyn, brother of the last native Prince of Wales, was executed there in 1283. That was also the year when Shrewsbury Castle was the meeting place of the first English Parliament in which the Commons were properly represented.

Derelict for more than 100 years after the Civil War, the castle was restored by Thomas Telford in 1790 for his wealthy patron Sir William Pulteney, the town's Member of Parliament. Its main building has been the town council's meeting place since 1926.

It is impossible to walk more than a few paces in central Shrewsbury without seeing a memorable building. The Old Council House near the castle is where the Council of the Marches met and was visited by Charles I and James II. Its neighbour, about 120 years younger, is thought to have been used as a prison by the Court of the Marches. On the opposite side of the street a statue of Charles Darwin, Shrewsbury's most famous son, stands outside the buildings where Shrewsbury School was founded in 1552. The school moved to its present site beyond the river in 1882, the year of Darwin's death.

Other fine buildings include the 600-year-old Abbot's House in Butcher Row, Ireland's Mansion in High Street – built in the late 16th century by a wealthy wool merchant – and Rowley's House in Hill's Lane which is now one of the town's many museums.

At the lower end of Mardol is the King's Head, a 15th-century inn whose upper storeys project over the pavement. Magistrates dispense justice in the Old Market Hall of 1596 which stands in The Square near a statue of Robert Clive – 'Clive of India' – who was born near Market Drayton in 1725. He was Mayor of Shrewsbury in 1762 and the town's MP from 1761 until his death in 1774. Clive House, his home on College Hill, is now a museum.

Holy Cross Abbey, beyond the English Bridge, was founded by Roger de Montgomery and is where he

KEY TO THE MARCHES
Embraced within a loop of the Severn that closes to a bottleneck no more than 300 yds across, it is not difficult to appreciate Shrewsbury's appeal to the old Norman warlords. They built a castle to block the bottleneck and a wall as a second line of defence within the loop, so creating a formidable barrier on the route into mid-Wales. The medieval town grew up behind the wall, and many of its buildings remain. So, too, does its spirit, as such curious street names as Murivance and Dogpole, Shoplatch and Wyle Cop bear witness.

pillars, Regency elegance, ornamented Victorian, and here and there, odd bits of the Middle Ages poking through. This is a fair summary of the rest of the town, though there are also some grand Georgian houses in Long Street, and grandest of all in Newland. The great mansion there was built by Henry Seymour Portland in 1720, apparently as a Dower House to be inhabited by his wife after his death. But she regarded it as being 'no more than an inn', and sold it. About a century later, it was bought by George Macready, the famous Victorian actor-manager, and now it houses Lord Digby's School for Girls.

Lord Digby also owns Sherborne's two castles. The old bishop's castle was taken over by the Crown at the Dissolution and remained in royal hands until Sir Walter Raleigh, riding by one day on his way from Plymouth to London, gazed upon the old building in its lovely setting 'as Ahab did upon Naboth's vineyard', and fell off his horse in his delight at the scene. Or so it is said. At any event, he persuaded Elizabeth I to grant him a lease on the place. He did not enjoy it for long, however, since shortly afterwards, the queen discovered his secret marriage to Elizabeth Throckmorton, one of her ladies-in-waiting, and threw them both into the Tower of London. Nevertheless, when Her Majesty's irritation subsided, they returned to Sherborne, and built a new castle in the grounds of the old one, a pretty, pinnacled confection, designed far more for comfort than defence. There, Raleigh spent some of the few settled years in his stormy life, and after his execution in 1618, both castles passed into the hands of the Digby family.

died in 1094, three days after becoming a monk. The opposite end of Abbey Foregate is dominated by what is said to be the tallest Doric column in the world. Just over 133 ft high, it supports a statue of Lord Hill, a Shrewsbury-born soldier who became one of the Duke of Wellington's most trusted commanders.

St Mary's Church occupies the highest ground in Shrewsbury and dates from the 12th century. Three hundred years later its Norman tower was topped with a steeple whose tip is 222 ft high. An inscription on the tower records an ill-fated attempt to fly over the Severn from St Mary's in 1739.

The classical building next to St Mary's was built in 1826–30 as the Royal Salop Infirmary. After serving as a hospital for nearly 150 years, it was converted to flats and shops. Another old building which has found a new role is the Church of St Julian which is now a colourful craft centre. It was rebuilt in 1750 by Thomas Farnolls Pritchard, the Shrewsbury architect who also designed the world's first iron bridge, which still spans the Severn at Ironbridge Gorge, a few miles downstream from Shrewsbury.

The old towpath which follows the river round most of central Shrewsbury passes through The Quarry, a spacious park whose focal point, The Dingle, has all the charm, colour and tranquillity of a private garden. For many years it was the domain of Percy Thrower, the local government employee who became one of Britain's best-known gardeners.

SOUTHWOLD *Suffolk*

Lying between low marshlands and the browny-grey North Sea, Southwold's principal occupation nowadays is that of seaside resort. Its general aspect is as crisp and fresh as a spring morning, an impression that is enhanced by the glistening white lighthouse that rises with charming incongruity from a group of colour-washed houses in the middle of the town. It can be seen from far out to sea, paired with the 100 ft high tower of St Edmund's Church, while in the town itself, its presence is so dominating that its lantern of gleaming, latticed glass, topped by a golden weathervane, seems to follow one about the streets.

Strolling is a rewarding occupation in Southwold. The greens – nine of them – are well-shorn and tended, the architecture refreshingly varied, with here and there a touch of Dutch to remind the visitor that this is the closest part of Britain to the coast of Holland; in this context see especially the attractive Dutch Cottage that houses the town museum. In the High Street and in the triangular Market Place there are distinguished Georgian hotels, The Crown and The Swan, tea-rooms galore, and many fascinating old shops. Altogether a serene and happy town, whose air of assurance, it would seem, must stem from centuries of easy prosperity.

Nothing could be farther from the truth. Though Southwold has had its prosperous times, most of its long history has been one of endless – and sometimes despairing – struggle against the whims of the sea and, not infrequently, the caprices of men as well.

For centuries the seaport of Dunwich to the south was far more important – until the tide lifted shingle across the mouth of the Blyth at Dunwich, causing the river to seek new exits, ever closer to Southwold.

At the same time, Dunwich town was being eroded. Churches, houses and port gradually collapsed into the North Sea, yet the Dunwickers, desperate for the harbour dues that were their ancient right, continued to fight for them. At the turn of the 14th century they sank a number of ships anchored in Southwold Bay and murdered a Southwold crew. But in 1328, a great storm sealed off Dunwich harbour for ever, and Southwold's star rose in consequence. By the middle of the 14th century, the period of the great rebuilding of its church, it had become one of the most important fishing and trading ports on the east coast. Only 150 years later, however, a local pamphleteer was complaining that much of this business had been taken by the Dutch, not due to any lack of industry on the part of Southwold's seamen, but to the constant shifting and silting of the approaches to its 'naughty harbour'. It continues naughty to this day, and is at present suitable only for small boats and pleasure craft.

GROUP FLASHING FOUR
Nowhere in Southwold can one forget the sea. The figureheads of long-vanished ships pop up everywhere in the town, and looming over all, like some sailors' totem, is the sturdy white lighthouse. It was built in 1890, but has long been automatic. As every user of the North Sea knows, its beam is visible for 22 nautical miles, and makes a white group of four flashes every 20 seconds. Not so well known is that the source is a football-sized bulb of 3,000 watts pushing forth a 24,000 candlepower light.

It is remarkable how many clues to the town's ups and downs lie just skin deep beneath its modern, placid exterior. Several of its green, open spaces, for example, cover the foundations of houses burned down in the great fire of 1659 which virtually destroyed medieval Southwold and left more than 300 families destitute. Collections were taken up throughout the land and rebuilding started immediately, but it was many years before the town made anything like a full recovery. Then, there cannot be many British teashops that have played a major part in a naval battle, but Southwold has one, the pretty Sutherland House that, during the Dutch Wars of the late 17th century, was the headquarters of the Lord High Admiral, James, Duke of York, later King James II.

On May 27, 1672, there were 158 ships of the French and British Fleets – France was an ally on this occasion – anchored in Sole Bay, just north of the town when, early in the morning, the topsails of 138 Dutch men-o'-war lifted over the horizon. The wind was light, which was just as well, since it permitted four hours' grace before battle was joined, which time the Duke used to complete his plans and, even more important, recover his crews from the alehouses where they had spent the previous evening. The ensuing battle lasted all day until the Dutch Admiral de Ruyter pulled his battered ships out of action. Casualties were heavy on both sides, but who was the victor is a matter of contention, for although the Dutch withdrew, the Allies lost more ships.

Not far off is Gun Hill, so named from the six cannon installed there, so it is said, by the Duke of Cumberland in 1745. The town had long wished for defences to counter attacks by pirates, and finally gained them by cheering Cumberland when he arrived from Flanders at the beginning of his campaign against Bonnie Prince Charlie and his Jacobites.

If some of the things to be seen about the town recall its sadder days, the church at least gloriously tells of its bright medieval summer. It is dedicated to East Anglia's special saint, Edmund, king and martyr, who was murdered by the Danes in 869. It represents not only the wealth of the 15th-century town, but the exuberance of its spirit too, from the lovely south porch to the incredible ceiling, with its great carved angels reaching out from the rafters. Above the chancel they are painted in delicate pinks, reds and greens, standing against a ceiling-sky of deepest blue, studded with golden stars. The pulpit survived the Reformation and so too, by an even greater miracle, did the 15th-century screen. On its panels, saints and prophets are portrayed in glowing colours, surrounded by exquisitely painted sprays of flowers and other decorations. From a distance, the whole thing looks like an enormous illuminated manuscript, only slightly marred by the erasure of the faces of some of the saints, presumably by Puritan zealots. Children visiting the church are fascinated by Southwold Jack, a brightly painted oaken automaton dressed as a man-at-arms. He strikes the bell beside him with his sword at the beginning of services and at weddings, when the bride enters the church.

STAMFORD *Lincolnshire*

If anyone should suggest a trip to Stamford, please go, for it is a collector's item among country towns. It has half a dozen medieval churches, a considerably larger number of ancient inns and pubs, one of the finest of England's great Elizabethan houses, a history that reaches back to the early days of the Roman occupation, and architecture that would grace a cathedral or university city of several times its size.

At one time, Stamford, with its narrow, stone bridge, was a notorious bottleneck on the A1, but now that the road has swung away to the west, the town is better able to breathe. Nevertheless, the approach to the town from the south is just as imposing, and as

TRAVELLERS' REST *For two millennia, until the great road to the north was diverted, Stamford was a stopping-place for travellers. The George, however, with its famous gallows sign, is still a reminder of the time when 40 long-distance mail coaches a day ('20 up and 20 down') used to stop at Stamford. But hospitality was dispensed at the site long before then; the present cellars were the crypt of a hospice of St John, that 800 years ago sheltered pilgrims on their way to Jerusalem. Beneath the lovely tower of St Martin's, at the top of the hill, lies Lord Burghley, Elizabeth I's Treasurer and friend.*

charmingly unexpected, as ever. The road, the old A1, sweeps down in a steep curve, with greenery on one side and the bastion of Burghley House estate on the other, then through another bend, and all at once there is the town, piled layer on layer, ahead. Beyond the bridge over the River Welland, buildings climb the far slope in alps of pale gold stone, with here and there the loftier peaks of the churches, the closest being the broad-shouldered tower of St Martin's and the bold, 14th-century spire of St Mary's. Those not at once arrested by the architectural splendour will be halted anyway by The George of Stamford, a handsome inn whose sign spans the road on a gallows that was erected, so they say, to welcome honest travellers and threaten highwaymen.

Close by The George is the Town Bridge over the dark olive and near stationary Welland. Ermine Street, the Roman road to the north, crossed the Welland at a ford about 700 yds west of the Town Bridge. Later the Saxons called it Stane or Stone Ford, so naming the settlement that grew up beside it.

But the town's position also conferred great advantages. The junction of river and road swiftly made it an important trading centre, for its own products, as well as other people's – Stamford cloth was well known as early as the 12th century. It was also a convenient stopping place on the pilgrim routes to the south, and hospitals and guest houses were set up by various monastic orders to accommodate them.

Many of the ecclesiastical buildings disappeared

after the Dissolution, but their spirit of charity and hospitality lingers on in the town's many old alms-houses – most notably in the handsome Browne's Hospital in Broad Street, built in the 1480s by William Browne, 'a merchant of very wonderful richnesse', to succour ten poor men and two poor women. The churches also remain, spectacular in their number and in their individual attractiveness. All Saints, in Red Lion Square, is mostly 13th century, and contains some wonderful carving and monuments to the Browne family, including William. Stamford School has a medieval church of its own – St Paul's – as the school chapel. St George's, in St George's Square, was rebuilt in the mid-15th century. Another medieval church, St John the Baptist, is small, intimate and immensely cheerful with an entire Heavenly host of carved archangels, angels and cherubim supporting the roof, but the very pinnacle of the town is the spire of St Mary's, triumphantly soaring to the sky.

Most visitors, however, probably go first to St Martin's, to see the splendid stained glass and the monuments to the Cecil family. Paramount among them is that to Lord Burghley, Elizabeth's High Treasurer. He died in 1598, having spent most of his life as Elizabeth I's closest confidant and adviser. Those requiring further monuments should see the various charitable institutions he bestowed upon the town, and most especially visit the palace-like Burghley House, the home he built for himself.

Though the monastic theologians have long departed, there is still about Stamford an air of measured calm – especially noticeable at weekends, when the traffic has wandered off, and it is possible to see the town on foot. The effect is enhanced by the dignity of stone, of which the town is almost entirely composed. It varies in colour from charcoal grey to pale gold, depending on age or cleaning, and it precisely suits the gracious severity of the largely Georgian architecture. Enlivened throughout by gaily painted doors surmounted by pretty fanlights, Stamford presents one of the most satisfying townscapes in Britain.

STORNOWAY *Isle of Lewis*

The metropolis of the Outer Isles has a population of about 5,500, including a few adventurous, Gaelic-speaking Asian shopkeepers, one set of traffic lights, a colony of grey seals in its fine natural harbour, and Sunday. Or rather, in a sense, it does not have Sunday. Apart from a stirring about Kirk time, nothing moves, not a car nor a bicycle nor a fishing boat all day. You cannot come to Lewis on a Sunday, nor leave it – and there is no entertainment but to watch the seagulls.

For the rest of the week, however, it is a busy, bustling place, whose life centres upon the harbour. It has about 40 fishing boats of its own, a mere shadow

PORT AT THE WORLD'S EDGE *Ancient navigators believed that the world came to an end a little beyond the Western Isles, and at sea in winter this may still seem a reasonable proposition. But in Stornoway, stout walls and tight roofs keep winter at bay.*

of the 1,000-strong fleet that used to sail from Stornoway, but there are usually a number of foreign boats – from France, perhaps, or Germany, the Faeroes or Scandinavia – tied up as well. An oil rig, like a science-fiction monster, looms over the construction yard, but it is a happy omen of increased employment, as is the boat repair yard on the islet near by. In contrast, and as a reminder of the islanders' long struggle against the sea, is the cairn on Holm Point, at the harbour's entrance. It stands above The Beasts of Holm, a group of rocks on which, in 1919, the Admiralty Yacht *Iolaire* foundered. She was carrying Lewis ex-servicemen returning from the First World War, and 207 of them drowned within sight of home. On the other side of the harbour, beside the oil-rig yard, there is another monument. This is to Prince Charles Edward, who spent several unhappy days as a fugitive on Lewis in 1746. Perhaps he would have been touched by the idea of the monument, but he received little enough help from the islanders at the time, though they did not hinder him either.

On the Eye Peninsula, more or less a suburb of Stornoway and locally called The Point, there is the airport, shared by civilian and NATO traffic, and close by, yet another monument. This is the derelict, 14th-century church of St Columba, and the cemetery of Ui, in which 19 MacLeod chieftains are buried.

The mock-Tudor Lewis Castle, now a technical college, on the outskirts of the town is, in its way, the most poignant memorial of all. It was built about 1840 by Sir James Matheson, who imported huge quantities of soil in which to plant the trees that surround the

HOW MUCH A LEG? *Since 'time out of mind', Stow-on-the-Wold's fairs have been famous, assured by the town's position at a major crossing of Cotswold highways. In the Middle Ages, sheep, wool and horses were the major commodities and, later, at the Hiring Fairs, farm servants sought new masters there. Some trades have departed, but the horses still return for the Horse Fair on May 12, as do half the gypsies and 'travelling people' in England.*

house, and spent a fortune on land improvements, schools and new industries to improve the lot of his neighbours. But the islanders did not wish to be improved, and the scheme came to nothing. Then, in 1918, Lord Leverhulme purchased the estate, and half the Outer Hebrides with it, and set about turning Stornoway into the greatest fishing port and fish processing plant in Europe. He started the retail firm of Mac Fisheries as an outlet, and began to build roads, docks and kippering sheds. But he, too, met the unchangeability of the islands, as gentle, courteous and eternal as their summer twilight, and he, too, gave up and went away. The dock installations, the factories and the roads remain in exactly the same half-finished state as on the day that he left.

STOW-ON-THE-WOLD
Gloucestershire

It used to be said that the town's site was so inhospitable that even the elements shunned it. There was no earth, or at least only 5 in. of it before the bedrock was reached, no fire because there was no wood for fuel, and no water on the hilltop. There was no air either, they said; only the wind.

However, things improved a bit after the enclosures of the mid-18th century, when erosion was reduced through the planting of hedgerows and of the beech windbreaks that are still the glory of the approaches to the town. Water, though, remained a problem for many a long year, and well into the 19th century it was still sold in the market at a farthing a bucket.

The town is built upon the site of Mauger's Bury, one of nine Iron Age hill-forts that were constructed in about the last century BC to cover the Severn. The ancient track of the Fosse Way, which the Romans straightened and paved, runs by the town's edge and, altogether, eight roads met there, including the Roman roads bearing metals from the mines of Wales and salt from Droitwich. Where the roads joined there seems to have been a settlement, partly Roman and partly Celtic. Then, at some unspecified moment in the Saxon period, according to legend, there lived on the site a hermit named Edward, and the place came to be known as St Edward's Stow, or the Place of St Edward; 'on the Wold' simply means on the hill.

For centuries before and after the Norman Conquest, the Manor of Stow belonged to the Abbey of Evesham, which had the right to hold a weekly market and two annual fairs. The meeting of the roads and Cotswold wool guaranteed success, and it is said that 20,000 sheep used to change hands every fair day. The fairs continued long after the Dissolution of the Monasteries, first as Hiring Fairs – an early and rural form of Labour Exchange – and later as Horse Fairs, a role that continues to this day. They are held in May and October, and colourful events they are too, with gypsies, dealers and all the fun of the fair.

Outside of fair and market days, Stow is a quiet little place – it still possesses a set of stocks – and is actually smaller than it was in its medieval heyday. Still, it is an attractive town, mostly composed of Cotswold stone, which is usually described as 'warm' or 'mellow' but can in fact look fairly bleak in driving rain, a not infrequent phenomenon in Stow winters. Apart from High Street, Church Street and Digbeth Street, access to the Market Square is through narrow alleys known as 'tures', which were probably a means of forcing sheep into single file to facilitate counting. The Market Cross is mostly medieval, as are a number of buildings about it; the old Grammar School, for example, now the Masonic Hall, and the higgledy-piggledy Crooked House. The Talbot and Ross House belong to a century or so later. The most imposing building, the Gothic St Edward's Hall, however, dates only from 1878. It is the civic centre.

Of the many inns that served the drovers and coaches in the old days, only a few remain, or at least only a few that are still recognisable as inns. Among them is the King's Arms, said to have been licensed in 1548 by the boy-king Edward VI who, despite his youth, considered it the best pub between London and Worcester.

The great 15th-century tower of St Edward's Church is a legacy from the wool days, and a number of wool merchants are buried within the building, their tombs distinguished by carved wool bales.

STRATFORD-UPON-AVON
Warwickshire

Literary pilgrims have been visiting Stratford-upon-Avon since the 17th century, and William Shakespeare's birthplace in Henley Street now attracts more than 500,000 visitors every year. Interest in the playwright tends to submerge the fact that Stratford is a lovely old town in its own right, rich in character, history and timber-framed buildings. It deserves to be savoured at leisure, not devoured in a few hasty gulps.

Treasures not directly concerned with Shakespeare include the 15th-century Guild Chapel whose nave has a mural depicting Judgment Day. Harvard House was the home of a butcher's daughter who married Robert Harvard. Their son John, born in 1607, emigrated to America and founded the university named in his honour. The White Swan in Rother Street has a 16th-century mural depicting the story of Tobias and the Angel, and what used to be a church in Shakespeare Street now houses a museum filled with some of the world's most exotic vintage cars.

Weekly markets have been held since Richard the Lionheart's reign, and the annual Mop Fair in October has been a lively event in the town's calendar for nearly 800 years.

The timber-framed house where John and Mary Shakespeare's first son was born in 1564 changed hands for just £210 in 1806. Forty-one years later it was sold to what eventually became the Shakespeare Birthplace Trust for £3,000. Sale posters described it as 'the most heart-stirring relic of the greatest genius that ever lived'.

New Place, at the junction of Chapel Street and Chapel Lane, was Shakespeare's home from 1597 until his death in 1616. Queen Henrietta Maria, wife of

Charles I, stayed there in 1643 as the guest of Dr John and Susanna Hall, Shakespeare's son-in-law and daughter. New Place was demolished in 1759, but the foundations have been uncovered and now form part of a tranquil garden overlooked by the Guild Chapel. Nash's House flanks the garden, and houses a museum whose exhibits go back to prehistoric times.

The River Avon flows past the Collegiate Church of the Holy Trinity where Shakespeare was buried. Its oldest parts date from the 13th century and the church is a fine building by any standard. Soft, multi-coloured light streams through the stained-glass windows and the choir has a superb set of 15th-century misericords. Carved from black oak, they depict flowers, foliage, birds, animals, a naked woman riding a stag, the capture of a unicorn and a woman beating her husband over the head with a saucepan.

Shakespeare's bust in the chancel shows him holding a quill in his right hand while the left rests on a sheet of paper. His gravestone on the floor is carved with a plea followed by a stern warning:

> 'Good friend for Jesus sake forbeare
> To digg the dust encloased heare
> Bleste be ye man yt spares thes stones
> And curst be he yt moves my bones.'

Hall's Croft, a short walk from the church, is a lovely old building whose oak frame, numerous gables and

SO HONOUR'D A GRAVE *One of the few ascertainable facts about Shakespeare is that he was buried in the chancel of the Church of the Holy Trinity, Stratford-upon-Avon, in 1616, when he was about 52 years of age. Though much honoured by his contemporaries, he owed his privileged place of burial not to his fame as a poet, but to the fact that he was a lay rector in the lovely old church.*

I KNOW A BANK… *In his boyhood, and in his few years of retirement, William Shakespeare must have known a view very similar to the one on the following page. The spire reaching over the willows flanking the River Avon is that of the Church of the Holy Trinity, Stratford-upon-Avon, in which the playwright was baptised and buried.*

THE SHAKESPEARE CONNECTIONS
'Bardolatry', the worship of all to do with Shakespeare, is something of an industry in Stratford. Among its shrines is Mary Arden's House (above), the birthplace of Shakespeare's mother at Wilmcote. Others include his own probable birthplace (bottom), and Anne Hathaway's Cottage, his wife's family home (below).

Anne Hathaway's Cottage

Shakespeare's birthplace

tall chimneys are complemented by the beauty of a spacious garden. It was John and Susanna Hall's home before they moved to New Place in 1616, and is now preserved by the Shakespeare Birthplace Trust.

Judith Quiney's House, now the town's information centre, became the home of Shakespeare's younger daughter when she married Thomas Quiney two months before her father's death.

Anne Hathaway's Cottage nestles beneath a thatched roof in Shottery, 2 miles from the centre of Stratford. Richard Hathaway's daughter was born there in 1556 and married 'William Shagspere' 26 years later, only seven months before their first child's baptism was recorded.

Despite the playwright's fame, Stratford's first Shakespeare Memorial Theatre was not built until 1879. It burned to the ground in 1926, and its controversial replacement was opened six years later. It was faced with red brick because the original proposal to use Cotswold stone was rejected as too expensive. A play watched by official guests from many nations makes an appropriate *grande finale*, when formal homage is paid to Shakespeare's memory every year. The event is generally held on the Saturday nearest to April 23 – St George's Day and almost certainly the dramatist's birthday.

Shakespeare is also commemorated by the lofty Gower Memorial which stands between the theatre and the bridge built by Hugh Clopton, a wealthy Stratford merchant and benefactor who became Lord Mayor of London in 1492. The monument has a seated figure of Shakespeare and includes life-size bronze statues of Hamlet, Lady Macbeth, Falstaff and Prince Hal. They symbolise philosophy, tragedy, comedy and history – themes which Shakespeare handled with a genius that no writer has come close to matching.

SWAFFHAM *Norfolk*

Since this is a working town serving a working countryside, vast lorries piled high with carrots are more often seen about the streets than antique shops. It is not a place that has ever sought to be pretty, but casually, over the years, a certain handsomeness has overtaken it.

Market Place is the heart and life-force of Swaffham, just as it has been for centuries, perhaps as long ago as the days of the Swabians, or Swaefas, the Saxon tribe that settled in the area when the Roman legions departed, and bequeathed its name to the town.

Wedge-shaped rather than square, Market Place's focal point is the graceful Market Cross that was given to the town by Horace Walpole in 1783, for some reason that is not entirely clear. It consists of eight columns supporting a lead-sheathed cupola upon whose summit stands a statue of Ceres, the Roman goddess of agriculture. Once, butter sellers used to shelter beneath the dome of the cross, but now it stands empty, and the traffic breaks about it as though on a reef.

Near by are the old, red-brick Assembly Rooms, built in 1817, when Norfolk landowners and woolmen were a power in the land. Swaffham was never a Bath or a Tunbridge Wells, but the balls that took place in the rooms were every bit as elegant as those described by Jane Austen. There are also a number of fine Georgian buildings about the market, of which the best is probably the grammar school with great white ornamental vases set upon its gate piers. The school was founded in 1736, and still occupies the same buildings. Such graciousness rather shows up the glum Victorian Corn Exchange, but mingles well with the stately, three-storey flint house opposite.

When in the market, spare a moment for a glance into Plowright Place where a double row of ancient cartmakers' and wheelwrights' workrooms have been converted into an attractive arcade of small shops. Plowright, incidentally, is the name of the firm that was making carts in Swaffham as long ago as 1700, and they flourish still as agricultural engineers.

No one knows when Swaffham's first church was built, but most of the present structure belongs to the 15th century. Its chief glory is the great double hammer-beamed roof supported on the shoulders of a cloud of angels – 200 of them in all – and even from the floor of the nave, 51 ft below, the delicate carving of their chestnut wings is apparent. When they were restored in the 1880s, a large number of bullets were found embedded in them. As usual, Cromwell's troopers were blamed; more likely the bullets were fired to dissuade birds from nesting among the high beams. And besides, Cromwell's maternal grand-mother, Catherine Steward, is buried in Swaffham church and presumably even he would have drawn the line somewhere.

TEWKESBURY *Gloucestershire*

In a country that is liberally sprinkled with the sites of battles long ago, there are only a few to which an aura of ancient despair still clings. Flodden is one, Bosworth another, and Sedgemoor a dreary third; but despite the loveliness of its setting, Tewkesbury must also stand high on the list. The decisive battle of the Wars of the Roses was fought on Saturday, May 4, 1471, in the fields about Gupshill Manor just to the south of the town. The protagonists were the Lancastrians, under the nominal command of Queen Margaret of Anjou, wife of the deposed Henry VI, and their son, the Prince of Wales, and the Yorkists, led by Edward IV and his two brothers, the Duke of Clarence and the Duke of Gloucester (later Richard III). The issue was not long in doubt. Due to the Yorkists' superior military skills, and possible treason, the Lancastrians were swiftly crushed, but it was the aftermath of the fight that gave the day its peculiar horror. All Wars of the Roses battles were bitter, but at Tewkesbury no quarter at all was given. Some of the fleeing Lancastrians were killed as they tried to cross the river at Abbey Mill, and many more were butchered at a place still called Bloody Meadow. While those who sought sanctuary in the abbey were cut down in the aisles.

Among those who died was the young Prince of Wales, despatched, so it is said, by the daggers of the Dukes of Gloucester and Clarence, while any Lancastrian who had held even a minor military command was summarily tried for treason and executed at the Market Cross. The Prince of Wales was buried in the abbey, and so, a few years later, was one of his supposed killers, the Duke of Clarence.

Such drama was the very stuff of the Middle Ages. But equally so is the setting, Tewkesbury's glorious Abbey Church of St Mary, whose only peers in Britain, cathedrals apart, are Westminster Abbey and Beverley Minster. Purchased by the townspeople at the Dissolution, it is very nearly all that remains of the great Benedictine monastery inaugurated by Robert Fitz-Hamon in about 1100, and even after 900 years its majestic columns and fan-vaulted ceiling, the stained-glass portraits of men-at-arms, the massive tower and the 65 ft high west window are things to marvel at. The names on the monuments are a roll-call of medieval chivalry – FitzHamon and de Clare, Despenser, Beauchamp and Montacute.

About the church is the yellow-stone Tudor Gatehouse and Abbey House, a pretty patchwork of stone and brick that was the Abbot's Lodging and is now the vicarage. With one or two exceptions, such as the Town Hall, these form the sum total of all stone buildings in Tewkesbury. As can be seen from the top of the church tower, having recovered from the ascent

MOCK AND TUDOR *Like most of Tewkesbury's town centre, its High Street was virtually completed by the late 1300s. Since then, the street's pattern has been one of piecemeal rebuilding, replacing and refacing, making the entire thoroughfare a fascinating review of English domestic architecture over seven centuries. The dark green and white No. 124 is flanked by a pair of Georgian houses and shops and fronted by an early Victorian notion of a Tudor façade. The building behind it, however, is genuinely Tudor, with fine panelling and a beam inscribed DEV: REG: AMIC – 'For God, Queen and Friends'.*

LITERARY TOWNSCAPE *The delicate ironwork of Tewkesbury Abbey's gateway frames The Bell Hotel in which, while lunching there in 1852, Mrs Craik was inspired to write her long-term bestseller,* John Halifax, Gentleman. *The inn figures in the novel as the house of Abel Fletcher, while her hero's name was taken from a gravestone in the churchyard opposite. Largely rebuilt in 1696, The Bell stands on the site of an ancient abbey hospice; but old though it is, it is but one of a number of equally venerable inns in the town.*

of 205 steps, most of the town is medieval plaster and timber or Georgian brick. Another thing that is apparent from this vantage point is the town's curious shape, gathered tight-packed about the Y of its three main streets. The reason is its position – jammed between old monastic lands and the junction of the Avon and Severn rivers. It was a compressed place, even from the beginning, which accounts for its alleys, medieval space-savers, that lie behind the main streets and are so narrow that the opposing upper storeys practically embrace each other. Projecting upper storeys are a particular feature of the medieval and Tudor buildings in Tewkesbury; some, as on The House of the Nodding Gables in the High Street, seem to be defying gravity.

It is remarkable how many really old buildings have survived in the town. Abbey Cottages in Church Street is a complete row of merchants' houses built about 1450 and lovingly restored. Number 41 has been converted into a museum, The John Moore Museum of the Countryside, named after the author of *Brensham Village*; he was a native of Tewkesbury and died there in 1967. There are a number of other old buildings, such as Warwick House, Cross House and Ancills Court, and the attractive Berkeley Arms, whose oak timber framing was set up in the early 15th century. There is also the intriguingly named restaurant, 'The Ancient Grudge', in the High Street. It is said to date from 1471, the year of the battle; hence the name, presumably. It sells pots of Tewkesbury Mustard, a powerful brew that has been famed since the Middle Ages.

These buildings and their contemporaries reflect the town's medieval prosperity as a market and wool town, just as Tewkesbury's other major architectural style, Georgian brick, tells of its later importance in the malting, leatherworking and stocking-weaving industries.

THURSO *Highland*

Holborn Head and Dunnet Head shelter Thurso from the fury of the Pentland Firth, a wild stretch of water between Scotland's spectacular northern coast and Orkney. Thurso Bay and the mouth of the River Thurso provided an ideal anchorage for the Viking settlers whose power reached its height in 1040 when Thorfinn the Mighty, Earl of Orkney, defeated an army commanded by King Duncan of Scotland's nephew. The town's name is probably derived from the Norse for 'Thor's River'.

The broad bay is overlooked by a town whose age is belied by a rectangular street pattern neat enough to delight the most demanding drill sergeant. The 'new town' is a lasting tribute to Sir John Sinclair, a far-sighted landowner who was Member of Parliament for Caithness from 1780 until 1811. He also introduced the Cheviot sheep to the Thurso area and was responsible for *The Statistical Account of Scotland* which surveyed and documented the entire country.

Sir John is commemorated by a statue in the square named after him in 1893. The figure is dressed in the

uniform of the Rothesay and Caithness Fencibles, a regiment of volunteers which Sir John raised during the Napoleonic Wars.

A plaque in Wilson Street marks the house where one of Thurso's most famous sons, Robert Dick, lived from 1830 until his death 36 years later. Dick was a self-educated baker who contributed much to the sciences of geology and botany. The town's museum has a section dedicated to the man and his work. Other exhibits include a cross carved with Viking runes.

Thurso's harbour, now used by a few small fishing boats and private craft, was a busy trading port for many hundreds of years. In the 19th century it was used by vessels which shipped polished flagstones from local quarries to destinations all over Europe and as far afield as Australia. The quays share memories of Thurso's past with Old St Peter's Church, which dates from the Middle Ages and has not been used for public worship since 1832. It is thought to have been

founded by Gilbert Murray, Bishop of Caithness, in the first half of the 13th century. Faint traces of the bishop's residence, Scrabster Castle, stand on a cliff to the west of the town, high above the great sweep of Thurso Bay.

Thurso Castle, on the opposite side of the harbour, was built in 1660 and became the Sinclair's family seat in 1719. A nearby tower is said to mark the burial place of Earl Harald the Younger who ruled parts of Caithness, Orkney and Shetland. He died in battle in 1196.

Thurso is the British mainland's most northerly town and stands nearer the Arctic Circle than Moscow, parts of Alaska and much of Hudson Bay. It is not quite in the 'Land of the Midnight Sun' region, but midsummer nights amount to little more than two or three hours of semi-darkness. Midnight golf, tennis and bowls matches are a feature of Midsummer Week.

The town is an ideal centre for exploring a magnificent stretch of wave-lashed coast between Cape Wrath and Duncansby Head, whose clifftop vantage point provides superb views over the Pentland Firth to the scattered islands of Orkney. Car ferries sail to Orkney from Scrabster, a five-minute drive from Thurso. In 1916 HMS *Hampshire* sailed from the harbour at the start of a voyage to Russia with Lord Kitchener on board. He lost his life when the ship went down off Orkney's main island after either striking a German mine or being hit by a torpedo.

TOBERMORY *Isle of Mull*

Most people land on Mull at Craignure, where the ferry comes in from Oban. It is not much more than a pier and a few houses and shops, but behind it looms the gaunt, fairy-tale Castle of Duart, a very suitable mood-adjuster to the whole magical island. Mull is not at all like the common expectation of the Hebrides; it is green and jolly and youthful, with the merry glint of little lochs always at the corner of the eye. The road to

Tobermory runs north, following the Sound of Mull the whole way, the shoreline punctuated by beaches of white sand.

The island's capital is just as unexpected. A backdrop of steep oakwoods surrounds the fine natural harbour and its piers, which are sheltered from the Sound by Calve Island. Almost all there is of Tobermory is slung one street deep around the curve of the bay. The buildings are stone and slate, but there is nothing of the usual greyness here, for they are colour-washed blue, primrose, pink, buff, magenta or emerald green, with window and door surrounds picked out in dazzling white. There is a shop that sells fishing tackle, guns and paperbacks; another that purveys everything for the yachtsman and the skin diver; a sweet-scented bakery; and places where the visitor may buy smoked or fresh trout one at a time or by the box. Mingled with these delights, there are little hotels and restaurants that hold seafood festivals that commence with clams with green noodles, then move via lobsters and the like to honey and cinnamon-flavoured pears. Ruminating upon these things, one can at the same time contemplate the gracious swell of Ben Hiant – the Holy Mountain – on the mainland, and should the outer world beckon, it is possible to catch ferries to such faraway places as Coll and Tiree at the pier. The most imposing building in the little burgh, the distillery apart, is a church with a spire so weatherbeaten that small trees have taken root in the cracks between the stones. Actually the building no longer has an ecclesiastical function, but houses the Craft Centre instead. Some hotels and houses on the terraces above Main Street, a gaggle of yachts bobbing in the harbour, a few fishing boats tied up at the pier, and that is about all there is visible of Tobermory.

Tobar Mhoire – the Well of Mary – takes its name from the Well and Chapel of St Mary, an ancient Christian settlement whose remains can still be seen in the old cemetery. The town itself, however, is by no means ancient, having been created all of a piece in the 1780s, though the excellence of the harbour was noted long before. When James Boswell and Dr Johnson came there on their tour of the Hebrides in the 1770s, they observed more than a dozen vessels at anchor, and were told that sometimes as many as 70 or 80 sail might take shelter there at once – merchantmen, mostly, making their way to or from the Baltic.

However, the town, when it was finally built, was designed not to serve merchant ships, but the fishing industry. It was built, together with Ullapool and Lochbay in Skye, by the British Fisheries Society, as a means of encouraging settlement in the Highlands.

The one thing that everyone knows about Tobermory is its galleon, a creature almost as exasperating and elusive as the monster in Loch Ness, though there seems to be no doubt that a straggler of the storm-

driven Spanish Armada of 1588 does indeed lie in the bay, some 300 yds off the end of the pier. The problem is, what is she? It has always been believed, with unshakable optimism, that she is the *San Francisco*, one of the ships that carried the fleet's pay chests. It seems, however, that the *San Francisco* eventually got home to Spain, though in a sorely battered condition, and a more likely candidate for the hole in the sea-bed off Tobermory is a troopship with the resounding name of *Santa Maria de Gracia y San Juan Bautista*.

Nevertheless, the legends of treasure remain as insistent as ever. Yet despite more than 50 attempts by successive Dukes of Argyll, who own the salvage rights, nothing of note has ever been recovered.

TOTNES *Devon*

As Troy burned, so it is said, Brutus, great-grandson of Aeneas, led the survivors of the garrison to the ships, and sailed across the known world until they came to the River Dart. The Trojans pulled the galleys upstream until they came to a fording place, at which point Brutus jumped out on to a rock and said:

'Here I am and here I rest
And this town shall be called Totnes.'

By way of proof, the rock can still be seen in Fore Street, and important proclamations are made from it to this day. More prosaic historians, however, ascribe the town's origins to the Saxons.

Either way, after the Norman Conquest, the flourishing little manor and several dozen more were presented to a Count Judhel, one of William's Breton allies. As was the practice of overlords of the day, he at once flung up a great earthen motte or mound, and built a timber fort on top. Practical matters thus settled, he then, for his soul's sake, presented the patronage of the church at Totnes to the Abbot of Angers, who established a Benedictine priory there. Only a few fragments of the Norman church survive in the fabric of the present building, but Judhel's motte still stands proud and high, its summit crowned with a stone keep that was built to replace the timber one about a century after his death. The keep is no more than a hollow shell, but it is well worth climbing to the top for the view that the battlements afford over the town and surrounding countryside.

The most remarkable feature, and one that can be seen for miles about, is the red-sandstone exclamation mark of St Mary's church tower. Or not quite an exclamation mark, since it is topped with four delightful little pinnacles, very typical of Devon churches. Like the rest of the building, it is the result of the enthusiasm of several successive mayors in the 1400s, and the hard work, enthusiastic or not, of the parishioners. All in all, it was a magnificent effort for a town that for most of its history never had a population that exceeded 4,000. Just the same, it was usually prosperous. It was, and is, the market town for a rich farming area.

Close by the church is the Guildhall, dating from 1553, with a pillared walkway and, within, the Court

Room and Council Chamber with some plasterwork that is unexcelled in any small town in England. Despite its ancient foundation, the 16th century is really the keynote in Totnes, the best example being at 70, Fore Street, a merchant's house of 1575, now the town museum. It contains a large local history collection and an exhibition devoted to the work of Charles Babbage, a native of the town who, in the 19th century, invented a calculating machine from which modern computers were evolved. The building, however, is white plaster and black timber, which is not really typical of Totnes. The favourite material for cladding both roofs and walls is slate, hung in overlapping square tiles, in diamond or rounded patterns or painted over. It is a remarkably effective material, especially in the steeply plunging Poultry-walk and Butterwalk where the shops are sheltered by overhanging upper storeys supported on pillars.

The late 17th and the 18th centuries were also comfortable times in Totnes, and are well represented by a pretty, dotty little 'Gothick' house just off Fore Street, a couple of gravely imposing inns – The Seymour Hotel and The Royal Seven Stars – the old Grammar School, and some good, formal rows, like Devon Place.

ARCH ACROSS THE AGES *East Gate is one of two surviving gates in Totnes's medieval defences, though as can be seen from its pretty and unmilitary front, it was considerably altered in 1837. At the gate, Fore Street, which takes its name from the houses built before, or outside, the walls, becomes High Street. Fore Street, which runs down to the River Dart, harbours one of the town's dearest possessions, the stone on which Brutus, the legendary founder of Totnes, stood to harangue his fellow-survivors of the Siege of Troy.*

TUTBURY *Staffordshire*

No one could miss the strategic importance of the mount that rears over the old town by the River Dove, and, since the Iron Age, few have. Celts, Saxons, Mercians and Normans all built fortifications upon it, the Norman Earl Ferrers adding a further artificial mound or motte, on which he erected the usual wooden keep. Within a few years, he or his son replaced it with a stone one, though it has little to do with the romantic ruin that crowns the mound now. This was built just as it is in 1777 by Lord Vernon, as an improvement upon history and on the view from his house at Sudbury, 5 miles farther up the Dove.

The remainder of the buildings and ruins, however, the hall, gatehouse and towers, belong to the 14th century and are largely the creation of the Earls of Lancaster and of John of Gaunt, the first Duke of Lancaster. His son, Henry Bolingbroke, ascended the throne as Henry IV in 1399 and Tutbury, as part of the estate of the Duchy of Lancaster, has belonged to the Crown ever since. This was part of its attraction for Elizabeth I who twice imprisoned Mary, Queen of Scots in the castle.

Long after her death at Fotheringay, her son, James I, stayed at Tutbury, as did his son, Charles I. During the Civil War the castle was twice besieged, in 1643 and 1646. On the last occasion, the Royalist garrison held out for three weeks before surrendering, where-upon the Parliamentarians, to avoid further repetition, dismantled the building to its present state.

The Church of St Mary, Tutbury's chief glory, also stands above the town. It was part of a priory, also founded by the Ferrers in the 1080s, and a remarkable amount of the original church remains, though the monastic buildings have long disappeared. The west doorway is something worth travelling a long way to see. It is almost 15 ft high, and consists, in the Norman fashion, of six arches of diminishing height, all wonderfully carved into representations of demons, flowers, birds and beasts. The second innermost arch is of alabaster, the earliest known use of this stone in England. Nevertheless, it is not surprising that it should appear there, since it is the local stone, and alabaster and gypsum, its ground-down form used in fine cements and filters, has been a mainstay of the town for centuries. In the church, a carved altar-piece recalls a tragic sidelight of the industry, for it commemorates not only the fallen of both World Wars, but those who died in the Fauld mine explosion of 1944 as well. The disaster had nothing to do with usual mining hazards. An abandoned gypsum mine had been taken over by the RAF as a dump for bombs, and in November of that year, 4,000 tons of them erupted in an explosion that was heard in London and registered on seismographs in Switzerland. People, buildings and livestock simply vanished, leaving in their stead only a gigantic crater.

On a more cheerful note, the church also preserves a notice warning parishioners against the further pursuing of treasure that rightly belongs to the Duchy of Lancaster. This recalls a happy moment in 1831 when workmen, digging by the bridge, unearthed a vast, 500-year-old hoard of silver coins. Almost certainly this was the pay chest of the army of Thomas, Earl of Lancaster, which he deposited there when he fled from the Battle of Burton Bridge in 1321, and was shortly after executed at Pontefract. Tens of thousands of coins were said to have been recovered by the townsfolk, but they must have hung on to most of them, since only 1,500 ever found their way to the coffers of the Duchy.

Tutbury has grown considerably in the last decades, due not only to the growth of the alabaster and plaster industries, but to one that is very nearly as ancient, the manufacture of crystal glass. Most of the new building is tucked away, however, and old Tutbury, at the foot of the castle hill, is still a pretty, old-fashioned place. There are some handsome Georgian houses, and among them the rather surprising black-and-white timbered Dog and Partridge Inn, which is said to date from the 14th century and was once a town house of the Curzon family. The interior fittings are even more surprising, since they originally figured in a cruise liner.

ULLAPOOL *Highland*

Magnificent mountains plunge down to the shores of Loch Broom, a beautiful anchorage whose waters reflect the trim, whitewashed buildings lining Ullapool's main street. The tiny town is the focal point of a huge Highland parish where 400 square miles of land are inhabited by fewer than 1,500 people. It is nothing more than a small village by southern standards – but ranks as a large community among the tiny settlements scattered along Scotland's spectacular northwest coast.

Visitors who follow the long road to Ullapool – farther from Edinburgh than York is from London – are richly rewarded by splendid moorland and mountain scenery before they reach the tiny town. Many then take the ferry to Stornoway on the Isle of Lewis and enjoy even more spectacular views as the ship passes the Summer Isles with their backcloth of mountains.

Loch Broom was famous for herring in the Middle Ages, but Ullapool dates from 1788 when the British Fishery Society spent £10,000 on a pier, warehouse, inn and other essential buildings. The pier is a lively and colourful focal point first thing in the morning when trawlers transfer their catches to waiting trucks while seals bob up and down in search of titbits. The town echoes to the clamour of wheeling, swooping seagulls.

Ullapool is the gateway to some of the most majestic coastal scenery in Europe, and attracts many tourists during the holiday season. It also has a great reputation as a sea-angling centre whose launches take fishermen out in search of cod, conger and many other species, including huge skate which often tip the scales at well over 100 lb. Freshwater lochs within easy reach of the town are stocked with trout while salmon and sea-trout are caught in local rivers.

Mountains with magical names – Ben More Coigach, Beinn Dearg, Sgurr Mor and Stac Polly – have challenged and delighted many generations of hardy walkers. The main road north of Ullapool also passes within walking distance of Eas coul Aulin, Britain's highest waterfall with a drop of 658 ft. Smaller, but more spectacular, are the Falls of Measach, 12 miles south-east of the town.

FISHERMAN'S TOWN *Seen from the narrows of Loch Broom, Ullapool seems a haphazard huddle of white houses. A closer look, however, reveals a neat grid street pattern of the late 18th century when the place was laid out all of a piece by the British Fishery Society. The harbour is still used by home based trawlers and those from eastern Europe. Sporting fishermen flock to Ullapool too, competing for rooms in the hotels and boarding houses with tourists bound for the wild and mountainous Inverpolly Nature Reserve to the north.*

WANTAGE *Oxfordshire*

Long before the place had a name, or any name we know, there must have been a settlement on the spot, for it was the meeting place of some of the oldest of man-made things in Britain – the great trackways and immigrant routes that were ancient when the first farmers arrived here from the Continent in the wake of the retreating Ice Age, 10,000 years ago. Some took the route over the high chalk – the Ridge Way – while others bravely took what is now the Icknield Way, through the then marshy and forested Vale of the White Horse; but either way, they passed very close to the site of Wantage.

The tracks are now the main roads from Oxford to Andover, and from Cirencester to Reading. The Romans used some of the trackways and metalled them. After the legions departed, the invading Saxons fought a great battle not far from Wantage, against a Romano-British leader who might or might not have been the legendary Arthur. The Saxons won, and swiftly carved kingdoms out of the conquered island. One such kingdom was Wessex, with Wantage at its heart, and it was there that its greatest king, Alfred, was born in 849. Tradition says that he was born in a palace that once stood at Belmont, about half a mile north of the town centre, or possibly in the area now occupied by the Market Place. At any rate, this is where his statue now stands.

Wantage's position at the centre of a web of roads assured it of a gentle prosperity as a market town, and this is the air it wears still, with its vast, irregularly shaped Market Place, wrapped about by Georgian houses in the blue and red brick very typical of this part of the country, and the imposing Bear Hotel, an old coaching inn. Georgian, with a dash of pretty, Victorian Gothic, is also the keynote for the rest of the town, though there are some 17th-century houses and almshouses growing out of the edges of its older, cobbled streets. But nowhere is there a hint of the town's stormy, early history, nor, indeed, of the brief period in the early 19th century when it was known as 'Black Wantage', from its notoriety as a haven for thieves and cutthroats, and its inns as places of nightly riot. Its easy access seems again to have been the root, married to unemployment caused by agricultural depression and regular invasions by navvies who were digging canals in the vicinity. But by Victoria's reign, law and order were once more established, and Wantage was serene again.

From its appearance, the 13th-century Church of St Peter and St Paul, just behind the Market Place, has never been anything else. It is the ideal of the small town church, gathering years and parishioners into itself, and the odd eccentricity, like the silver plate that is supposed to have belonged to the Russian Emperor, Peter the Great; if it did, no one seems to know how it got there. The splendid old choir stalls bear carvings of eagles and pelicans, and there are monuments to the Fitzwarin family, into which London's Lord Mayor, Sir Richard Whittington, married. Most touching is the monument to John Stamp and his wife, with their

child between them; they died in the early part of the 18th century.

Just along Church Street, the recently opened Vale and Downland Museum picks up the story of the town and the surrounding countryside, and shows their long development from the arrival of the farmers of the New Stone Age, through invasions and medieval prosperity to a vivid summing up of the changes our own century has brought. But perhaps the overriding message is how very little, in truth, this ancient landscape has changed at all.

WARE *Hertfordshire*

The best known thing about Ware is no longer there – its Great Bed, 11 ft 1 in. by 10 ft 8 in., which was made in the town in 1463. Its creator, a local carpenter named Jonas Fosbrooke, intended it for the personal use of Edward IV, but for some reason or other it was never delivered, and came instead to be owned by a succession of Ware innkeepers. It brought considerable fame to the town, and even Shakespeare made laboured jokes about it; also, it was useful on market days when, apparently, as many as 12 couples could be accommodated in it. But for many years now the bed has been a feature of the Victoria and Albert Museum in London.

Another thing missing from Ware is the torrent of traffic that used to thunder down the High Street before the by-pass was made on the Cambridge road. It can hardly be called quiet now, but at least the gracious old houses with their high arches, designed to permit the passage of coaches-and-fours, are no longer shaken by passing juggernauts. But they are still more tranquil when seen from the rear, where their gardens' run down to summer houses and gazebos balanced on the banks of the River Lea.

Ware was, and to some extent still is, a malting and milling town, though some of the maltings with their tilted conical flues have been converted to other uses, and the scores of grain barges that used to ply up and down the Lea (or Lee) between Ware and London, run no longer. Nevertheless, 40-odd miles of waterway may be explored, using Ware as a base, while beyond the Lea and Stort systems there is access to the Thames and the canals of half of England.

So important was Ware in the brewery trade that Hertford – the county town – was once known as Hertford-by-Ware, but when the major breweries took their business elsewhere, or did their own malting, Hertford gained the ascendancy. Still, despite the scars of industry old and new, Ware's general aspect is that of a pretty, country town. In High Street, Baldock Street and in unexpected lanes and alleys, Georgian, 16th-century and Victorian buildings mingle in pleasing harmony. There are also a number of more ancient structures, such as the basically 15th-century priory and the 14th-century Place House in Bluecoat Yard. Originally the Manor House of Ware, it was the home of the Bluecoat School from 1674 to 1761.

The parish church of St Mary was founded in the 10th century, but much of the present building

NATIVE SON *Alfred, King of Wessex and hammer of the Danes, was born in Wantage, perhaps on the site of the Market Place where his statue now stands. It was erected slightly more than 1,000 years after his birth, and has the hairy, beefy look that the Victorians liked to ascribe to prophets and heroes. Nevertheless, it reflects the town's pride in its son, and perhaps its gratitude too. After a single horrendous sacking, the Danes, and history generally, passed it by.*

belongs to the 14th. Tradition says that Joan Plantagenet, the 'Fair Maid of Kent' and wife of the Black Prince, paid for the rebuilding, and there are a number of sculpted Plantagenet portraits on arch terminals to support the story.

No visitor to Ware should miss Scott's Grotto in Scotts Road, an 18th-century folly created by John Scott, the Quaker poet and owner of Amwell House. When the grotto was built, it lay in Amwell's gardens, but the area is covered by modern housing now. The odd structure, consisting of six rooms linked by underground passages all lined with sea-shells, remains as Scott's monument.

WARWICK *Warwickshire*

The names of the people who created Warwick ring like a roll-call on some medieval field of battle. Beaumont and Beauchamp, Plantagenet, Dudley and Greville; most of these were Earls of Warwick, but before them came William the Conqueror, who raised a mound and tower on the site of the present castle, and before him, King Alfred's formidable daughter, the Lady Ethelfleda. In the year 914, during her struggle with the Danes, it was she who first appreciated the strategic importance of the low, rocky hill above the Avon, and threw an earthwork about it, whose lines are more or less followed by the walls of the medieval town.

Most of what is visible of the castle, however, or at least of its exterior, belongs to the 14th century, and is, without doubt, one of the great castles of Europe. For mass, majesty and theatrical domination of the landscape it is equalled in England only by Windsor, and from some points of view, from down by the Avon, say, and framed by trees, Warwick may even excel it. It is a tremendous sight, and doubly so, since it is reflected with hardly a shake in the stilly waters of the river.

But once inside the walls, the fortress practically vanishes and gives way to what is more or less a palace of sumptuously decorated state apartments, brimming with the garnishings of many an 18th-century Grand Tour, and with the splendid collections of furniture and paintings that successive owners have assembled down the years.

Warwick itself began as a garrison town – Smith Street, for example, was where the castle's armourers throve – and then grew to later importance as a market. The old part of the town is largely of two very distinct periods, medieval and 18th century, due to a fire that devastated the town centre in 1694. The medieval buildings that survive were then on the periphery of the town – like the old timbered houses in Mill Street and Castle Street that were shielded from the flames by the castle's bulk, and those by the town's ancient portals, East and West Gate. West Gate itself dates in part from the early 12th century, and has an attractive little Victorian chapel perched on top. Next to it is a group of splendid timbered buildings that from about 1383 to 1546 housed the Town Guilds. For 25 years after that they housed the Corporation

Council and the Grammar School, but since 1571 it has been the Lord Leycester Hospital. It was founded by Elizabeth I's life-long friend, Robert Dudley, Earl of Leicester as an almshouse for 12 Brethren who would be 'such poor and impotent persons as shall hereafter be maimed or hurt in the wars in the service of the Queen, her heirs and successors', and it shelters ex-servicemen – and the museum of the Queen's Own Hussars – to this day.

St Peter's Chapel over the East Gate was reconstructed in the reign of Henry VI, and Landor House, close by, in 1692. It is now part of a girls' school, but in 1775 it was the birthplace of the poet Walter Savage Landor, who spent a considerable fortune in raising and equipping a regiment which he led against the forces of Napoleon in the Peninsular campaign. During his poverty-stricken old age, he was maintained by his fellow-poet, Robert Browning. Other old buildings include the Elizabethan Oken's House, which now contains a delightful collection of old dolls and toys, St John's House, ornately Jacobean and the home of the Royal Warwickshire Regiment's Museum, and the Market Hall, of a slightly later period, which houses the County Museum.

By way of contrast, there is Northgate Street, perhaps the finest Georgian thoroughfare in the Midlands, with the mid-18th-century Shire Hall as its focal point. Below ground, and a little to the north of the Hall, there is a dungeon that was part of the town gaol from 1680 until about 1820. A hell-hole if ever there was one, it is an octagon 21 ft in diameter, fed with a trickle of water and supplied with a cesspit in the centre. Light and air came through a grating in the roof, and the prisoners – 59 of them on one recorded occasion – were shackled to a single, heavy chain whose scar can still be seen, cut deep into the steps.

One of the casualties of the conflagration of 1694

PROUD WARWICK *A list of the builders and custodians of Warwick Castle is like a roll-call of English chivalry – Beauchamp, Neville, Plantagenet, Dudley, Greville – and their creation still stands as one of the greatest and best-preserved castles in Europe. This view from Guy's Tower looks over the gatehouse with its giddy wall walk between turrets, to the piled galleries and firing positions of Caesar's Tower. This was completed in 1356, just in time to house a large number of French prisoners captured at the Battle of Poitiers. Though the castle changed hands on several occasions, it was usually through marriage or because its owner had become involved in a fatal controversy elsewhere. Only once was it besieged, in a half-hearted way, during the Civil War.*

was the Collegiate Church of St Mary. The nave and the tower were both destroyed, though the chapter house, the vestries and the choir all survived. So too does the astonishing Beauchamp Chapel, with its exquisite fan-traceried ceiling and medieval glass. There, all warfare and intrigues at an end, lie the Earls of Warwick. It was built first to house the tomb of Richard Beauchamp who died in 1439 and whose monument is one of the finest of its period in the country. His effigy, with its thin, humorous face and slim, upraised hands, lies beneath a cage of hoops designed to support a funeral pall. Around him are the tombs of his descendants and successors, among them, Robert Dudley, Elizabeth I's favourite, and his wife, Lettice Knollys. Close by is the tomb of their son, whose epitaph reads: 'Here resteth the body of the nobele impe, a child of great parentage, but of farre greater hope and towardness. Died (age 3) 1582.'

WHITBY *North Yorkshire*

Gulls clattering and endlessly, raucously protesting about the unfairness of life; the mingled tangs of diesel, fish and smoke from the curing sheds borne on the edged breeze off the North Sea; children, sand-dusted and with sunburned noses clambering up from the beach. All these things are Whitby, the immortal-looking red-roofed town piled and jammed between the River Esk and the cliff, on top of which stands the ethereal ruin of the Abbey of St Hilda, etched against the sky.

A lantern of the Dark Ages, the abbey was founded by King Oswy of Northumbria in fulfilment of a vow made before his victory over the heathen King Penda of Mercia in 655. Hilda, the first abbess, presided over a community of both monks and nuns, and the place swiftly gained a reputation for piety and learning. Caedmon, the greatest poet of the age, was a farm-worker on abbey lands, and was apparently inspired by an angel to compose and sing a great hymn to the Creation. Hilda, hearing of his prowess, persuaded him to take up the monastic life.

But the present abbey is not the one that Hilda and Caedmon knew; that was destroyed by the Danes in 867, and the site was abandoned until a few years after the Norman Conquest, when the abbey was re-founded and rebuilt by the Benedictines – this time monks only. Apart from the occasional Norse raid, and a stern episcopal warning to the monks to stop hunting, the abbey flourished until the Dissolution.

Balancing it to the north of the abbey, and reached from the town by 199 gruelling steps, is the Church of St Mary, one of the more remarkable of English parish churches. The shell dates largely from the 12th century, but the furnishings – the galleries and box

THE GREAT DIVIDE *The swing bridge across the River Esk divides the two communities of East and West Whitby – each a jumble of narrow streets where fishermen still mend their nets. On the river itself, fishing boats ride the waters where the great explorer Captain Cook learned the art of seamanship.*

Whitby-built ex-colliers, which he regarded as being the most seaworthy craft afloat. Models of his ships can be seen in the museum in Pannett Park, and his statue stands high on West Cliff, looking out to sea.

The old town contains the Market Square, bright with stalls on Saturdays and centred upon the Town Hall, built by the Cholmleys in 1788. There are some old houses and among them, at the top of the square, a building that was a chapel until its conversion into a house at the time of the Reformation. Jet jewellery can still be purchased in this part of the town, though it is not so fashionable as it was. Whitby jet – actually fossilised monkey-puzzle tree – is mined locally and sometimes found on the beaches. It has been carved into ornaments since prehistoric times, though the Whitby jewellery industry did not really get under way until about 1800. It received a tremendous boost when Queen Victoria began to wear the black neck-laces and beads as part of her mourning ensemble, but in the end she may have done it a disservice; even today people still associate the semi-precious stone with death.

About Market Square are the narrow, jumbled streets that give East Cliff its character, and below them the harbour which covers more than 80 acres. A dredger seems to be almost permanently at work clearing the channel and carrying Esk silt out to sea, as it must, for Whitby handles a large number of cargo vessels plying to and from the Continent. Among them are the traditional craft, the offshore fishing fleet of keel boats, and the little cobles, unique to the north-east, used for inshore fishing. Descended from Viking longships, they are clinker-built, with high bows and low, sloping sterns, while their tough construction makes them ideal for launching over beaches.

Across the swivel bridge which dates from 1909, though its ancestors date back to the 14th century, is West Cliff. About the bridge on the western shore there are more ancient streets, including Flowergate which has the rare distinction, for a street, of being mentioned in Domesday Book. It was called 'Flore' then, and is now a shopping thoroughfare. At the bottom, there is a studio exhibiting the works of F. M. Sutcliffe, the photographic pioneer whose photo-graphs of the fisherfolk and the daily life of the north-east coast in the 19th century are now world-famous.

A LIVING LEGEND The picturesque ruins of Whitby Abbey (above) look down on the scene of one of Whitby's oldest customs (below). There, on the eve of Ascension Day, the Horn Garth, or Penny Hedge, is built. The custom originated as a penance imposed by the abbot in 1159 on three hunters who killed a hermit. Their lives were spared on condition that each year they and their descendants built a hedge on the foreshore that would withstand three tides.

pews designed to seat 2,000 people – are pure Georgian, put in at the period when the town was growing rich from whaling. The galleries are reached by extraordinary staircases and the building is illumi-nated by skylights exactly like those of an early 19th-century man-o'-war, which is not surprising since they were constructed by ships' carpenters. There is no altar; instead, there is a plain Communion table placed there under an ordinance of Elizabeth I and which no one has seen any reason to remove since. The three-decker pulpit is a masterpiece.

The town is spread out below, with the twin piers at the mouth of the Esk roughly facing due north. The river makes a sharp boundary between the medieval town on the East Cliff, and the largely 19th-century creation called West Cliff. Some of the streets in East Cliff, those about Church Street, for example, are getting on for 1,000 years old and cover sites that were occupied at the time of the first abbey. There is Grape Lane, formerly called Grope Lane because it was so dark, all higgledy-piggledy buildings and bowed shop-fronts. A plaque on one of the houses announces that this was the lodging of the great circumnavigator and cartographer, Captain James Cook. The ships that carried him on his explorations of the Pacific, the *Endeavour*, the *Resolution* and the *Adventure*, were

WICK *Highland*

Rocky headlands shelter Wick Bay from the full fury of North Sea storms and encouraged this small, solid town's development as a busy fishing port at the end of the 18th century. In 1786 the British Fishery Society founded what became known as the Burgh of Pultney-town on the south bank of the River Wick. Its broad, straight streets and tree-lined squares were planned by Thomas Telford, the civil engineer best known for his roads, bridges and canals.

Telford also built a river-mouth harbour that was later modernised by Thomas Stevenson, one of whose breakwaters failed to survive an exceptionally violent storm. Scathing criticism may well have prompted the engineer's son, Robert Louis Stevenson, author of *Treasure Island*, to label Wick as 'the bleakest of God's towns on the bleakest of God's bays'.

Pultneytown merged with Wick in 1902, creating what was then the largest town in Scotland north of Inverness. Wick has been a royal burgh since 1589, but its roots go right back to the Viking era. The town's name means 'bay' in the old Norse language.

Andrew Carnegie, the great Scottish philanthropist, helped finance the library and museum which bear his name. The museum's exhibits include an effigy believed to depict St Fergus, Wick's patron saint. The figure came from the old parish church when it was demolished in 1830.

A monument on South Head recalls James Bremner, the 19th-century engineer born in the tiny village of Keiss, halfway between Wick and John o'Groats. His round-fronted house overlooks the harbour, and was built by raising a single-storey building to make way for a ground floor.

The clifftop path can be followed down the coast to the Castle of Old Wick, a medieval ruin perched on a narrow finger of rock flanked by deep, wave-lashed ravines. Brig o'Trams, a few hundred yards away, is a sea-carved arch 300 ft high.

The road to John o'Groats skirts Sinclair's Bay, a long sweep of sand overlooked from the south by Noss Head and its lighthouse. On the cliffs are the ruins of Girnigoe and Sinclair castles.

WINSLOW *Buckinghamshire*

Were it not for a notice at the entrance that tells how Winslow is twinned with the town of Cours-la-Ville in France, the newcomer might easily think he was coming into a pretty and not over-populous village. The effect is strengthened by a group of very village-like cottages, some thatched, some pantiled and with little flights of steps running up to the front doors. There are a lot of chestnuts and poplars, and, peeping through and over them, the topmost windows of a fairly substantial manor house.

A closer glance reveals that 'fairly' is not the qualification for the substance of Winslow Hall. It is very grand, very formal – so much so that all by itself it dispels any notion that its town might be a village. Only lightly guarded from the road by a creeper-covered wall and a front garden that would be no larger if the house were in a city, it rears its gracious red-brick front with the three rows of immaculately placed windows topped by four tall chimney stacks, that from a certain angle makes the building slightly reminiscent of a turn-of-the-century liner. It is simple and, despite its size, restrained; a gentleman's residence, as a discreet inscription over the front door proclaims. It reads: 'William Lowndes, 1700', or rather, 'AD MDCC'. Sir William Lowndes, Secretary of the Treasury under a number of monarchs, was described by Britain's first Prime Minister, Sir Robert Walpole, as

STILL WATERS *Only the lonely cry of the gulls and the whispering creak of the moored fishing boats disturb the stillness of Wick harbour. But before this stillness descends the harbour is bustling with activity as heavily laden fishing boats discharge their catches. The fish are then packed in ice and despatched to the southern markets – and a still beauty enwraps the harbour.*

being 'as able and honest a Servant as ever the Crown had', and a glance at the house he built would seem to confirm the accolade. Very likely the architect was Christopher Wren and, if so, it is the only example of his country houses to have survived unaltered.

As befits so small a town, everything – apart from the Hall – is in miniature. All of one end of the Market Square is occupied by a single shop, a saddler's and horsey sports shop with notices pasted on the door offering stabling, ponies, hay and Jack Russell terriers for sale. A baker's shop and an estate agent's, both bow fronted, and a bank or two, just about completes the commercial centre, a lovely mixture of strawberry brick, patterned tiles and cream plaster. Just off the Square, however, there are a couple of old pubs, almost cheek-by-jowl: The Bell, black and white, and with big, welcoming windows, and The George, with a fantastical, wrought-iron balcony.

Just down the road is the Church of St Laurence, of worn, pale stone, and with paths and fences economically composed of old gravestones. It contains some medieval wall-paintings, and, on the hour, its clock sweetly chimes a hymn tune over the lanes of black-and-white and old red-brick cottages that surround it. Buried among the lanes is the Cattle Market – again small – and next door, off Bell Alley, is Keach's Meeting House, which is miniscule. Built as a Strict Baptist Chapel between 1625–95, its stern but cosy interior remains practically unaltered. Keach, its founder, published a collection of hymns and introduced the idea of community hymn singing.

WIRKSWORTH *Derbyshire*

Jammed high up in a corner of the Ecclesbourne Valley, Wirksworth has been described as lying 'in a bottom eternally overhung with smoke from the lead and calamine works, the principal covering being here and there broken into pillars of white smoke from smelting mills'. At least, this was how it appeared in 1806, by which time its mining industries were already on the wane, and textiles, including the manufacture of Government red tape (used to tie up bundles of official papers), were already beginning to replace them. But now the smoke has blown away, and some of the ancient prosperity too, and present-day Wirksworth appears as a slightly faded stone market town, attractively stacked on rising levels, and with a maze of ancient lanes climbing anyhow up the hillside beyond the Market Place.

The countryside about is honeycombed with tunnels and dotted with old spoil heaps. Some of them are very old indeed, for the Romans mined lead in the area, and sent it home – drainpipes made from Derbyshire lead have been discovered in Pompeii. All through the Dark Ages, and through all history, in fact, almost until the last mine closed in 1827, lead from Wirksworth was a product vital not only to the town, but to the nation as well. But cheaper, imported ores killed it in the end, and now all that remains of the industry is the Moot Hall, where the Barmote Courts were held. These adjudicated in the curious mixture

of laws and customs that ruled the lives of the peakrills – the lead miners. Also in the Moot Hall is a standard lead-measure of Henry VIII's reign; it holds 14 Winchester pints, a Winchester pint being twice as much as the usual kind.

But one kind of mining – limestone quarrying – continues to flourish in the area, as is apparent from the yawning chasms bitten into the hillside above the town. In addition to its role in industrial development, Wirksworth was a centre of Christian worship as long ago as the 7th century, as is apparent from the Saxon coffin lid on show in the glorious 13th-century cruciform Church of St Mary. It was discovered beneath the chancel in 1820, and is covered with vivid depictions of episodes from the life of Christ.

Then, too, there is the town centre, the Market Place and the major streets about it, a collection of disciplined Georgian houses and inns in weathered but unwearying local stone. This is the part of the town in which Richard Arkwright kept a shop before he invented his spinning machine, and in which George Eliot set her best-known novel, *Adam Bede*.

Each year at Whitsuntide, Wirksworth's continuity is celebrated at its Well Dressing Ceremony, a custom it shares with other Derbyshire towns and villages.

WISBECH *Cambridgeshire*

In the flat landscape of the fens many towns and villages choose to signal their presence with a tall church tower or lofty spire. Not so Wisbech, with the result that from whichever direction you approach, you are in the town almost before you know it. And, if the approach is along the Peterborough road in spring, you emerge from blossom-decked orchards alongside a broad, grassy-banked river from the far shore of which rises the mellow brick of one of the finest Georgian streets in England.

The river is the Nene. The street is the North Brink. This is no formal terrace of symmetrical look-alikes, as can be found in Bath. Its delight is its variety, a subtle blend of three and four-storey structures, low windows, sash windows, mellow-toned stone and brick with tall 18th-century warehouses at the town end, and cottages at the other. Beyond the cottages, the tall building with an imposing pediment is the local brewery, which dates from 1790.

But of all the buildings on the North Brink – or indeed the whole of Wisbech – pride of place goes to Peckover House. It was built in 1722 and is named after the family who owned it from the end of the 18th century until 1948, when the Honourable Alexandrina Peckover presented it to the National Trust. It was a particularly appropriate gift, since one of the founders of the National Trust, Octavia Hill (1838–1912), was born in another Georgian house – marked by a plaque – on South Brink, almost facing Peckover House.

The Brinks come together at the Town Bridge, which is overlooked by an ornate Victorian memorial commemorating Thomas Clarkson (1760–1846), the Wisbech-born campaigner for the abolition of slavery.

Standing under a 68 ft high canopy and spire, he looks rather like Prince Albert under his canopy in Kensington Gardens – which is not surprising, since both memorials were the work of the same man, Sir Gilbert Scott. It is a fine Victorian monument to a fine Victorian man. His contemporaries – who knew a good man when they saw one – rated Clarkson at least the equal of William Wilberforce, his co-leader of the abolitionist movement.

With his back to the river, Clarkson looks over the centre of the town to the Crescent with the church beyond. The Crescent, together with Union Place and Ely Place, forms an oval of Regency houses surrounding a central garden and a large Regency villa called The Castle. Villa and garden occupy the site of Wisbech Castle, built by William the Conqueror. It was from this castle that King John set out on his fateful journey across The Wash in which he lost the crown jewels and contracted the fever from which he died.

Opposite The Castle is Museum Square, which leads to the churchyard. The museum, which dates from 1847, owes its lopsided look less to age than the fact that it stands on the filled-in moat of William's castle which has suffered a certain amount of subsidence. The church may not tower over the town, but it certainly spreads itself, being nearly as broad as it is long. It dates mainly from the 14th century and looks it – particularly from the outside. Inside is a brass of 1401 commemorating Sir Thomas de Braunstone. It is

9 ft long, one of the biggest in England.

A few yards east of the church is the Market Place, one of two. The market is busy all week, becoming super-busy on Saturdays when shoppers from the surrounding countryside throng to its colourful stalls.

On the other side of the river, at the eastern end of the North Brink, is the open space known as the Old Market, where produce auctions are held on Saturdays.

Two markets are not too much for a town surrounded by the most fertile land in Britain, if not the world. With such riches available, it is not surprising that over the centuries every effort was made to export them. Consequently, Wisbech has been a port since Norman times – at first on the Ouse, and later on the Nene. The name Wisbech, incidentally, means town on the Wise (or Ouse) bece, *bece* being Old English for stream. The switch from Ouse to Nene occurred not because of any movement on the part of the town, but because the rivers changed courses – or had their courses changed by one or other of the indefatigable improvers seeking fame and fortune by draining the fens.

Today, in spite of its name, Wisbech stands firmly on the Nene. And just north of the Old Market, on the opposite bank of the river, is the Corporation Quay, nearly a mile long, where seagoing ships dock after a 9 mile voyage upstream from The Wash and the North Sea. Ships of up to 2,000 tons trade into Wisbech, mostly from northern Europe.

ELEGANCE ON THE BRINK
Peckover House, on the North Brink of the River Nene in Wisbech, was purchased by the Peckovers, a family of Quaker bankers, in the latter half of the 18th century. As befits its former owners, the exterior is elegant and solid, with no aristocratic fripperies, which makes the exuberant and elaborate carving and plasterwork of the interior all the more breathtaking. The garden is a rare Victorian survival, with borders, summerhouses, oranges fruiting under glass and one of the largest and oldest maidenhair trees in the country. Peckover House now belongs to the National Trust, and is open on certain days of the week in summer.

JOHN RUSKIN

The first thing an event in life by my nurse of Friar's Crag, on

I remember as was being taken to the brow Derwent Water.

SECULAR GLASS Stained glass is not exclusive to churches. This portrait of John Ruskin is in the Royal Oak Hotel, Keswick.

LIVING HISTORY IN OUR STREETS

A guide to some of the interesting and curious works of man that over the centuries have given character to the country towns of Britain.

ALMSHOUSE

Private charity has provided almshouses as homes for the poor, and usually old, in Britain for centuries. Although the poor laws of the 18th and 19th centuries, and the creation of the National Health Service in 1948, supplemented the services of almshouses, many still operate, and new ones are still being founded.

The first almshouses may have been set up in Saxon times. In the Middle Ages they were founded by monarchs, nobles and the Church, but after the Reformation the guilds, individual wealthy merchants and others endowed them, too. A plaque carrying the history and purpose of the foundation is set on the wall of many almshouses.

Almshouses were among the first buildings to be constructed as terraces, which helped keep down building costs.

The oldest almshouse still functioning in England is the Hospital of St Cross in Winchester, Hampshire, founded in 1136 by Bishop Henry of Blois, brother of King Stephen. Some of its pensioners still wear a uniform of black gowns and medieval caps, while others wear mulberry-coloured gowns, commemorating Cardinal Beaufort, who enlarged the institution in 1445.

Browne's Hospital in STAMFORD, Lincolnshire, was endowed by a rich wool merchant in the 15th century to care for 'ten poore men and two women'. Also in Stamford are the Burghley Almshouses, originally founded by Benedictine monks in the 11th century, but refounded and enlarged in the 16th century by Lord Burghley, Elizabeth I's treasurer.

In 1549, Elizabeth's favourite, Robert Dudley, refounded the almshouses built by the guilds in WARWICK, Warwickshire, in 1383, and they are still known by Dudley's title – the Lord Leycester (Leicester) Hospital. The Maison Dieu (or Bede House) at MELTON MOWBRAY, Leicestershire, and the Matron's College for widows of the clergy in Salisbury, Wiltshire, are examples of 17th-century almshouses.

AQUEDUCT

For 80 years, from the 1760s until the arrival of the railways, canals were the arteries of the Industrial Revolution, the cheapest way of transporting raw materials and manufactured goods in bulk. The first major canal in Britain opened in 1761. It was built by the millwright turned engineer James Brindley for the 3rd Duke of Bridgewater, to move coal from his mines at Worsley, Lancashire, to Manchester, and named after the duke.

Aqueducts, iron troughs supported on a series of arches, conveyed the canals, and the craft plying them, across valleys.

One of the most impressive canal engineering feats is the 1,007 ft long Pont Cysyllte aqueduct near LLANGOLLEN, Clwyd. Designed by Thomas Telford and William Jessop, it opened in 1805 and carries the Llangollen branch of the Shropshire Union Canal on 18 stone piers 127 ft above the valley of the River Dee.

A three-arched aqueduct takes the Peak Forest Canal 100 ft above the River Goyt at Marple, Greater Manchester. In the same area, the unique swing aqueduct at Barton upon Irwell carries Brindley's Bridgewater Canal over the Manchester Ship Canal. It pivots from an island in the ship canal to allow ships on that waterway to pass. The present aqueduct, completed in 1894, replaced Brindley's original, the first in Britain.

Just west of BRADFORD-ON-AVON, Wiltshire, the elegant 300 ft long Avoncliff aqueduct, designed by John Rennie in 1804, carries the Kennet and Avon Canal over the River Avon.

ARCH

The simplest way of building a doorway or window is by post and lintel, two uprights with a beam across the top. Until the development of modern building materials, the opening could not be very wide, because the weight of the walls and roof above thrust directly downwards and could collapse the doorway. The Greeks and other ancient peoples partly solved the problem by supporting the lintels with load-bearing pillars placed at intervals underneath, but the Romans found a more elegant solution – the arch. The curve at the top of the arch transmits the weight it bears sideways as well as downwards, reducing the strain. The discovery of that principle enabled the Romans to build large dome-roofed structures, and bridges with spans 100 ft long.

To make an arch, masons built up accurately cut stone blocks over a round-topped wooden frame. Wedge-shaped blocks covered the top. The last to be put in place was the keystone, in the top centre. It locked all the blocks together so that the wooden support could be removed.

Arches have altered in shape over the centuries as a result of developments in building techniques and changing fashion. Each style is associated with a particular era, so a glance at the doors and windows is a good guide to a building's age. Churches and castles may, however, mix several styles, reflecting rebuilding, restoration and additions.

Six main styles are common in Britain:
Saxon (600–1066) The arch is narrow and the stones are roughly hewn and often of uneven sizes. The top is semicircular, occasionally made from a single stone. There is a good example of a Saxon doorway at Brixworth Church, Northamptonshire.
Norman or Romanesque (1066–1190) The arches are rounded, elaborately

FOR THE OLD *The Elizabethan almshouses at Audley End, near Saffron Walden, are still lived in.*

carved and built of small, trimmed stones. Canterbury Cathedral has a Norman porch and stairway.

Early English (1190–1300) Graceful pointed arches and tall, narrow 'lancet' windows distinguish this style. There are multiple lancet windows in Hereford Cathedral.

Decorated (1300–1490) The arches are large, pointed, elaborately carved and ornamented. Each large window is divided into several smaller ones by tracery work – delicate bars of stone running horizontally or vertically, or shaped to form patterns. There are good examples in Exeter Cathedral.

Perpendicular (1380–1490) Arches are still pointed, but less markedly than in previous styles. Windows are larger, and tracery is at its most ornate. York Minster has windows with Perpendicular tracery.

Renaissance (1550–1830) Church arches are once again rounded. Windows, usually rectangular, are framed by raised and prominent surrounds, sometimes heavily carved and decorated, sometimes austerely classical.

FRAMED *A Georgian arch frames the courtyard of Clifton House, King's Lynn.*

AREA

In the 18th and 19th centuries, whole streets of tall terraced houses were designed, building upwards to make most use of the ground space and to obtain light. The ground floor was often raised above street level to obtain a better outlook and perhaps fresher air. This arrangement allowed more light into basements, which had a paved area in front, approached by a flight of steps from the street. A gate at the head of the steps formed part of the iron railings which divided the house from the street, and extended to the front door on either side of a set of steps. The basement was the powerhouse of the Victorian dwelling – the place where the servants heated water, laundered, cooked and cleaned, and from which they answered bells to supply the needs of the family above.

ARMS

The earliest coats of arms were embroidered on cloth surcoats worn over the armour of knights in the Middle Ages. They identified the wearer in battle or tournament, and were then, as now, prized, because the right to display a coat of arms was granted by the monarch.

Arms often commemorated some personal quality or daring deed of their bearer or his ancestors. Many of the proud possessors displayed their arms in stone on the outside of their houses or of churches on their lands, or had them painted on huge wooden panels inside.

PEEBLES' PRIDE *Tweed salmon feature in the town's coat of arms.*

After the Reformation in the 16th century, large representations of the Royal Arms began to appear in English churches, as a reminder of royal authority over the newly founded Church of England.

From the 15th century, the award of coats of arms was no longer linked only to military prowess. Many guilds of craftsmen, and towns and cities were given the right to bear arms, which were displayed on guildhalls, and on town halls as at ARUNDEL, West Sussex, and PEEBLES, Borders.

ASHLAR

Square-edged, smooth-faced stone, cut with precision and usually laid in close-fitting regular courses, is called ashlar. The Saxons built with uncut or roughly hewn stone, but after the Norman Conquest higher standards of masonry were introduced from France. Their arrival paved the way for the magnificent achievements of the craftsmen who built the Gothic churches and cathedrals from the 12th to the 16th centuries.

Bricks were widely available from the 16th century onwards, but ashlar was still chosen for many kinds of building, because of its elegant appearance and its strength. Often, it was used as a facing to cover brick or other materials.

Examples of fine ashlar work include the impressive limestone spire of the 14th-century tower of All Saints Church in OAKHAM, Leicestershire, and the ashlar-faced Georgian church of St Peter and St Paul, built to John Bastard's design in 1748 in BLANDFORD FORUM, Dorset.

BARGE BOARD

Wooden boards known as barge boards, verge boards or gable boards are fixed beneath the eaves of gables and following their slope to protect the ends of the rafters from the weather. Most barge boards are plain, but many older ones are carved with scrollwork and or pierced designs. Some end below in decorative pendants and above in finials, or spikes.

Decorated barge boards appear frequently on the timber-framed buildings of the west Midlands and the north-west. The 15th-century Feathers Hotel in LUDLOW, Shropshire, has fine examples, each capped with a beautifully carved wooden finial. So do Rufford Old Hall, Lancashire, and Bramall Hall, Greater Manchester.

BOLLARD

Originally, bollards were posts of wood or iron on quays, to which ships' mooring ropes were secured. But the word has come to mean similar posts set up inland as barriers to keep vehicles out of pedestrian areas, away from buildings or monuments, or to mark the limits of road islands.

In 1746, bollards were put at either end of the narrow, cobbled Church Lane in LEDBURY, Hereford and Worcester, to protect people on foot, and the fine Tudor black-and-white houses, from the heavy coaches of the day.

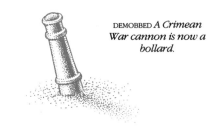

DEMOBBED *A Crimean War cannon is now a bollard.*

Early in the 19th century, the fear that Napoleon might invade Britain led to the production of cannon on a huge scale. Once the scare was over, many of the cast-iron cannon barrels were removed from service and put to new use as bollards. In ROTHESAY, on the Isle of Bute, Strathclyde, Battery Place was the site of a shore battery during the Napoleonic Wars. Muzzles from three of the cannon have been turned into bollards to protect one of the approaches to the pier.

In Bristol, Avon, there are four bronze bollards outside the 18th-century Exchange building. They are called 'nails', possibly because of their shape. Once merchants had concluded a transaction, money was placed on top of one bollard – which gave rise to the expression 'payment on the nail'.

BOND

See brick.

BOUNDARY MARKS

Between the 5th century and 1066, the Saxons drew much of the map of England as we know it. They created the parishes and shires, and their successors the Normans kept the Saxon system, eventually extending it to Wales and Scotland.

Often, the limits of a parish were designated by inscribed stones, such as the one at the top of the High Street in Cookham, Berkshire, or by an existing landmark such as a milestone.

Ancient customs to assert these boundaries still survive; the Rogationtide ceremony of 'beating the bounds' is one of them. Clergy and officials walk round the edges of the parish, and landmarks showing its limits are beaten with long willow canes by children of the church choir or church school, as a reminder to participants and onlookers of where the boundaries lie.

The West Saxons set up the first shires in the 7th century, and the idea spread throughout the country from Wessex. Often the shires were based on old kingdoms – for instance, Kent, Sussex (land of the South Saxons) and Essex (land of the East Saxons). Devon corresponded to the old Celtic kingdom of Dumnonia.

The Saxon and Norman shire boundaries lasted until new administrative counties were created in the 19th century. Many of the original names have been kept, though others – such as Middlesex –

officially disappeared after further reforms in 1972. Some old county boundary marks still exist, including the Four Shire Stone off the A44 just east of Moreton-in-Marsh, Gloucestershire; it marks the spot where Gloucestershire, Oxfordshire, Warwickshire and Worcestershire met before the counties were reorganised. An ancient stone pedestal with a domed top beside the B2080 between Tenterden, Kent, and RYE, East Sussex, denotes the old Kent-Sussex border.

In Scotland and northern England, monarchs often gave land to a community in recognition of its loyalty in war. These Common Lands, with their attendant rights, were jealously guarded by townsfolk and burghers. Common Riding ceremonies still take place, for example, in Selkirk, Borders. They include the 'riding of the marches', in which local officials ride on horseback around the boundaries (marches) of the Common Lands, to emphasise their extent.

BRICK

The Romans were Britain's first builders in brick, but the art of brickmaking disappeared following the collapse of the Roman Empire in the 5th century. It was reintroduced to England in the 14th century by Flemish refugees or agents of the Hanseatic League of merchants in East Anglia, where it was often used in combination with flint for major buildings. Tattershall Castle, Lincolnshire, built in the 15th century, is one of the most splendid and important examples of medieval brickwork in Britain. Stone is used only for window and door frames, and a little for decoration.

By the 16th century, brick was rapidly replacing timber-frame construction as a means of building homes. It was much more resistant to the fires that regularly destroyed large areas of towns, and as timber had become scarce, it was almost as cheap. Burghley Almshouses in STAMFORD, Lincolnshire, were rebuilt in brick at that time.

Sometimes the timber frames were kept and bricks were used only as infilling between the timbers, in place of highly combustible and fragile wattle-and-daub. This was known as brick nogging, and examples include houses in Grope Lane, SHREWSBURY, Shropshire. Often, the bricks were set in a herring-bone pattern.

Over the next 300 years or so, the use of brick spread inexorably, and even the

Brick Taxes imposed between 1784 and 1850 could not halt its advance. By 1880, brick had become almost the universal building material in England and Wales.

A brick laid so that only an end appears on the wall face is called a header. One laid so that its side can be seen is a stretcher. The arrangements of bricks in courses or layers are called bonds. In all types of brickwork, the courses are laid so that the vertical edges of the bricks in one course do not line up with those in the courses above or below. That form of interlocking means there are no vertical joins more than one course high to weaken the wall or make it unstable. English bond consists of courses entirely of headers alternating with those entirely of stretchers; it is the strongest bond. The more decorative and popular Flemish bond has alternating headers and stretchers in each course. Header bond is laid entirely as headers, and stretcher bond, similarly, has only stretchers. Bricks with ends specially fired to give them a metallic colour are used with other bricks to produce the diamond patterns of diaper bond.

Roman and medieval brick building usually have random patterns of bonds, and the bricks themselves vary considerably in size – anything from 6×6 in. to 12×8 in. After 1477, there were attempts to standardise bricks at various lengths and widths, but height was rarely controlled. In 1936 the British house brick was standardised at $8\frac{3}{4} \times 4\frac{3}{16} \times 2\frac{5}{8}$ in. Since metrication the standard has been $215 \times 102.5 \times 65$ mm.

BRIDGE

Place names such as Bideford, Devon, Woodbridge, Suffolk, and Tonbridge, Kent, are reminders that many of the earliest settlements grew up around river crossings. Britain's oldest surviving bridges – some of them were built 2,000 years ago – are simply massive natural stone slabs laid on piers of piled-up stones.

Pack-horse bridges are made of stone and are supported by one or more rounded arches. They got their name because, until the canals and railways of the Industrial Revolution, most goods in bulk that needed to be transported long distances were carried by teams of pack-animals. The Romans introduced this form of bridge to Britain, and it was still being built until the 18th century. The fine 17th-century Holme Bridge on the outskirts of BAKEWELL, Derbyshire, is typical. It is narrow, with low parapets that would not obstruct the load-carrying panniers of the pack-animals, narrow humped arches, and triangular recesses into which pedestrians could duck if they encountered a pack-train while crossing.

Many notable stone bridges were built in Britain in the Middle Ages by the Church or private benefactors. Old London Bridge (1176–1209), with its tunnel-like 'street' of five-storey shops and houses resting on 19 pointed arches, though frequently 'falling down', lasted for more than 600 years, until it was replaced in 1831. The 14th-century bridge over the River Dee at LLANGOLLEN, Clwyd, was constructed for a Bishop of St Asaph, and is called one of the Seven Wonders of Wales.

A small chapel in which travellers could pray was a feature of the more important medieval bridges. One survives on the Town Bridge at BRADFORD-ON-AVON, Wiltshire, whose two central arches date from the 14th century.

PACKHORSE BRIDGE *Laden horses took precedence on narrow medieval bridges.*

When the first tollgate was authorised by law in England in 1346, the custom of levying tolls to raise money for bridge maintenance was already a time-honoured practice. The 13th arch from the City end of Old London Bridge was a tollgate, and there was another above, so river traffic under the bridge and road traffic over it could be charged.

Bridge-building was revolutionised in the 18th century by the use of iron. Its strength and durability allowed bridges made of it to carry heavier loads than those traditionally constructed of stone, and it could be used over distances previously too wide to span. The world's first all-iron bridge opened in 1780, and gave its name to Ironbridge, Shropshire. It was built in just three months by local ironmaster Abraham Darby, and still soars over the River Severn.

The principle of suspension bridges has been understood since prehistoric times, but it is only in the last 200 years or so that

IRON BRIDGE *The graceful bridge at Craigellachie was built in 1815 by Thomas Telford.*

MODERNISED *Bakewell's 600-year-old packhorse bridge has been widened to take modern traffic.*

it has been used for structures capable of carrying heavy traffic. In modern versions, the roadway, or deck, is suspended by steel hawsers from cables which pass over towers to anchor-points on the ground. One of the most unusual suspension bridges in Britain is at CONWY, Gwynedd. It was built by Thomas Telford and opened in 1826, and it has castellated support towers to harmonise with Conwy Castle near by. Close to it is Robert Stephenson's railway bridge, built in 1848 and made of two 424 ft wrought-iron tubes forming a single span. The fine three-arched stone bridge over the Severn at BEWDLEY, Hereford and Worcester, is another of Telford's many bridges, and dates from 1798.

Modern cantilever bridges, in which girders project from central piers to meet midway between them, or to support another section of bridge, were developed in the 19th century.

The Forth Railway Bridge, near Queensferry, Lothian, was built of iron between 1882 and 1890. It has main spans of 1,700 ft, which were the longest in the world when it was opened. All-steel bridges were first built in the 1870s, and concrete structures are a 20th-century innovation.

BOOTSCRAPERS

In the days of horse transport and unmade-up roads, even in town centres the bootscraper near the front door of a house was an essential piece of street furniture – the more so since no organised street cleaning was carried out until about 1850. These useful appliances took many forms, standing on pavements, or beside stone steps, fixed across a cavity in the wall of a house, or decoratively cast as part of an elegant set of railings.

BUILDING STONE

The great variety in colour and character of building stone is seen at its best in old country towns where stone buildings of

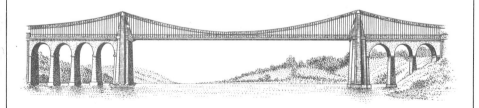

SUSPENSION BRIDGE *Thomas Telford completed the Menai Bridge in 1826.*

many periods stand in close proximity, often mellowed by time and weather. The main building stones are those derived from the limestones, sandstones and granites, with their many regional types, while other stones such as marble, slate and flint all have their special uses in building. Stones such as the fine-grained sandstones and limestones that can be cut easily at an angle are known as freestones.

Limestone A sedimentary rock consisting mainly of calcium carbonate. A great band of it, laid down in Jurassic times (135–190 million years ago), stretches across England from Dorset to Cleveland. It makes several fine building stones, such as the warm yellowish Bath stone, the paler Portland stone from Dorset, Ancaster stone from Lincolnshire, and Ketton stone, quarried near STAMFORD and used for many great houses. Oolitic limestone (or oolite), named for its resemblance to fish roe, is another Jurassic limestone. It is easily worked and good for precise cutting, shaping and carving, as in several Oxford colleges, and its honey colour gives a warmth to the Cotswold towns. The older limestones of Wales, central Scotland and the Pennines are harder and greyish in colour. Marble, a limestone which has been altered by great heat and pressure, is harder still and variously marked. It takes a high polish, and is used in sculpture and for facing buildings.

Sandstone A sedimentary rock made mainly of quartz, and widespread in Britain. It is often coloured reddish-brown by iron oxide, and its various reds, pinks and browns give a distinctly regional character to buildings made of it. Millstone Grit, quarried in the Pennines and South Wales, is a hard, durable sandstone, once used for millstones. It is difficult to cut, giving rise to stark, grey, plain-cut stone buildings. Sarsen stones are blocks of extremely hard sandstone left scattered over the chalk Downs following erosion of overlying rocks. They were used by the prehistoric megalith builders, as at Stonehenge, and are now used largely for footings and floors.

COTSWOLDS *Gold-tinted limestone is the traditional fabric of Cotswold houses.*

CORNWALL *Granite walls and slate roofs are typical of houses in Cornish towns.*

Granite The hardest of building stones, usually cut into massive blocks or slabs. It is generally a coarsely crystalline rock formed from molten rock deep in the earth's crust, and consists mostly of quartz and feldspar, with some mica. Aberdeen, the 'Granite City', is built largely of granite from the 450 ft deep Rubislaw Quarry in the west of the city. In Cornwall the traditional style of house has granite walls and a slate roof. Several exceptionally fine granite building stones from the county include Penryn Granite. This has been used in many parts of the world. For instance, for the Fastnet Lighthouse off southern Ireland, and in the docks and harbours of Calcutta and Singapore, as well as in Britain. London's Penryn Granite buildings include the Old Bailey.

Slate A rock formed from clay or volcanic ash under pressure and heat. It cleaves easily into thin sheets for roofing material,

and is a particular feature of many Welsh towns, and of houses in Devon, Cornwall and the Lake District, all areas where it is quarried. In the 19th century, slate was a relatively cheap fireproof roofing material, and it came into widespread use with the great expansion of building, especially in the large industrial areas. Other rocks that split easily into sheets thin enough for roofing are loosely called slates. They include Cotswold slate, a hard, durable Jurassic limestone, and some flagstones or tilestones, both types of sandstone.

Ragstone (*or rag*) A hard, rubbly sedimentary rock used roughly cut for building. For example, Kentish Rag, found in the Weald of Kent, was used for walls of early cottages and farm buildings there. See also cladding; flint.

BUILDING STYLES

Before the 16th century most town houses consisted of a timber framework with the spaces between the timbers filled with wattle and daub – a web of sticks plastered with clay and bonded with straw. Timber-framed houses continued to be built into the 18th century. Many fine examples, dating from the 15th century onwards, can be seen in towns such as Ledbury and

REGENCY *A plain stucco façade with wrought-iron balconies typifies the Regency style.*

GEORGIAN *Sash windows and porticoed doors mark these late Georgian houses at Farnham, Surrey.*

DURHAM *The local gritstone is the traditional building material of north-east England – even Durham Cathedral was built of it.*

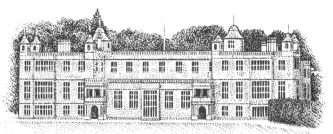

JACOBEAN *Audley End, near Saffron Walden, is one of Britain's finest Jacobean buildings.*

PEEBLES *Neidpath Castle, near the town, is a 14th-century Border tower house.*

Saffron Walden. Brick and stone came into increasing use during the 17th century, and building styles began to show more variety. The grand houses of the late Elizabethan and Jacobean periods were distinguished by elaborate roofs decorated with turrets, cupolas and balustrades, and by tall, mullioned windows. In the Stuart period, which followed, classical influences took hold – doorways were embellished with columns and porticoes and crowned with pediments. Next came the Georgian period, at first marked by a widespread use of moulding, carving and other decoration. But, as the 18th century advanced, styles became more restrained, retaining only the symmetry of classical design. Stucco, which came into increasing favour at this time, flourished to become one of the hallmarks of the subsequent Regency period.

CANNON

Old cannon stand sentinel in castles and museums and on town battlements all over Britain. Most date from the Napoleonic Wars, but some are much older. Those at SOUTHWOLD, Suffolk, are 16th century, and the mortar (short-muzzled wide-bore cannon) known as 'Roaring Meg' at Castle Green, Hereford, Hereford and Worcester, was used by Cromwell's troops against Goodrich Castle, near ROSS-ON-WYE, during the Civil War.

In most essentials, cannon changed little between the 14th century, when they were first used in Europe, and the 19th century. But then a whole series of improvements led to the development of the 'modern' field gun. Unlike earlier forms of artillery, it is loaded by the breech at the barrel end nearer the gunner, instead of by the muzzle, and fires an explosive shell. Such field guns were in service by the mid-1860s, and superseding other types.

Many outdated cannons then became memorials to the success of local regiments. For instance, at CAERNARFON Castle, Gwynedd, in the Royal Welch Fusiliers Museum, there is a gun captured in the Crimean War at the Battle of Alma in 1854.

CARTOUCHE TABLETS

Memorial tablets, surrounded by scrolls in highly ornamental baroque style, are often seen on the inside and outside of churches and on tombstones. The finest examples date from the 17th and 18th centuries and are usually carved in marble. The round or oval centre plaque is convex, and inscribed with fine Roman lettering. The surrounds are lavishly carved with intricate strapwork and embellishments of flowers, foliage and seashells, and often incorporate armorial crests and military emblems. Cartouche tablets commemorating local families or notable parishioners are often seen on the transept walls of larger churches.

CASTLE

Castles were virtually unknown in Britain before the Norman Conquest, but in the following 500 years about 2,000 were constructed. Many were built close to existing settlements, either to protect them or control them, others became the focus of new settlements. In some cases the settlement, too, was fortified and encircled by walls linked to those of the castle, as at CHEPSTOW, Gwent, and CONWY, Gwynedd. The first Norman castles were known as motte-and-bailey castles – the motte was a flat-topped earthen mound on which stood a wooden tower, while the bailey was a courtyard protected by a ditch and timber stockade. Stone began to replace wood in the century following the Conquest: the

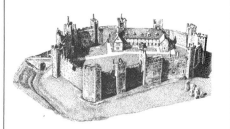

FRAMLINGHAM *This castle has no central keep, instead there are 13 wall towers.*

tower became a stone keep and the stockade was replaced by the curtain wall – its gate protected by gatehouse, drawbridge and portcullis.

CHIMNEYS

Iron-Age huts and other primitive buildings relied simply on a hole in the roof to carry away the smoke from fires. Chimneys only began to appear in medieval times. The earliest examples usually consisted of a single stack built on to the outside of the building, keeping as clear of the thatch as possible. Building with brick made for safer houses, with brick chimney stacks built into the pitched roof. By Tudor times, in larger houses the chimney came into its own, becoming a prominent feature of the vertical style of the time, often with simple spiral designs. In Elizabethan houses chimney stacks became larger and highly decorative, with intricate zig-zag, diamond pattern and barley sugar designs, and ornately shaped chimneys. With classical styles of building, chimney stacks generally became plainer and were usually squared, with a projecting ridge at the top. In many 18th-century houses a parapet gave a classical outline to the building, concealing the chimneys. Prominent stacks came into fashion again in Victorian times, when chimney pots also became popular. They were a major product of the potteries industry and were fitted to the growing armies of terraced town houses requiring several high stacks and a separate pot for each flue, to disperse the smoke from coal fires.

CLADDING

An extra layer of suitably weather-resistant material on the outside of a building gives it added protection in Britain's changeable climate. Over the centuries, craftsmen have devised many forms of this cladding.

Plain plastering Tough plaster, made of sand and lime mixed with oxhair, was spread all over the exterior of a timber-framed building from the late Middle Ages onwards.

Pargeting (or parging or parge work) From the reign of Elizabeth I until the mid-18th century, plain plaster was often worked into highly decorative patterns by using moulds or sharp-pointed implements on it before it dried. The technique is called pargeting, and it is common on

PARGETING *Decorative plasterwork of this type is an East Anglian craft.*

SHIP-LAGGING *Cladding with overlapping planks is common in the Kentish Weald.*

TILE-CLADDING *Houses like this are found in Lewes and other Sussex towns.*

timbered buildings in eastern England. Good examples include the Ancient House in Ipswich, Suffolk, built in 1567, and houses in Church Street, SAFFRON WALDEN, Essex, and High Street, Ashwell, Hertfordshire.

Rough casting When rough casting was developed in Tudor times, two coats of plaster, mixed with bullock's or goat's hair to stop cracking, were spread over the building's walls. The outer layer was roughened by throwing on fine shingle mixed with lime. Pebble dash is a modern version. The animal hair is left out, and pebbles or stone chips are sprayed on to the second coat of plaster before it sets.

Weather-boarding Wooden boards nailed or pegged horizontally on the outside of buildings appeared in the late 16th century. At first, oak or elm was used. Later, those woods were replaced by cheaper imported pine or fir. Often the boards overlap, and sometimes the lower edge of each one is rabbeted (or rebated) with a step cut along it to receive the upper edge of the board below. Weather-boarding was particularly popular in the 16th century, and it can be seen on many buildings in Woodbridge, Suffolk, and Winchelsea, East Sussex. Sometimes the boarding covers only the upper storeys, and the ground-floor walls are faced with brick.

Ship-lagging (or ship-boarding) A form of weather-boarding in which both the upper and lower edge of each board is rabbeted. As its name suggests, it was copied from ship-building, and it was used on many Georgian houses – for instance, in Tenterden, Kent.

Clap-boarding An East Anglian technique. The boards overlap and are feathered – wider at the bottom than at the top. Their lower edges are often chamfered to round them.

Plain tile-cladding Plain roofing tiles hung on laths nailed or pegged to the wall-timbers gave good protection to the wattle-and-daub infilling of half-timbered buildings, and the idea spread rapidly once tiles were produced on a large scale, from the 17th century onwards. Scalloped lower edges and the use of different colours were later refinements. On buildings where the upper floors overhung the street, those storeys were often tile-clad, and a brick wall was added to protect the ground floor. La Trobes in the High Street at Reigate, Surrey, is a fine tile-clad, timber-framed 18th-century house. Mathematical tiles (or mechanical tiles or brick tiles) were moulded to imitate brick walls. They

were introduced in the mid-18th century and used throughout south-east England into the next century, as at LEWES, East Sussex. They were cheaper than bricks, and also avoided the Brick Taxes levied between 1784 and 1850.

Slate-cladding In areas where slate was plentiful, such as the Lake District, parts of Wales and Cornwall, it was used as a substitute for tile-cladding. Many slate-clad buildings still survive.

CLOCKS

Mechanical clocks were first used in churches and cathedrals probably as early as the 12th century and were without dials. They were timekeeping machines to give the signal for bells to be rung for prayers and curfew. Later they were adapted to ring a bell as well. Clocks with dials came later. The earliest ones have only one hand and show the hours and quarters only on the clockface. Mechanical figures, known as 'Jacks', or 'Jack of the Clock', became popular in the 16th century and were often mentioned by Shakespeare. At RYE, East Sussex, two gilded cherubs, known as 'Quarter Boys', were added to the 16th-century church clock in 1761. This is one of the oldest clocks in the country still functioning. At Wimborne Minster, Dorset, a grenadier which strikes the quarters with a hammer is mentioned in a poem by Thomas Hardy. Another famous figure, the 15th-century carved oak man-at-arms known as 'Southwold Jack', strikes a bell before services at St Edmund's Church, SOUTHWOLD, Suffolk. The invention of the pendulum in 1657 led to great improvements in the accuracy of clocks, and opened the way to a great era of clockmaking in the 18th century. Many clocks were installed in church towers, and turret clocks were built on guildhalls and market buildings. In the 19th century, the spread of factory working and the advent of railway travel put greater emphasis on accurate timekeeping. Public clocks appeared on civic buildings, office premises and shops, and as commemorative clock towers in town centres and parks. Many clocks were erected to mark such national events as Queen Victoria's Jubilees of 1887 and 1897. A fine example is the clock tower of 1887 at NEWMARKET, Suffolk.

COACHING INNS

The stage-coach system, which had its heyday in the early 19th century, could not

SERVICE ENTRANCE *Coaches drove through the tall gateway to the stable yard.*

have developed without a network of staging posts – coaching inns where tired teams of horses could be changed for fresh ones, and coach travellers obtain shelter, food and drink. Many of these inns remain largely unchanged. A wide arch leads from the street to an inner courtyard, with galleried rooms on one side of it, and stables on the other.

At the four corners of the entrance arch, set into the wall, are spur-stones, a type of circular bollard which protected the building from the stage coach's iron-rimmed wheels. The Norfolk Arms at ARUNDEL, West Sussex, the Three Swans at MARKET HARBOROUGH, Leicestershire, and the 15th-century George and Pilgrims at GLASTONBURY, Somerset, were all prosperous coaching inns. So was the 300-year-old Green Man at ASHBOURNE, Derbyshire, which has an unusual inn sign spanning the street.

By 1840, fast, regular stage-coach services linked Britain's main towns and cities. Six coaches a day left London for York, and the 197 mile journey took only 28 hours; road improvements had helped to cut the time from one week in 1700. The Royal Mail was carried by coach from 1784 until 1846, when the railways took over. The mail coach, with only four passengers inside and no passengers or luggage on top, achieved great speed, and became a byword for regularity. On Thomas Telford's London-to-Holyhead road, mail coaches covered 100 miles in under 12 hours. The Post Office schedules allowed a time of five minutes for a change of horses at a coaching inn. Frequently, the switch took less than two minutes.

COAL-HOLE COVERS

Coal delivered in horse-drawn carts to Victorian terraced town houses was usually tipped from the sack straight into the basement coal cellar through a coal-hole in the pavement outside each house. The coal-hole, of about a foot in diameter, was covered by a heavy cast-iron lid with a raised pattern on the top, which gave it a non-slip surface. Some of these covers advertised the name of their manufacturer. Others displayed a pattern only. But these patterns are so varied and decorative that they have created interest among lovers of Victorian design and have been the subject of exhibitions of rubbings and of the covers themselves.

COB

This primitive building material was common in the Middle Ages and continued in use into the 19th century. A mixture of clay and chopped straw, sometimes including gravel and sand too, was built up layer by layer. Each layer was allowed to dry out thoroughly before the next was put on top of it.

However, the cob easily became weather-worn and crumbled. Because of that, and because most cob houses had no timber supports, the walls had to be thick – more than 2 ft wide – to last.

BASIC MATERIAL *The rounded look is typical of old cob-walled cottages.*

They were built on a stone or brick base that was often tarred on the outside, and covered with an overhanging, light roof, usually of thatch. There is an old saying in Devon: 'All cob wants is a good hat (roof) and a good pair of shoes (base).'

Cottages of cob abound in the West Country and in parts of the Chilterns, particularly Buckinghamshire. They are usually lime-washed to give added protection against weathering. Dockacre House in LAUNCESTON, Cornwall, is an example of larger cob building of the 17th century.

COBBLE

See flint, cobble and pebble.

COLUMN

The vertical pillar which supports the cross-members in classical architecture consists of a base and a cylindrical shaft topped by a capital. The decorative styles of these columns represent the different orders of classical architecture introduced by the Greeks, and later added to by the Romans. The first three, devised by the Greeks, are the Doric, Ionic and Corinthian. The Doric, the earliest in origin and the least ornate, is the most widely used. The Ionic, often with fluted shaft, is probably the most elegant. The Corinthian, which came from Athens, is the most

TO GOD'S GLORY *Norman carving on column capitals in Sherborne Abbey.*

florid. The Romans adapted these orders to their own ideas and added two more – the Tuscan, a simplified version of the Roman Doric, and the Composite, a mixture of Greek Ionic and Corinthian, which is the most elaborate. The capital, or head of the column, is the main distinguishing feature of each style. The Ionic is decorated with a scroll turned over at each end; the Corinthian has acanthus leaves, while both are combined in the Composite. These five orders were established in a book published in Italy in 1540, which laid down proportions and decorations in detail and set the standards for Renaissance and Neoclassical architecture.

COMMEMORATIVE PLAQUES

Plaques are fixed to houses and other buildings in which famous people lived or with which they were associated. In 1866 the Royal Society of Arts began the practice of setting up the now familiar blue plaques. There are about 400 in London alone, where the Greater London Council now looks after the scheme. In Britain as a whole there are hundreds more blue plaques, as well as many other tablets and inscriptions set up by local bodies.

CROSSES

Missionaries brought Celtic Christianity from Ireland to Wales and Scotland, and from Brittany to Cornwall, in the 5th century. Roman Christianity arrived in Kent with St Augustine in 597. As the faith spread, stone crosses became a feature of Christianised Britain. Some were fashioned from prehistoric standing stones, such as the one at Rudston, near Bridlington, Humberside. Others were put up to mark holy ground or boundaries, or the site at which a monk regularly preached. They were also set up as memorials to individuals or great events.

By late medieval times, every churchyard had a cross, and people often met around it to buy and sell goods. As markets became larger, they moved away from churchyards to other sites, such as town squares, and crosses were put up there, too.

CELTIC CROSSES *Carved stones in Wales and Scotland often record the deeds of kings and saints in the Dark Ages.*

Celtic crosses Elaborate crosses, with a circle representing eternity linking the four arms, are among the finest examples of Celtic art. St Columba landed from Ireland on the island of Iona, Strathclyde, in AD 363; Iona once had 360 Celtic crosses, but only three remain. The 14 ft Celtic cross at Carew, Dyfed, records the death in battle of an 11th-century Welsh ruler.

Pictish crosses The Picts of northern Scotland, who united with the Celtic Scots to form the Kingdom of Scotland in the 9th century, put up crosses, and fragments of some of them survive. The best-preserved is in the churchyard at Aberlemno, Tayside. It is a 6 ft slab from the 8th century, and has carvings of animals on one side and a battle scene on the other.

Saxon crosses Monumental crosses, up to 18 ft high and dating from the 7th and 8th centuries, are found mainly in northern Britain. The finest examples are those at Ruthwell, Dumfries and Galloway, and Bewcastle in Cumbria. They are carved with vine-leaf decoration and figures of Christ and the saints, and carry inscriptions in runes, the Anglo-Saxon alphabet.

Wayside crosses In the Middle Ages, stone crosses were often put up beside roads, at places where coffin-bearers rested on their way to a churchyard and prayers for the dead were said. The most famous are the Eleanor crosses, set up by Edward I between Harby, Nottinghamshire, and Westminster Abbey, to mark the resting-places of the funeral cortège of his wife Eleanor in 1290. There were once 12, and three have survived with restoration: at Geddington and Hardingstone, Northamptonshire, and Waltham Cross, Hertfordshire. They are ornately carved Gothic columns, topped by spires. There was an Eleanor cross in the forecourt at Charing Cross station, London (Charing is a corruption of the French *chere reine* – 'beloved queen'), but the present monument is Victorian.

Market crosses By the 13th century, many markets that assembled round a cross in a town street or square had acquired a roof. They were the forerunners of the stone or brick-built pavilions of the 15th to 18th centuries, which kept the name of market crosses.

MARKET CROSS *The octagonal cross at Chagford, Devon, is a Victorian replica.*

The octagonal market cross at MALMESBURY, Wiltshire, built around 1490, has ornate carvings, buttresses and statuettes.

Names such as Butter Cross or Poultry Cross recall specialised markets. The Butter Cross in the market square at OAKHAM, Leicestershire, is a fine example.

Market crosses became more elaborate with time. Open-air markets were eventually replaced in many towns by market houses or halls. These had open, arched ground floors where goods were sold, upper chambers for civic meetings, and sometimes a gaol for miscreants. There are market houses at CHIPPING CAMPDEN, Gloucestershire, built in 1627, LEDBURY, Hereford and Worcester, completed in 1655 and supported by 16 pillars of Spanish chestnut, and ROSS-ON-WYE, Hereford and Worcester.

BUTTER CROSS *Dairy produce was sold under the cross at Bingham, Nottinghamshire.*

MARKET HALL *Chipping Campden's Cotswold stone hall dates from 1627.*

Many crosses were rebuilt in neo-Gothic style in the 19th century. One was the cross, commemorated in the nursery rhyme, at Banbury, Oxfordshire. It was destroyed by Puritans as being 'Popish' in 1600, and replaced by the present six-sided monument in 1859.

Mercat crosses In many burghs in Scotland the Mercat cross (mercat is an old form of the word market) was a central place for meetings and proclamations from medieval times. The Mercat cross in the High Street, CRIEFF, Tayside, probably dates back to the 10th century. Its red sandstone is carved with interlacing patterns. The Mercat cross in Kirkcudbright, Dumfries and Galloway, was put up in 1610.

Churchyard crosses In many churches, processions through the churchyard are part of certain ceremonies, for example, Good Friday. The churchyard cross is often the destination. It is also a symbol of the holiness of the church ground and, in modern churches, a memorial to the dead

ELEANOR CROSS *The best of the three surviving royal crosses is at Gedlington, Northamptonshire.*

POULTRY CROSS *Salisbury poultry market was held at this cross.*

of two World Wars.

The crosses normally stand near the south porches of churches. Many old ones were destroyed, either by weather or during the Reformation or Civil War, but often the original steps up to the cross survive.

Plague crosses These rare churchyard crosses commemorate deliverance from plagues. One, in the churchyard at ROSS-ON-WYE, Hereford and Worcester, was erected by thankful survivors of an epidemic in 1637, and the inscription records the burial of 315 victims in a communal grave near by.

CRUCK FRAMING

Before England's forests largely disappeared, cut down to make ships, cruck framing was a widespread simple way of building, in use from the Middle Ages. Pairs of heavy, curved timbers, called crucks, were raised and set together to form arches. The tops of the arches were connected by a beam to make the ridge of the roof. Each cruck was cut from the trunk of a carefully chosen tree, to match when in position. The walls were then infilled, usually with wattle and daub, and the roof was thatched.

In the simplest cruck-framed cottages and barns, the shape of the building is determined by the cruck at each end. In more elaborate houses, the crucks support a framework of vertical wall timbers and pitched rafters that give a conventional shape.

Crucks were used for the upper storeys of some buildings until the 19th century. Most examples of cruck framing are found where the forest persisted longest: in northern and central England, and in Wales. The 15th-century Old Grammar School in LEDBURY, Hereford and Worcester, and the mid-14th-century hall of the White House in Aston Munslow, Shropshire, are large cruck-framed buildings. Part of the Red Lion Inn in Weobley, Hereford and Worcester, was once a separate cruck-

SIMPLE ARCH *Naturally curved timbers formed the frames of cruck houses.*

framed cottage. Another is the Barley Mow Inn at Long Wittenham, Oxfordshire.

DOOR KNOCKERS

The earliest door knockers were used on church doors. They were often associated with the right of sanctuary and protection from arrest for those pursued by enemies or by the law. This is more symbolic than accurate since the right of sanctuary, abolished in 1540, applied to any part of consecrated ground and was defined by crosses and other marks. Church door knockers were decorated with a lion or monster's head, which was put there to keep evil influences away from the building. These designs were continued on the knockers made for dwelling houses, and the lion's-head pattern in particular was produced in large quantities by the iron foundries at the end of the 19th century. Georgian and Regency door furniture produced door knockers in classical style including many in the shape of urns, another traditional pattern still much used. After 1840, with the Penny Post, letterboxes were added for the first time to many doors. At first they were usually vertical below the door knocker; the horizontal type came later, probably after 1856 when the slot in pillar boxes was also changed from vertical to horizontal.

WAY IN *Letterboxes, cast in iron or brass, first appeared in the 1840s.*

DOVECOTE

Until the 18th century, when root crops were first planted on a large scale as winter feed for cattle and other livestock, pigeons provided a prized source of scarce fresh meat during British winters. Landowners – including religious foundations – often had a dovecote (in Scotland, doocot) in which breeding pairs were kept. The adult birds were not normally eaten, but their unfledged young, called squabs, were. So were surplus eggs.

FRESH MEAT *Young pigeons were bred in dovecotes for winter meat.*

There were some 25,000 dovecotes in medieval Britain, housing more than a million pigeons and their offspring. Many were round buildings of brick or stone, with rows of nesting holes inside and a lantern-shaped entrance for the birds on top. In some, the nests containing squabs could be reached for collection from a ladder revolving round a central pole inside.

The Knights Templar built the round dovecote at Garway, Hereford and Worcester, in 1326; its 4 ft high walls enclose 666 pigeon holes. The rubble-built 16th-century Phantassie Doocot at East Linton in Lothian is beehive-shaped and has 544 stone nests. Another 16th-century dovecote, at Willington, Bedfordshire, is rectangular, with a stepped roof and 1,200 nesting sites arranged in tiers. The magnificent 17th-century dovecote on the Erddig estate near Wrexham, Clwyd, has been restored to working order complete with revolving ladder.

DRINKING FOUNTAINS

Many drinking fountains were set up in the streets of Britain's towns in the 19th century. They were often paid for by philanthropists or temperance societies, to allow people to slake their thirsts with water rather than beer or other forms of alcohol. Generally they are built of granite, marble or cast iron. Some are set against walls, while others are free-standing columns with a basin around the foot to provide a drinking trough for animals. Today, few are in working order, and most have lost their original iron cups on chains. Designs vary widely, severely classical to ornate. The fountains may commemorate a great event or a notable citizen, and many carry a morally uplifting inscription, such as the fountain in the Rothermarket at STRATFORD-UPON-AVON, Warwickshire. It was given to the town by Gordon Childs of Philadelphia, USA, to commemorate

Queen Victoria's Golden Jubilee in 1887, and bears a quotation from Shakespeare's *Timon of Athens*: 'Honest water which ne'er left man i' the mire.'

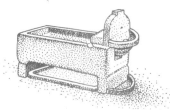

DOUBLING UP *The combined trough and fountain catered for man and horse.*

FOURSOME *Four people at a time could drink at this Victorian fountain.*

DRY *A canopy protects the fountain at Middleton in Teesdale.*

FIRE MARKS

These marks, which can be seen on the walls of some old buildings, are the symbols of the first fire insurance companies, which were founded at the end of the 17th century, after the Fire of London. The marks, which are made of metal, were fixed to the front walls of houses whose owners had insured against fire. They identified the house to the company's

firefighters, and included the insurance number of the owner. The symbol might be a bird with flaming wings (the Phoenix Fire Office), or a radiant sun with a human face (the Sun Fire Office), the clasped hands of the Friendly Society of Edinburgh or the thistle of the Caledonian Insurance. These and other companies developed the first organised fire-fighting services using mobile hand and foot-operated pumps during the 18th century. By 1800 they had horse-drawn fire engines and steam pumping equipment. It was not until the 1860s that fire services became the responsibility of local government.

FLINT, COBBLE AND PEBBLE

Locally available materials characterise the building styles of particular regions. Useful, but difficult to build with, these three types of local stone have been used in building from medieval times, often in combination with hewn stone, and later with brick. Usually the corners, and door and window frames of the building are of brick or stone, and the flints, cobbles or pebbles set in clay.

FLINT *Cut or whole flints are used for building in the chalk country.*

Flint nodules Lumps of silica (quartz) in which the crystals are so small that they cannot be seen with the naked eye occur, often in layers, in the chalk of southern and western England. They were used for building mainly in East Anglia and Hertfordshire, where there is little other local building stone. They formed hard, durable walls, and were either knapped (split) to give a flat outside face to the wall, or used whole. Flint often appears between courses of brick or stone, or in overall chequerwork, in which squares of stone or brick alternate with squares made of flint. Notable examples of flint chequerwork are the 15th-century Guildhall and Victorian town hall in KING'S LYNN, Norfolk, and the Church of St Edmund at SOUTHWOLD.

Cobble and pebble Rounded, usually water-worn stones, were used in much the same way as flints. Cobbles, more than 2½ in. in diameter, were frequently laid in courses. Cobbles were also used for road-paving, and Mermaid Street in RYE, East Sussex, and Church Lane in LEDBURY, Hereford and Worcester, are among the many fine examples that survive.

GABLE

A gable is the triangle-shaped flat area between the sloping sides at each end of a pitched roof. But it has also come to mean any similar ornamental feature, for example over a door or a dormer window. In the 16th century, the crow-stepped gable was introduced from Europe. Instead of being straight, the sides of 'triangle' rise to the apex in a series of narrowing steps. They extend beyond the edges and ridge of the roof, giving extra protection against wind and rain, as well as adding architectural interest. In Scotland, where such gables are common in many areas, they are called corbie steps, from the Scots word for a crow. Over the centuries, projecting gables became more elaborate. The Dutch gable has curved sides topped by a pedi-

CROW-STEPPED *This style of gabling, popular in Europe during the Renaissance, is common on stone-built houses in many parts of Scotland.*

DUTCH *Houses gabled in Dutch style are a feature of the Lincolnshire fens. This Dutch influence arose from trading links over the centuries.*

ment. It is found on 18th-century and later buildings in Lincolnshire and East Anglia, evidence of the area's long-standing trading links with Holland. Shaped gables have sides formed into a series of curves and, often, a rounded top. The ornate style may have been copied from the Low Countries, too. A hipped gable slopes backwards at the top to join the ridge of the roof.

GABLE BOARD

See barge board.

GARGOYLE

BEAUTY AND THE BEAST *This fantastic creature protects the magnificence of Oxford's 15th-century Magdalen College.*

MORE HUMAN *A less demonic-looking gargoyle sits atop Scotland's ruined Melrose Abbey.*

A grotesquely carved waterspout projecting from a roof or parapet. On cathedrals, churches and other great buildings of the Middle Ages, gargoyles demonstrate the imagination, skill and humour of the stonemasons, who created fantastic open-mouthed demons, birds, beasts and other creatures, and less alarming figures holding upturned pitchers. The gargoyles' main job is to direct rainwater from the roof clear of the walls. But they may have been given their bizarre appearance in the belief that they would frighten evil spirits away from the building. A company of gargoyles gapes down at the market square from the Church of St Lawrence in Lechlade, Gloucestershire, and there are other fine examples on BEVERLEY MINSTER, Humberside, the Lady Chapel of GLASTONBURY Abbey, Somerset, and ROMSEY Abbey, Hampshire.

GATES

Many country towns were once enclosed by defensive walls with fortified watchtowers and gatehouses. Heavily reinforced oak doors gave the only access to the town, and after a curfew was sounded these could be closed at night. Many remains of medieval and Tudor gatehouses still stand. Some towns, such as CAERNARFON and CONWY, in Gwynedd, also have substantial remains of the walls themselves. In others, street names such as Stonegate, Castlegate or Westgate are reminders of former fortified town gates. The 15th-century Hotspur tower at ALNWICK, Northumberland, the three remaining gatehouses of the 13th-century walled town at Winchelsea in East Sussex, and gatehouses at TOTNES, in Devon, and LAUNCESTON in Cornwall, are among those still to be seen. Not all town gates were defensive. Some were erected to control traders going in and out of the town and to collect market dues. Such is believed to be the case with the North Bar at BEVERLEY, Humberside. Within many old towns there are more ancient gates to castles, abbeys and medieval houses, such as the Brasenose Gate at STAMFORD, Lincolnshire, and the Norman gateway to the 16th-century Latin school at BUCKINGHAM, Buckinghamshire.

Lych gates The Anglo-Saxon word *lich*, meaning 'corpse', gave the name to these small covered gateways to many church-

ROOFED GATEWAY *The lych gate at Winfrith Newburgh adds charm to the Dorset village.*

yards. They marked the division between consecrated and unconsecrated ground. There the pall bearers would stop with the corpse – in the coffin or shrouded – until the priest arrived to perform the first part of the burial service which prepared the body for entry to the church. While many lych gates have been restored or rebuilt, some medieval examples still stand. Others date from the 17th century. An unusual lych gate at Clifton near ASHBOURNE in Derbyshire has a church clock set into its gabled roof.

Kissing gates These are small wooden or cast-iron gates to fields, churchyards and footpaths which turn inside a curved enclosure allowing only one person at a time to pass through. Since they cannot be left open, they are often used on farmland to prevent animals from straying from or entering forbidden areas.

Ornamental gates Some of the best examples of wrought-iron work are the massive sets of gates that mark the approaches to many country and town houses, castles and churches. Some of the finest are on the borders of North Wales, at Plas Erdigg near LLANGOLLEN, Clwyd, Chirk Castle and Wrexham Church. These were made in the early 18th century by the Davies brothers of Bersham. But there are fine examples in Scotland and in other parts of Britain, some of which incorporate coats of arms and heraldic emblems.

MEDIEVAL GLORY *The imposing gatehouse shows the scale of Thornton Abbey.*

LAST BASTION *The gateway at Rye, Sussex, is all that remains of the medieval walls.*

BY THE SEA *The seaward gate of Beaumaris Castle leads to an inner fortress.*

DIVIDER *The restored 15th-century East Gate in Totnes, Devon, divides Fore Street from High Street.*

SOLE SURVIVOR *Fisher Gate, on the quay, is the only survivor of the medieval gates that once guarded the cinque port of Sandwich.*

GAZEBO

These small one or two-storey buildings, built for the purpose of sitting and enjoying a view, usually stand on a high point in a garden or country estate. Sometimes they were built into a wall to command a view of the outside, perhaps to watch for approaching carriages and visitors. They were mainly built in classical style during the 18th or early 19th centuries.

Similar lookout rooms at the top of large town houses are known as belvederes.

BACK IN TIME *The 16th-century gateway at Chepstow leads to steep medieval streets.*

Several can be seen above the 18th-century houses on the Brinks in WISBECH, Cambridgeshire.

GEORGIAN

See building styles.

INN SIGNS

Inn signs are pictorial history, charting the centuries of change in everyday life, work and leisure in town and village. The earliest inn sign is believed to be the bush, which hung outside Roman wine shops, and much later gave rise to such names as the Bull and Bush. In the Middle Ages, when few could read, a distinctive trading sign gave visible guidance to places where travellers could find rest and refreshment. Later it became a legal obligation for inns to display signs, and by the 18th century they were widespread and often elaborate. Some spanning streets became so cumbersome and dangerous that they were restricted by law.

Inn signs are of two main kinds – those in which the emblem or picture is painted on a board, which either projects over the street or is fixed against the wall of the building, and hanging signs in which the symbol or emblem is cut out in metal or wood or fashioned as a three-dimensional model. In many cases the supporting brackets are fine examples of the most intricate wrought-iron work. In all their immense variety, a number of main groups stand out in the names of inns and their signs.

Pilgrim inns In the 12th century, inns were set up by the monasteries to accommodate

CRUSADER'S ENEMY *The Saracen's Head depicts the Infidel Turk in the Crusades.*

pilgrims and travellers. Names like the Mitre, Cross Keys, the Anchor (all Christian symbols) are reminders of this era. Their visitors included knights on the way to fight under Richard I in the Third Crusade, a campaign commemorated in names such as the Trip to Jerusalem, the Turk's Head, the Lamb and Flag, representing Christ with the banner of victory, and the Saracen's Head.

Royal signs After the Dissolution of the Monasteries in the 1530s many inns adopted royal titles and symbols – the Crown, the King's Head and the Rising Sun, a royal device from the badge of Edward III. The numerous Royal Oaks recall the hideout of Charles II after the Battle of Worcester in 1651.

Echoes of war Battles, military and naval commanders, as well as the rank and file, claim a large share of inn signs. Besides numerous reminders of Nelson and Wellington are such figures as the Marquis of Granby, remembered not so much for his success as a cavalry commander in the 1760s, as for the fact that he set up many of his disabled NCOs after the wars as landlords of inns from Surrey to Derbyshire.

Heraldic emblems Symbols from royal badges and heraldic arms of the nobility provided many signs, easily seen and remembered. Both Red and White Lions are royal emblems, as are Greyhounds (the Tudor kings), Unicorns (Scottish kings) and White Horses (the Hanoverians). Emblems from the arms of local families, probably owning the land on which the inns stand, are numerous, such as the Bear and Staff (Warwick), the Eagle (Derby), the Blue Boar (Oxford), and many others. These often have earlier origins in medieval religious symbolism, the Unicorn symbolising the Virgin Mary. Other signs with religious links include the lily (the Fleur-de-Lys) symbolising purity. The Vine, or Grapes, and the Rose (long before the Wars of the Roses) were also Christian symbols.

CHANGE *Originally a Christian sign, the bull later depicted a site for bull-baiting.*

Mitre

PILGRIM'S SANCTUARY *The Mitre indicated a monastic inn for pilgrims and travellers.*

SAFETY *Popular in seaports, the anchor symbolised safety from the storms of life.*

KNIGHT'S REFUGE *In this sign for a monastic inn the lamb represents Christ and the flag the cross of the Crusaders.*

Trades, crafts and professions Farmers, farm workers and rural craftsmen claim a vast army of signs. Many crafts are represented by the arms of their guilds, which may have met at the inn, such as saddlers, carpenters, cordwainers (shoemakers), brewers, smiths, farriers, and flint knappers who prepared flints for muzzle-loading guns. These are succeeded by inns christened in an industrial age with the arms of steelworkers, bricklayers, miners and railwaymen. Railways also gave rise to station hotels and railway inns.

Sport and leisure There are reminders of inns which once catered for brutal sports, where bulls were baited by bull terriers and fighting cocks were set against each other. At the Dog and Duck, dogs raced across a pond to be first to reach a pinioned duck. The Bird in Hand related to falconry. The Bat and Ball at Hambledon, Hampshire, marks the birthplace of the first cricket club, founded in 1750.

Transport signs With their close connection with road travel, such signs as the Coach and Horses, Horse and Groom, or the Dover Stage recall the stagecoach services of the 17th and 18th centuries.

There are few aspects of national life which are not featured in this gallery of inn signs. Personalities, both famous and infamous, real and legendary, have a whole portrait gallery to themselves – from Robin Hood to Dick Turpin, from Nell Gwyn to Grace Darling. Local landscape and townscape features, such as the Castle, the Ferry, the Bridge or the Windmill, appear everywhere – the inn identified with the place. Coastal inns cover every branch of maritime history and activity – the Smugglers, Pilots, Lobster Pots and Lifeboats, and innumerable Ships. And there is a vast miscellany of the curious, the unusual, the humorous or satirical, and the obscure. Many refer to local legends or events long forgotten. In other cases their original names have been transformed by common usage and time into something totally different, resulting in such examples as the well-known Pig and Whistle, believed to be based on the Saxon *piggen*, 'a pail', from which the ale was served, and *wassail*, meaning 'good cheer'.

JACOBEAN

See building styles.

JOUGS

See stocks.

KEYSTONE

The central, uppermost stone or brick of an arch, shaped like a wedge, which links the whole structure together. When an arch is used decoratively, over a Georgian doorway or window, for example, the keystone may be raised and embellished with a carved ornament. The other wedge-shaped stones making up the arch are known as voussoirs.

KILN

An oven or furnace for burning, baking or drying materials such as clay, grain, hops or lime. The most common type of kiln is the bottle-oven, a furnace used for firing bricks or pottery at a minimum temperature of about 900°C (1,650°F). These kilns were once a part of the Staffordshire skyline, but they gradually disappeared as gas and electricity replaced coal fires in the potteries, and now only a few remain.

BYGONE AGE *The bottle-oven kilns gave a distinctive skyline to the Potteries.*

LANTERN

An appropriately named turret on the top of a domed building or a room. Apart from its ornamental value, a lantern has the purpose of ventilating and providing light. If only light is required, the turret, often octagonal, will have glazed windows. In other cases the sides will be open. It is often surmounted by its own small dome, a cupola, capped by a cross or weathervane. Lanterns are often seen above the dome of a church in classical style, or on a country house or market cross. A fine example is on the County Hall at ABINGDON, Oxfordshire. In some 18th-century houses a lantern tower may form a small room used as a lookout or a retreat, commanding a fine view of the surrounding countryside.

LOCK-UPS

Most towns and villages used to have a lock-up for the detention of petty offenders. The lock-up was usually a small round or octagonal stone-built prison cell with a domed roof. It was usually under the control of the parish constable, the main law-keeping officer before police forces came into being after the Police Act of 1828. Sometimes called cages, or blindhouses because of the absence of windows, they were used either for a short period of corrective imprisonment or as an overnight cell for an offender being brought before the local Justices. In some cases they consist of a small, heavily barred room in a town hall or market building, since market days often led to arrests. Most

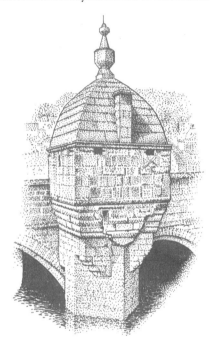

FROM GRACE TO DISGRACE *The lock-up on the medieval bridge at Bradford-on-Avon was once a chapel where pilgrims prayed.*

surviving lock-ups date from the 18th century when stone roundhouses replaced many earlier cells. A typical roundhouse of this period is one at Castle Cary, Somerset, built in 1799. A much earlier building, the 14th-century bridge chapel at BRADFORD-ON-AVON, Wiltshire, became a town lock-up in the 17th century. At ALDEBURGH in Suffolk, the cells are on the ground floor of the early 16th-century Moot Hall. In Scottish towns, the lock-up was usually called the tolbooth. There is a 17th-century example at KIRKCUDBRIGHT, Dumfries and Galloway, in which John Paul Jones, the American naval hero, was once held.

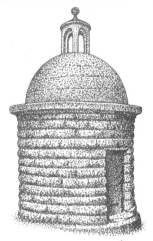

STONE CAGE *Lawbreakers in Alton, Derbyshire, were housed in this lock-up.*

MARTELLO TOWER

A small, round fort with a gun mounted on a revolving platform on top. Martello towers, named after a similar fort at Cape Mortella in Corsica, were built as a precaution against invasion by Napoleon in the early 19th century. They were two-storey, brick-built, about 30 ft high and 25 ft in diameter. The lower part was for ammunition and stores, and the upper part housed a garrison of about 24 men.

FORT *Seventy-four Martello towers once guarded the coast from Folkestone to Seaford.*

MISERICORD

A projecting shelf, usually finely carved, on the underside of a hinged choir seat, which served as a support for a person when the seat was tipped up. Misericords were originally decorated with leaves and scrolls, but in the 14th century the carving became more elaborate and depicted biblical scenes, heraldic emblems and allegorical scenes from contemporary life. The name comes from the Latin *misericordia*, meaning 'pity'.

HEADDRESS *A misericord in Ludlow Church.*

MOUNTING BLOCK

Stone blocks of three or four steps, set against a wall or at the edge of the pavement, date from the 19th century or earlier and were used by those who had difficulty mounting a horse or getting into a horsedrawn vehicle – ladies with long skirts, the young, the short, and the old and the stiff-jointed. Mounting blocks are sometimes seen in the courtyards of old inns, where they were used by passengers to get in and out of stagecoaches. Carters also used them when loading and unloading, so there are a few examples still to be seen by old warehouses, especially in port areas. Some blocks have an iron ring for tethering horses.

LEG UP *A mounting block gave a step up to the saddle or into the coach.*

NOGGING

See brick.

PARGETING

See cladding.

PEBBLE

See flint, cobble and pebble.

PEBBLE DASH

See cladding.

PEDIMENT

The term is used to define the low-pitched gable that is so notable a feature of Classical Renaissance and Neoclassical, especially Georgian, architecture. Above a pillared portico, a pediment may run across the entire front of a building or, on a lesser scale, be employed as a decorative feature above a door or window. A classical pediment forming part of the frontage of a building may often contain, within the triangular area, an escutcheon or a small circular window known as an 'eye'. An open pediment is one in which a section of

the apex of the triangle is omitted. A broken pediment is one in which there is an opening in the centre of the base. In Renaissance buildings, when used for doors and windows, the arch of the pediment is often curved, particularly in Baroque architecture.

PILLAR BOXES

Rowland Hill's Penny Post was introduced in 1840, and the first street pillar boxes appeared in Jersey in 1852. Over the next ten years some 200 boxes were set up in London alone, and every town and village had at least one. The early cast-iron boxes were made in classical styles – Doric columns, hexagonal or fluted pillars with decorative motifs, and many were painted dark green. Today's red cylindrical boxes and the flat boxes set into walls are descended from the first national standard pillar boxes of the 1880s. Apart from the royal ciphers, they have looked much the same ever since.

EARLY POST *Vertical slots, used on early pillar boxes, went out in the 1850s.*

Some of the earliest pillar boxes, bearing Queen Victoria's VR cipher, are still in use, but they are becoming quite rare. There are two 1856 boxes, with vertical slots, in FRAMLINGHAM, Suffolk, while ILKLEY, North Yorkshire, possesses a hexagonal box of 1870; all are still in service.

PILLORY

In this form of punishment, introduced in Henry III's reign (1216–72), a criminal stood on a raised board in the street, with his head and hands clamped in holes between two planks, and was pelted with stones and refuse by passers-by. Daniel Defoe, author of *Robinson Crusoe*, was sentenced to imprisonment and to stand three times in the pillory for seditious libel committed in his pamphlet attacking the Church. Defoe's first day in the pillory – June 29, 1703 – was a triumph for him, as the crowd was sympathetic. But on the subsequent occasions, the public was hos-

tile and he was pelted and suffered greatly.

The pillory was the punishment for perjury and, in the Middle Ages, for profiteering or using false weights. From 1637 to 1815 it was also meted out to those guilty of printing books without a licence or of libelling the government.

In more serious cases, such as that of Titus Oates (1649–1705), whose perjury in 1678 led to the execution of more than 35 innocent Roman Catholics, flogging was part of the sentence. The pillory was not abolished until 1837.

In RYE, East Sussex, the pillory that once stood in Market Street is displayed in the town hall. A double pillory, which could hold two criminals at once, stands on Church Hill in Coleshill, Warwickshire.

PLASTERING

See cladding.

PORTERS' REST

In the days before the delivery van, porters were not confined to railway stations and markets. Any burden too small to justify the use of a cart was entrusted to a porter. Sometimes they carried considerable loads, and those same Victorian philanthropists who erected troughs for horses, put up rests for porters. The rest consisted of a shoulder-high bench on which a load could be eased without having to lower it to the ground.

RESTING PLACE *An old porters' rest survives in London's Piccadilly.*

PORTICO

The main entrance to a large house or other building may be protected by a portico – a covered area in front of the doorway, consisting of a roof supported by columns. In its simplest form the classical entrance portico would have a pitched roof faced by a pediment above the columns. In its more elaborate forms, the grand front to a large Georgian mansion, for instance, there may be a balcony above the doorway, and tall columns reaching several storeys to the top of the building. Other houses of the same period have a recessed, colonnaded area at the head of a flight of steps. High porticoes supported by Ionic or Corinthian columns make an impressive introduction to many of the Neoclassical churches of the late 18th and early 19th centuries.

PUBLIC LAVATORIES

The Romans built public lavatories as a matter of course, but after they left Britain such amenities were virtually unknown until the 1850s. Then, Victorian health campaigners demanded that public conveniences should be provided widely. George Jennings' company set up the first cast-iron version, near the Royal Exchange in the City of London, and made a reputation by creating the same facilities in Hyde Park for visitors to the Great Exhibition of 1851.

Over the next two decades, in towns all over Britain, Jennings' strong but delicately ornamented circular or rectangular conveniences were installed. George Bernard Shaw was among those who campaigned for more of these lavatories in London boroughs.

Mid-Victorian designs are now rare, because they were largely replaced by underground establishments in the course of street-improvement schemes early this century. Many underground lavatories have decorative iron railings and overhanging lamps at their entrances. A good example of a Victorian cast-iron urinal stands on Horfield Common in Bristol, Avon.

PUMPS AND CONDUIT HEADS

The communal water source – river, well or lake – was always a focal point of town life and, indeed, often the very basis of the town's existence. Pumps, however, seem to have arrived fairly late on the scene. Medieval seamen knew of them as a means of draining the bilges, but no one appears to have applied the idea to extracting water from underground until the 16th century. Most surviving pumps belong to the 18th and 19th centuries. They often replaced ancient wells, or at least drew water from the same deep spring. Many pumps are freestanding, often beside stone drinking troughs for horses, while some are covered in with small, open-sided roofed buildings or boxed in with wooden cases to cover the pumping gear. There are well-preserved pumps at BLANDFORD FORUM, Dorset, CHIPPING CAMPDEN, Gloucestershire,

and in many other country towns.

As town populations grew, many old water sources became inadequate or polluted, and water was sometimes pumped from deeper levels and retained in small reservoirs or conduit heads, quite substantial brick or stone buildings sited at the highest point of the town. The handsome 18th-century Water House, a masterpiece of 'header' brickwork, beside the churchyard at RYE, East Sussex, is a fine example. In the same century, one of the first piped public supplies was brought into ROSS-ON-WYE, Hereford and Worcester. These in turn gave way to the earliest house-to-house mains water supply systems, which began to make an appearance early in the 19th century.

QUOINS

Blocks of dressed stone at the corners of a building, which frame the outer walls, whether of stone or brick, are known as quoins, or coigns. In early stone buildings the blocks forming the corners are usually larger and better cut than those used in the walls themselves. From Tudor times onwards, quoin stones were generally laid so that they showed alternately short and long faces from each angle of the wall. The purpose of this was partly decorative, as well as to give strength to the corner.

RAILINGS

Iron railings have been protecting and decorating town houses, churches and other buildings since the 18th century. They reached their peak in the design of Georgian and Regency terraces, crescents and squares, and have remained a feature of town architecture ever since. Their spear-like points, with extra spikes around the doorways and gates, continued the tradition of the well-defended manor house – a necessary precaution both before and after the first organised police forces of the 1840s. On Queen Anne, Georgian and Regency houses other features in ironwork included lantern holders, link extinguishers and footscrapers – often decorated with elegant scrollwork. By the late 18th century, designs were becoming less menacing and more decorative, though the deterrent spike remained a standard feature, as it still is today.

REGENCY

See building styles.

OLD SCHOOL *Market Harborough's grammar school dates from 1614.*

SCHOOL

Until the Dissolution of the Monasteries in the 1530s, education was largely in the hands of the Church. This ended with the Dissolution, but the Tudor monarchs soon realised the deficiency, and some of the money realised by the Dissolution went into the founding of schools. As a result, England has a heritage of fine old grammar schools bearing the names of King Edward VI, Queen Mary and Queen Elizabeth. Wealthy individuals followed the royal example and founded similar schools. Many of the original 16th and 17th-century buildings they paid for survive, though few are now used for school purposes. An exception is the school at STAMFORD, Lincolnshire, founded in 1552. Other fine examples also exist at SHREWSBURY, Shropshire (now the museum and library), ASHBOURNE, Derbyshire, and MARKET HARBOROUGH, Leicestershire.

SHIP LAGGING

See cladding.

STAINED GLASS

Paintings, sculptures and, above all, stained glass were the media through which the medieval Church taught the stories of the Bible to illiterate congregations. Stained glass, in fact, evolved specifically for this purpose some time before the 11th century. The oldest surviving stained glass dates from about 1050, and is preserved in a church in Augsburg, Germany, while in Britain, York Minster has glass dating from about 1150. But hardly a church in England is without its quota of stained glass. GREAT MALVERN, Hereford and Worcester, and LUDLOW, Shropshire, are among towns whose churches have especially fine medieval glass.

STOCKS

From the early Middle Ages until the 1850s, stocks were used as a punishment for drunkards and other petty offences. The stocks consisted of two heavy planks shaped to allow the criminal's leg to be locked between them, and were sited in a public place so that passers-by could ridicule and throw missiles at the occupant. The pillory, in which the head and arms were restrained, was a more rigorous punishment, since people in the stocks could at least duck from things hurled at them, or stop them with their hands.

FOR ALL TO SEE *Humiliation was a major part of punishment in the stocks.*

Ancient stocks stand under the Butter Cross in OAKHAM, Leicestershire, and near the Old Tollbooth in the High Street at CRIEFF, Tayside. Those near Scots Gate in BERWICK-UPON-TWEED, Northumberland, were last used in 1840.

Sometimes the stocks were mounted on wheels, so that the miscreants put in them could be dragged through the streets to increase their disgrace and discomfort. A set of mobile stocks is preserved in the Old Guildhall in MUCH WENLOCK, Shropshire. Persistent or more serious criminals might be sentenced to a whipping as part of their punishment. There is a whipping-post, with wrist-irons to hold the offender during the flogging, beside the stocks in MALVERN, Hereford and Worcester. In Scotland, wrongdoers were put in the 'jougs', an iron collar at the end of a chain, and one is attached to the town cross in Kinross, Tayside.

STONE

See building stone.

STREET LIGHTING

Before 1800, those using the streets at night usually carried their lighting with them, or hired linkmen – lamp-carriers – to show them the way. The Elizabethans lit some busy thoroughfares with beacons, and a number of town authorities insisted that a proportion of householders should show candles in a window to light the street; 'Lantern and candle light!' was a traditional cry of the town watchman. Late in the 18th century, oil lanterns began to be placed on larger houses and in town squares. A number of fine examples can still be seen, set above doorways, gateways and on bridges, or suspended from wrought-iron brackets – though most survivors are now converted to electricity. Railings in some Regency squares still incorporate elegant lamp holders and conical link (torch) extinguishers.

Gas lighting was first demonstrated in Pall Mall in London in 1807, and within 20 years main streets in many cities and towns were gaslit. The lamplighter with his long pole became as familiar a figure on the evening streets as the watchman had been. Lamp-posts offered an artistic challenge to Victorian designers and ironfounders, who responded with street lamps supported by dolphins, bearing coats of arms and surmounted by intricately pierced coronets. Every style from Gothic to Art Nouveau was represented, and their lamp-posts, wherever they have been permitted to remain, still bring charm and variety to streets all over the country.

STREET NAMES

Some street names are common to many towns, having their origin in common institutions – the town's defences, its trades and crafts, its religious and social history. High Street, probably the most common of all, was part of, or leading to, a main highway or highroad. 'Street' was originally the term for any road – the Roman *via strata* (a paved way). Usually High Street was, and often is, the principal street of the town, as is Main Street in the USA. Former fortified and walled towns often have street names related to town gates or battlements – Castlegate, Foregate (the front or main gate), and often a Barbican, named after the outer tower or gatetower, and a Bailey or Bayliss Street, recalling the fortified enclosure of a castle. Trades and crafts feature in many common names. *Chep*, the Anglo-Saxon word for 'sale', is the origin of such street names as Cheapside and Eastcheap, and the names of market towns like CHEPSTOW, Gwent, and

CHIPPING CAMPDEN, Gloucestershire. Market Streets, Poultrymarkets and Buttermarkets are common in old towns, as are names recalling centres of finance and local government – The Mint, Exchange Street, Guildhall Street. Merchant and craft guilds may have had their headquarters in streets bearing names like Mercer Street (sellers of fabrics), Cooper Street (cask-makers), or in Roper Street, Brewer Street, Skinner Street or Silver Street. Fletcher Street may have housed the makers of arrows, and The Butts recalls medieval compulsory

AFT *People once had to feel their way along Shrewsbury's dark Grope Lane.*

archery practice. Many street names in old towns are reminders of the establishments of friars whose mission was among the poor in crowded cities and towns – the Grey Friars (Franciscan), White Friars (Carmelite), Black Friars (Dominicans) and Austin Friars (of the Augustinian order). The word friars (brothers) may also be connected with the powerful military orders of the Knights Templar or the Knights Hospitaller who had their headquarters in medieval towns. The 19th century produced many street names commemorating military campaigns and leaders – Wellington Street, Sebastopol Terrace and Alma Place, for example, or a royal event such as Queen Victoria's coronation or golden jubilee.

Small streets, connecting alleys and passageways in old country towns have several local names, peculiar to different parts of Britain. In Harrogate, and other towns in North Yorkshire, narrow streets are known as 'ginnels' and 'snickets', the latter relating to an old use of 'snick', to cut or slip quickly along a road. The word 'vennel' appears in Scotland. There is a Friars Vennel in Dumfries. More widely in use in Scotland is the word 'wynd', having its origin in the Old English *windan* (a winding path). There is a Cross Wynd and Kirk

Wynd at HAWICK, Borders, Lossie Wynd and School Wynd at ELGIN, Grampian, Coal Wynd in Kirkcaldy, and many in Dundee, Aberdeen and Edinburgh. In the south of England a narrow footpath, usually between walls, may be called a 'twitten', possibly from an old German word, *tweite*, meaning an 'alley'. For example, in LEWES, West Sussex, Church Twitten is one of the many linking passages between the steep streets of the old town.

STUCCO

Originally stucco meant any type of plasterwork, and it was popular with Roman builders who used it, indoors and out, for low-relief wall decoration and as a basis for wall paintings. Stucco was reintroduced in Renaissance buildings as an outside rendering of smooth lime-and-sand plaster. In Britain it became widespread in Georgian and Regency times, and was widely used by architects such as the Adam brothers and John Nash. Stucco, or later in the 19th century rendering, was often used as a cheaper substitute for stonework, when lines were traced on the surface to simulate the jointing of stone blocks.

SUNDIALS

Sundials and sun clocks of various kinds go back to ancient Egyptian, Persian, Babylonian and Indian civilisations. In Britain there are several Saxon sundials incised on the south walls of churches. The sun's shadow continued to be a main means of telling the time until the 18th century – later still in some places – and even after the development of mechanical clocks, sundials were used to check them. Old church sundials gave the hour at which bells were to be rung and services held. A fine example is at Kirk Dale, North Yorkshire, dating from about 1060 and inscribed: 'This is the day's sunmarker at each hour. Haworth made me, and Brand, priests.' The 17th and 18th centuries saw an immense variety of sundials. They range

SUN TIME *The sundial at St Gregory's Minster, Kirk Dale, N. Yorks, dates from Saxon times.*

from complex sun clocks which include moon dials and give the sun's altitude, to simple vertical dials on church and house walls, horizontal dials on low pillars and portable sundials. Many were mounted on columns of market crosses, such as the one in the town centre at APPLEBY, Cumbria.

TIE PLATE

The brick or stone walls of buildings and bridges often tend to bulge outwards over the years, because of the weight they bear, or shifts in the soil, or both. To stop that happening, they are tied with a metal rod which is run from one exterior wall to another on the opposite side of the structure. The rods are held in place by tie plates of wrought iron at either end, and it is the plates which are visible on the outside walls.

Usually, the tie plates are shaped as a cross or the letter S, but some are barshaped or round. Many old S-shaped plates have a serpent's head at one end and its tail at the other, a pattern that may be derived from a pre-Christian protective symbol. Tie plates are commonly seen on the gable ends of old buildings, because the pressure of the roof is heavier on those than on the side walls.

TILE

See cladding.

TOLBOOTH

See lock-ups.

TOLLHOUSE

One of the easiest ways of raising money is to impose a toll for allowing people to perform some simple function – such as selling their produce, using a road or crossing a bridge. Usually the toll-gatherer is expected to make some return for the money – to regulate a market or to maintain a road or bridge. Tollhouses were built to house the toll-collectors. The earliest ones – sometimes called tolseys – are those associated with markets. Both BURFORD, Oxfordshire, and LUDLOW, Shropshire, have ancient tolseys. But most tollhouses date from the great period of turnpike road building in the 18th and 19th centuries. They were built to house the gate-keepers, who collected tolls from those using the roads constructed by private enterprise under the Turnpike Acts.

ROAD TAX *Travellers once paid their dues at the tollhouse.*

TOPIARY

The idea of clipping evergreen trees and shrubs into the shape of birds, beasts and other forms may have originated in ancient Greece and passed to the Romans. The word topiary comes from the Latin *topiarius*, a man who laid out or tended ornamental gardens. The skill reached Britain from France and Holland in the late Middle Ages, became popular on the estates of great country houses in Tudor times, and reached its height in the reigns of William III and Anne in the late 17th and early 18th centuries. It then fell out of fashion, but the Victorians revived it, and took it to smaller gardens in both country and town. Close-growing yew and box are most suitable for topiary, but privet, juniper, bay, laurel and holly are also used.

Ancient churchyard yews that provided wood for longbows in the Middle Ages were later clipped into formal shapes, for example at Beaconsfield, Buckinghamshire. Plas Newydd, an 18th-century black-and-white house at LLANGOLLEN, Clwyd, also has a fine topiary garden.

ORNAMENTAL *Box, holly and yew trees lend themselves to the art of topiary.*

TOWN HALL

The town hall has been the focus of civic life – and civic pride – for centuries. Every town has one, though it may not always be called the town hall – moot hall, town house and guildhall are some of the alternatives. They range in size and appearance from the tiny, timber-framed moot hall of 1512 at ALDEBURGH, Suffolk, to imposing Victorian edifices. In between they come in various guises. Those of BERWICK-UPON-TWEED, Northumberland, and KESWICK, Cumbria (a moot hall), have both been mistaken for churches, while the Town House at LINLITHGOW, Lothian, looks like a nobleman's residence.

DOMED *The 18th-century town hall at Kelso dominates the market square.*

ORIGINAL USE *The council still meets in Aldeburgh's 16th-century Moot Hall.*

TOWN SIGNS

Directional signposts came into widespread use with the building of turnpike roads in the 18th century, but town and village signs only appeared in any numbers at the beginning of the 20th century. Their structure has varied little from the start – the town name is shown prominently, together with a decorative motif often depicting a local trade or a famous character or incident from local history or legend.

FAME *The sign shows John Chapman, a local pedlar who lives on in legend.*

TULIP TOWN *Spalding's town sign symbolises its association with flowers.*

TRADE SIGNS

Signs and symbols of a trade were once essential when only a small proportion of the population could read. A number of these old signs survive in country towns. Some are carved in stone above doorways, others are fine examples of 18th-century wrought-iron work. They usually represent

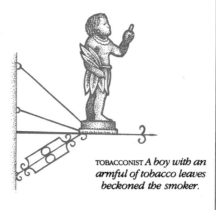

TOBACCONIST *A boy with an armful of tobacco leaves beckoned the smoker.*

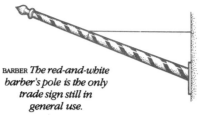

BARBER *The red-and-white barber's pole is the only trade sign still in general use.*

the product of the craft concerned and include elegant signs for hatters, bootmakers, tobacconists and furniture makers, and more down-to-earth signs for farriers, blacksmiths, locksmiths and chimney-sweeps. The red-and-white striped barber's pole is the most common, and is a reminder that barbers once carried out an additional role as surgeons and bloodletters.

OBVIOUS *To indicate their wares, locksmiths displayed a key and apothecaries a pestle and mortar.*

CHARM *Two elegant signs announce a cafe and hotel in Broad Street, Ludlow.*

VAULTING

One of the great glories of English church, abbey and cathedral architecture is its dramatic vaulting. These continuous structures of stone, brick or concrete form a self-supporting arched roof over a building or part of it. The Normans introduced vaulting to England as a more durable form of roof building to overcome the fire hazard of timber roofs. It reached its peak with such breathtaking effects as the fan vaulting in Henry VII's Chapel in Westminster Abbey, and in SHERBORNE Abbey, in Dorset. BEVERLEY Minster, Humberside, has a fine example of ribbed vaulting.

Barrel vault The simplest form of vault, and a component of Norman architecture. It consists of a long tunnel-like semicircular arch, and is also known as a tunnel vault. Some of the old tunnel vaulting in England can be seen in the crypt of the Priory Church at HEXHAM, Northumberland.

Groin vault In this type, vaults intersect at

Barrel vault

Norman vault

Early English vault

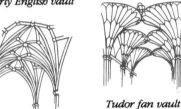

Tudor fan vault

Decorated vault

right-angles, the meeting arcs of intersection being known as groins.

Ribbed vault To overcome the heaviness of barrel vaults, 'ribbing' was introduced. Stone ribs criss-crossed the arches, and these supported relatively thin, lighter sections between. Extra ribbing was added in the Early English and Decorated styles for both support and decoration. The abbey presbytery at TEWKESBURY, Gloucestershire, has a fine roof in Decorated vaulting.

Fan vault A form of vault first used in the Perpendicular style of architecture (from about 1380). It has concentric curved ribs forming an inverted cone-like shape, and is also known as a conoidal vault. At the top, between the curved 'fans', the diamond-shaped areas are richly decorated. Some are hung with elaborately carved stone pendants. The abbey nave at SHERBORNE, Dorset, has a magnificent fan-vaulted ceiling.

VERGE BOARD

See barge board.

VIADUCT

Britain's basic railway network, which was laid down in the 1840s, required great feats of engineering to carry the lines across rivers, valleys and low-lying ground. The great aqueducts built for the canals earlier in the same century gave early experience in the type of construction needed to overcome such obstacles. The first great railway viaduct to be built was opened in 1830 and carried the Manchester to Liverpool railway on nine brick arches across the Sankey Valley. Others followed, includ-

RIVER CROSSING *This 1,476 ft viaduct spans the Ouse at Balcombe, Sussex.*

ing the largest masonry viaduct ever built, Robert Stevenson's 2,000 ft long Royal Border Bridge, which is carried on 28 arches across the River Tweed at BERWICK-UPON-TWEED, Northumberland. The boom in motorway building following the Second World War produced almost as many viaducts as the great age of railway building, including one 3 miles long on the M6 near Castle Bromwich, north of Birmingham.

WATERMILLS

From Roman times watermills have ground corn in Britain, far earlier than windmills, which did not reach Europe from Asia until the Crusades (11th to 13th centuries). The Saxons used watermills powered by streams, rivers or tidal waters, and the Domesday Book (1086) records more than 5,000 watermills in England, many of them grinding corn for the monasteries.

Depending on the site, the mills were built so that moving water struck the mill wheel from above (overshot wheel), or from the side or below (undershot wheel), different shapes of wheel being used for the different angle and direction of waterflow. Dams were frequently built upstream to control the flow of water, providing a steady supply even during summer drought.

WATER POWER *The waterwheel was once industry's main source of energy.*

Wooden waterwheels provided power for industry from the late 17th century, driving hammers to shape iron, and powering pumps, looms and spinning machines. The rural watermill, which began grinding corn, passed on its name to the cotton, woollen and steel mills of the Industrial Revolution. It was largely superseded by the steam engine in the early 19th century.

Well preserved watermills still in working order include a fine example on the River Avon at TEWKESBURY, Gloucestershire.

WATTLE AND DAUB

The timber-framed houses and cottages built throughout England and Wales from the 14th to 18th centuries usually had the gaps between the timbers filled with wattle and daub. Pointed staves were fixed between the horizontal timbers of the building to form a weaving warp. Then a weft of 'wattles' – pliable twigs, usually of osier or hazel – were interwoven on these. The woven panels were then daubed on both sides with a mixture of clay and dung, often with straw or animal hair added for bonding. A coat of plaster finished the panels, both inside and out.

In Lancashire, Cheshire, Wales and the north Midlands, the wattle-and-daub panels were whitewashed and the timbers pitch-coated to give striking, typical black-and-white buildings. Elsewhere the panels were usually colour-washed and the oak timbers left untreated, giving a quieter, warmer look.

WEATHER-BOARDING

See cladding.

WEATHERVANES

Knowing the way the wind is blowing has always been vital information as a simple form of weather forecasting. On towers, high buildings and other exposed places, weathervanes (or weathercocks) have been performing this service for centuries. Turning in the wind on a spindle above fixed points of the compass, they point towards the direction from which the wind is blowing.

The cock is the traditional emblem, and weathercocks probably date from a 9th-century pope's decree that all churches should display them as a symbol of St Peter's denial of Christ, and of the Church's authority and watchfulness. As well as the cock, the designs include biblical scenes, heraldic beasts or emblems, human figures, birds, fish and animals. They are usually cut from sheet iron or some other

INTO THE WIND *The weathervane at Bungay immortalises the town's notorious black dog.*

metal, and show the skill and ingenuity of a local blacksmith or metalworker. Many on churches have no cardinal points, as the altar is usually at the east end of a church.

There are examples of weathervanes in most country towns, such as the gilded fish above the Bridge Chapel at BRADFORD-ON-AVON, Wiltshire, known as the Bradford Gudgeon, and the three-dimensional sailing ship above the Town Hall at Farnham. At Bungay, a weathervane on a standard in the Market Place features a black dog said to have ravaged the church in the 16th century.

WELLS

The earliest wells were springs of running water. Many of them were connected with pagan worship and the cult of wishing wells sprang from this. Many became Christian holy places, sometimes associated with saints. In Derbyshire the custom of well-dressing with elaborate pictures of biblical subjects, made with flower petals embedded in clay, was well established by 1350. BUXTON has an annual well-dressing carnival. In WIRKSWORTH each May wells are dressed in thanksgiving for water itself.

Healing or purifying cults became associated with springs from earliest times, and 'spa therapy' began soon after at those with medicinal properties. The Romans first developed Bath in Avon for this purpose. Many became the focal points of fashionable spas in the 18th century, when their elegant pump rooms and assembly rooms became centres of social life, fashion and entertainment as well as for taking the waters. These buildings survive in Bath, ROYAL TUNBRIDGE WELLS, Kent, HARROGATE, North Yorkshire, MALVERN, Hereford and Worcester, and many other country towns.

Techniques for sinking wells to tap underground water came to England from France with Carthusian monks around 1100. However, old wells of simple stone or brick, complete with winding gear, rarely remain in towns, for the Victorians were great 'improvers' of wells – as of many town features. Often they installed a drinking fountain or, as in the case of the well at Southover Grange in LEWES, East Sussex, a pump and shaft cover to replace the old bucket on a rope.

WINDMILLS

Crusaders brought the art of building windmills to continental Europe from the Middle East in the 11th century. It reached Britain a century later via Germany and the Netherlands. For centuries after, windmills ground corn and supplied a vital source of power, especially in areas away from forests and coalfields. East Anglia was such a region, and in 1820 it had 700 windmills engaged in land drainage alone. Once the property of lords of the manor and monasteries who exacted tolls for grinding corn, from Tudor times windmills were privately owned by the miller. Besides serving the local community, he also bought grain and sold its flour to the growing towns and cities.

Static windmills were ideal in the constant winds of the Middle East, but the variable winds of northern climates demanded sails that could be turned into the wind. The earliest form was the post mill in which the whole millhouse was mounted on a central oak post and could be rotated by hand.

In the 17th century, a new, larger type of mill came on the scene. Only its top

WIND POWER *The eight-sailed windmill at Heckington, Lincolnshire, was moved from Boston.*

portion – the cap bearing the windshaft supporting the sails – could be rotated. There were two models: the weatherboarded smock mill and the brick-built tower mill. From about 1750 most windmills had 'fantails', circles of small vanes projecting on the opposite side of the mill at right-angles to the plane of the main sails. The fantail acted as an automatic steering device, and rotated the cap to turn the main sails into the wind.

Some of the best preserved windmills are in the eastern and southern counties of England. They include Saxtead Green Mill in Suffolk, a post mill with fantail dating from about 1700; Union Mill at Cranbrook in Kent, one of the finest smock mills in the country; there is a tower mill at Billingford in Norfolk and another, close to the town centre at WISBECH, Cambridgeshire.

ACKNOWLEDGMENTS

Front cover, Chipping Campden, Glos.; page 3, doorway at Richmond, N. Yorks.; pages 4/5, Gold Hill, Shaftesbury, Dorset; pages 6/7, town and castle, Richmond, N. Yorks.

The illustrations in this book were provided by the following artists, photographers and agencies.

Except where stated, credits read from left to right down the page. Work commissioned by Reader's Digest is shown in *italics*.

All the drawings are by Ray Burrows, with the exception of the following: 166 top and bottom, 171 bottom centre, 172 bottom centre, 175 bottom right, 177, 180 top left, top centre and bottom left, and 182 top right.

These were originally published in *Hand-Picked Tours in Britain, Book of British Towns* and *Illustrated Guide to Britain*.

Front cover: Adam Woolfitt/Susan Griggs Agency. Back cover: Colin Molyneux/Fotobank. 3 *Jon Wyand.* 4-5 Timothy Woodcock. 6-7 *Jon Wyand.* 8 Dennis Orchard/Bruce Coleman Ltd. 9 Andy Williams Photo Library. 10 John Bethell. 11 Roslav Szaybo/Susan Griggs Agency. 12 James Davis Photography. 13 Brian Shuel. 14 Eric Rowell/British Tourist Authority. 15 John Bethell. 17 both Adam Woolfitt/Susan Griggs Agency. 18 and 19 Andy Williams Photo Library. 20 Timothy Woodcock. 21 top, Sefton Photo Library; bottom, James Davis Photo Library. 22-23 CLI/Keystone. 24-25 James Davis Photo Library. 26 and 27 Spectrum Colour Library. 28 Airviews Ltd. 29 *Colin Molyneux.* 31 Colin Molyneux. 33

K. M. Andrew. 34 Spectrum Colour Library. 35 Clive Corless. 36 Mary Evans Picture Library. 37 James Davis Photo Library. 39 Andy Williams Photo Library. 40-41 John Bethell. 42 left, Nick Carter; right, Janet and Colin Bord. 43 Spectrum Colour Library. 44 and 45 Timothy Woodcock. 46 Northern Picture Library. 48 Timothy Woodcock. 49 Roger Scruton. 50 British Tourist Authority. 51 John Bethell. 52 Derek McDougall. 53 Peter Baker/International Photobank. 54 James Davis Photo Library. 55 Adam Woolfitt/Susan Griggs Agency. 56 Peter Baker/International Photobank. 57 Adam Woolfitt/Susan Griggs Agency. 58 Adam Woolfitt/British Tourist Authority. 59 left, Airviews Ltd; right, Bob and Sheila Thomlinson; bottom, British Tourist Authority. 60 Allan Davidson. 61 left, Adam Woolfitt/British Tourist Authority; right, Janet and Colin Bord. 62 Will Green (BPL). 63 left, Scottish Tourist Board; right, British Tourist Authority. 64 James Davis Photo Library. 65 Nigel Cassidy. 66, 67 left and bottom, Timothy Woodcock. 67 right, Janet and Colin Bord. 68 Brian Shuel. 69 British Tourist Authority. 70 Ron Oulds. 71 Adam Woolfitt/Susan Griggs Agency. 72 Andrew Beasley/Fotobank. 73 John Bethell. 74 Bob and Sheila Thomlinson. 75 Alex W. Hemmings/Spectrum Colour Library. 76-77 *Jon Wyand.* 78 Airviews Ltd. 79 *Jon Wyand.* 80 John Bethell. 81 Richard Jemmett. 82 Spectrum Colour Library. 83 British Tourist Authority. 84, 85 and 86 Sefton Photo Library. 87 Colin Molyneux/Bruce Coleman Ltd. 88 Aerofilms. 89 Kenneth Scowen. 90-91 Farrell Grehan/Susan Griggs Agency. 92

Derek Forss. 93 K. M. Andrew. 94 and 95 Janet and Colin Bord. 97 top, Spectrum Colour Library; bottom, Timothy Woodcock. 98-99 British Tourist Authority. 100 Spectrum Colour Library. 101 left, Ray Norton; centre, James Davis Photo Library. 102 John Bethell, 103 left, S. & O. Mathews; right, Ron Oulds/Fotobank. 104 Kenneth Scowen. 105 James Davis Photo Library. 106 Andy Williams Photo Library. 107 Scottish Tourist Board. 109 Spectrum Colour Library. 110 Derek McDougall. 111 Airviews Ltd. 112 top, Derek McDougall; bottom, K. M. Andrew. 113 Andy Williams Photo Library. 114 Derek McDougall. 115 Dennis Hardley/Wade Cooper Associates. 116 Peter Baker/International Photobank. 117 Roger Scruton. 118 Adam Woolfitt/British Tourist Authority. 119 Rich Newton. 120 CLI/Keystone. 121 Colin Molyneux/Fotobank. 122 Dennis Hardley/Wade Cooper Associates. 123 S. & O. Mathews. 124 CLI/Keystone. 125 Rich Newton. 126 left, Patrick Thurston; top right, CLI/Keystone. 127 John Bethell. 128 Rod Williams/Bruce Coleman Ltd. 128-9 Richard Jemmett. 132 Rich Newton. 133 Eric Rowell/British Tourist Authority. 134 Aerofilms. 135 Malcolm Aird. 136-7 Richard Surman. 138-9 Patrick Ward. 140 Adam Woolfitt/Susan Griggs Agency. 141 British Tourist Authority. 142-3 John Bethell. 144 Spectrum Colour Library. 145 Janet and Colin Bord. 146-7 K. M. Andrew. 148 John Watney. 149 Timothy Woodcock. 150-1 Dennis Hardley/Wade Cooper Associates. 153 and 154-5 CLI/Keystone. 156 Malcolm Aird. 157 Brian Shuel. 159 Richard Jemmett. 160 *Jon Wyand.*

Typesetting TRADESPOOLS LTD, FROME; Printing AMBASSADOR PRESS LTD, ST ALBANS; Separations LITHO STUDIOS LTD, DUBLIN, IRELAND
Paper TOWNSEND HOOK & CO. LTD, SNODLAND; Binding HAZELL WATSON & VINEY LTD, AYLESBURY

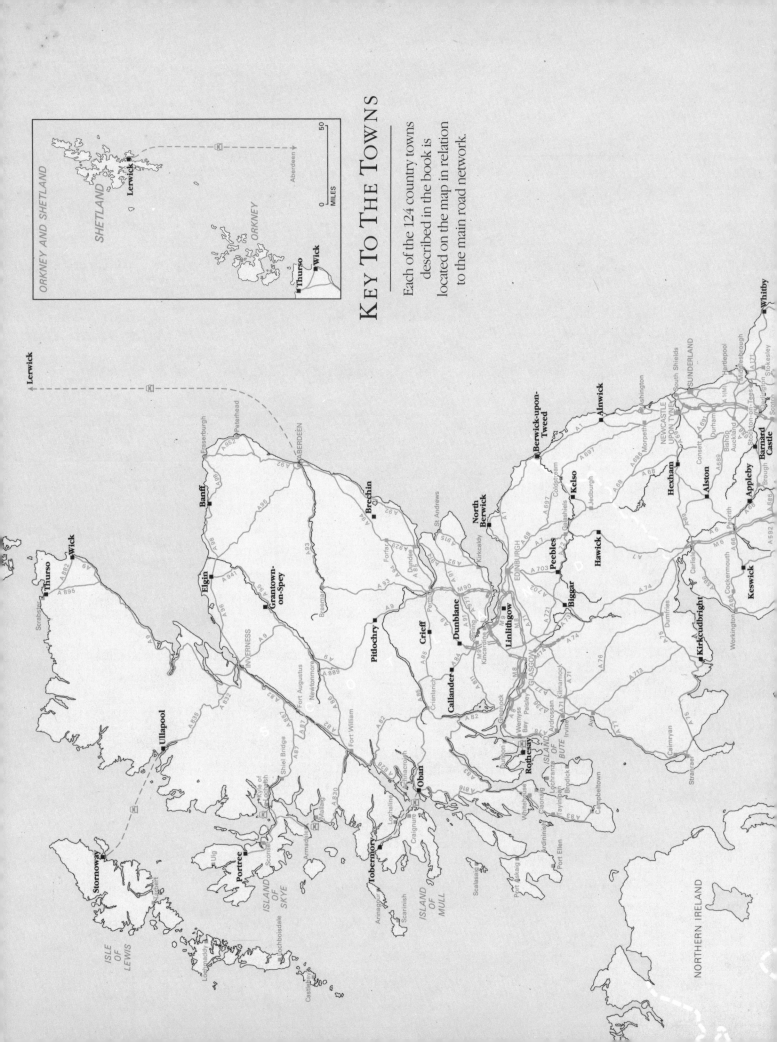

KEY TO THE TOWNS

Each of the 124 country towns described in the book is located on the map in relation to the main road network.

ORKNEY AND SHETLAND

SHETLAND

Lerwick

ORKNEY

Thurso **Wick**

MILES
0   50

Aberdeen

Lerwick

ISLE OF LEWIS

Stornoway

Wick
Thurso
Scrabster
Ullapool
Portree
ISLAND OF SKYE
Uig
Kyle of Lochalsh
Armadale
Mallaig
Fort William
Tobermory
ISLAND OF MULL
Oban
Craignure
Lochaline

Banff
Fraserburgh
Peterhead
ABERDEEN
Elgin
Grantown-on-Spey
INVERNESS
Fort Augustus
Newtonmore
Pitlochry
Brechin
Forfar
Dundee
St Andrews
Crieff
Dunblane
Callander
Crianlarich
Perth
Kinross
Linlithgow
Kincardine
Kirkcaldy
EDINBURGH
North Berwick
Berwick-upon-Tweed
GLASGOW
Paisley
Greenock
Wemyss Bay
Rothesay
ISLAND OF BUTE
Ardrossan
Brodick
Kilmarnock
Ayr
Campbeltown
Lochranza
Tarbert
Whitehouse
Claonaig
Ardminish
Port Ellen
Port Askaig
Cairnryan
Stranraer

Peebles
Biggar
Hawick
Jedburgh
Galashiels
Coldstream
Kelso
Hexham
Alnwick
NEWCASTLE UPON TYNE
South Shields
Ashington
Morpeth
Consett
Durham
SUNDERLAND
Bishop Auckland
Stockton-on-Tees
Middlesbrough
Hartlepool
Stokesley
Whitby
Dumfries
Kirkcudbright
Keswick
Appleby
Alston
Barnard Castle
Workington
Cockermouth
Carlisle
Penrith
Brough

SCOTLAND

ENGLAND

NORTHERN IRELAND